AN IMPROBABLE
FRIENDSHIP

AN IMPROBABLE
FRIENDSHIP

*The story of Yasser Arafat's
mother-in-law, the wife of Israel's
top general and their forty-year
mission of peace*

ANTHONY DAVID

**SIMON &
SCHUSTER**

London · New York · Sydney · Toronto · New Delhi

A CBS COMPANY

First published in Great Britain by Simon & Schuster UK Ltd, 2015
A CBS COMPANY

Originally published in the US in 2015 by Arcade Publishing,
307 West 36th Street, 11th Floor, New York, NY 10018

1 3 5 7 9 10 8 6 4 2

Simon & Schuster UK Ltd
1st Floor
222 Gray's Inn Road
London WC1X 8HB

www.simonandschuster.co.uk

Simon & Schuster Australia, Sydney
Simon & Schuster India, New Delhi

The author and publishers have made all reasonable
efforts to contact copyright-holders for permission, and apologise
for any omissions or errors in the form of credits given.
Corrections may be made to future printings.

A CIP catalogue record for this book
is available from the British Library

Hardback ISBN: 978-1-47115-459-1
Ebook ISBN: 978-1-47115-461-4

Printed and bound by CPI Group (UK) Ltd, Croydon, CR0 4YY

MIX
Paper from
responsible sources
FSC® C020471

Simon & Schuster UK Ltd are committed to sourcing paper
that is made from wood grown in sustainable forests and supports the Forest
Stewardship Council, the leading international forest certification organisation.
Our books displaying the FSC logo are printed on FSC certified paper.

To the memory of Jackie Kahn, whose friendship and encouragement inspired Ruth Dayan to tell her story.

"Only those who are capable of listening to the unforgetting silence of this tormented soil, from which everyone begins and to which everyone returns, Jews and Arabs, has the right to call it homeland."

—Meron Benvenisti

Contents

Acknowledgments

For her passion and belief in this book, my profound gratitude to my agent and friend Dorothy Harman. Without you, Dorothy, this book would never have been written. Esther Margolis, our partner, has also worked tirelessly and with astonishing energy to make this book a reality. My thanks to my publisher and editor at Arcade, Jeanette Seaver, who has more than lived up to her reputation as one of the great figures in publishing today. With her legendary sense of language and story, Jeanette fashioned a manuscript into a book. The rest of the team at Arcade, through the proofreading and design process, has done an extraordinary job in making this book complete. Finally, I want to thank Clare, my love, who accompanied me on this journey.

Prologue
A Secret Story

Sometimes it can seem that the only thing Israelis and Palestinians share is a common skepticism that there can ever be a solution to the conflict. As an American writer living and working in Jerusalem, this pervasive pessimism is what compelled me to write about Ruth Dayan and Raymonda Tawil. These two women, from the most prominent families of their respective nations, turned a chance encounter after the Six Day War into an improbable lifelong friendship that shows how, with empathy and common sense, the seemingly insolvable Middle-Eastern conflict can have an end.

Ruth and Raymonda did more than defy national taboos. At great risk and, on occasion, attracting dangerous attention to themselves, both women worked together for decades to address the underlying sources of the conflict. The more time I spent with these extraordinary women, the more I realized their story had to be told.

"How dare Ruth!" Raymonda said at the start of our Skype video conversation. She had just woken me up at 3 a.m. I was in my apartment in Jerusalem; she was at her home in Malta, where she lives with her daughter, Suha Arafat, Yasser Arafat's widow. After four years, I knew Raymonda well enough to distinguish between her emotions of anger, frustration, and hurt. She was clearly angry. I could see it in the way she kept slipping off her glasses and putting them back on again.

"I don't want to have a book now," she continued. "How can I put my name next to Ruth's? Do you know what she said to me?"

"Raymonda, calm down. Tell me what happened." Despite the early hour, the idea that my book on Raymonda and her best friend, Ruth Dayan, would suffer yet another setback made me break out in a sweat. I'd already abandoned a ghostwritten version of the story in favor of a straight dual-biography. Would I have to start over again from scratch?

"Anthony, I know how much time you've put in this book. But I just can't go on. Make it into a novel if you want. Turn it into an Agatha Christie murder mystery because I think I'm going to kill her. . . ."

"What happened?" I poured myself a cup of coffee.

"What happened? As usual, Ruth defended Moshe. Can you believe it, after all these years?"

From my experience, the two women's forty years of friendship and their basic agreement on the nature of the Israeli-Palestinian conflict, and on almost everything else, never prevented the occasional flare-up. Which was only to be expected because Raymonda Tawil was Yasser Arafat's mother-in-law, and Ruth is the widow of Moshe Dayan, the most celebrated Jewish general since Joshua and a man who spent much of his military career doing everything in his power to hunt down Arafat.

"Raymonda," I said to her, sipping my coffee. "Ruth was married to Moshe for decades, she had three children with him, she loved him — and still does. Okay, you think he was a psycho. But . . ."

She cut me off and insisted, with sniffles, that I call Ruth and tell her "*finito*! I'm pulling the plug on the book."

Ruth was awaiting my call. The woman nearly at the century mark has more energy than most college students. She, too, had the voice of someone who had just stopped crying.

"Hi, Ruth."

"Hi."

"I just got off the phone with Raymonda, and she tells me you've been quarreling."

"Quarreling? She screamed at me." Her voice was quivering.

"She says you yelled at her first."

"And what do you expect me to do when she sends me such an email?" This was the first mention of an email. "And it's all your fault." When I inquired why I was to blame, she explained that my interviews with Raymonda had dislodged memories, reopening old wounds. "She wrote terrible things. Just awful. I will NEVER speak with her again."

"Ruth, I've heard you say that a dozen times, and you two always reconcile. You love one another."

"This time I mean it. Just read the email."

"What does it say?"

Ruth got up and went to her office to read the email from the computer. Raymonda's message began with "My dear Ruthy, you are a great woman, you are compassionate, full of humanity, a woman I can call my best friend because you are your own army of love. While your husband was hunting down our best men, you were racing around Palestine looking for women to help. You are a feminist hero."

"C'mon Ruth, it's not such a bad letter."

"Why does she have to say that about Moshe?"

"My God, do you expect Raymonda to *like* Moshe?" Ruth, who downplays her own latent case of PTSD, doesn't fully appreciate how scarred the woman she calls her "soul mate" is after a life of exile and loss.

"Well, that's not the reason I'm finished with her," she snapped with the gravely voice of a longtime smoker. "Anyway, what can I do about Moshe and his wars? He's long gone, and Arafat too is already in the ground. And I'll be keeping them company soon enough. I'm not suited for this world any longer, what it's become. I want to go . . . to nowhere." Ruth, usually alive with the exuberance and vitality of a teenager, suddenly sounded weary.

"So Ruth, why are you angry if it's not because of Moshe? What else did Raymonda say?" When Ruth first contacted me to be her ghostwriter, never did I imagine I'd also need to be a psychologist and Middle East peace negotiator.

"She said I was a colonialist. Can you imagine? Me? She was up in arms because she said there was a 'Made in Israel' tag on some embroidery we made in Bethlehem thirty years ago." For decades Ruth ran a project for women in the occupied territories. "Those women had NO jobs." She raised her voice. "Would Raymonda have preferred that we let them STARVE?"

"Are you telling me that the two of you fought over a tag?"

"Sometimes you really are stupid. It's not just a tag. I spent the best years of my life working with Palestinian woman and here comes Mrs. Jane Fonda telling me I was an exploiter. I've never been more insulted."

I skyped Raymonda back to see if she had really called Ruth a colonialist, and she gave me a long lecture on how Palestinian embroidery was like handspun cloth for Gandhi in India. As she spoke I noticed the way she set her teaspoon down on a saucer and uncrossed her legs, like she was heading into a bruising fight.

After a few more minutes of explaining to me the symbolism of a "Made in Israel" tag, she grabbed a book Ruth wrote in the 1970s, *And Perhaps*, flipped it open, and read aloud a passage that made Ruth sound like the smug wife of the colonial administrator: "Palestinians are called the Jews of the Arabs. Villagers would work in an Israeli supermarket. I was so thrilled that ordinary people meet on an everyday level." With anger flaring up again in her voice, Raymonda then asked me to pass on the message to Ruth that she'd rather go hungry in her own country than work at the checkout aisle in an Israeli grocery store.

For the next two hours, I was on the phone now with Ruth, now with Raymonda, until a three-way Skype conversation left us all laughing. The tag was forgotten, the friends loved one another again, and the book about their friendship survived another crisis. Raymonda said goodnight by admonishing her dear friend to stay healthy. "We need you, Ruth. We love you. We still have so many things to do together."

"Okay, Raymonda. I'll keep going a bit longer." Ruth pressed the palm of her hand onto the computer screen: she was wearing a ring made from a Roman coin given to her by the iconic former mayor of Jerusalem, Teddy Kollek.

I first met Ruth at the end of 2008 after she rang me up and said I might be the right person to be her ghostwriter in recounting a "secret story" she had been lugging around for decades, and invited me to Tel Aviv. It was a bit like Barbara Bush contacting a historian with news of a "confession" she needed to get off her chest.

I had just moved from New York to Jerusalem to take up a job teaching literature and media at a program run by Bard College inside a hard-bitten Palestinian university in the West Bank village of Abu Dis, right next to the Israeli Separation Wall. All I knew about the Dayans was that General Moshe was probably the most iconic figure in the Israeli pantheon, a military genius people placed in the company of Hannibal and Admiral Horatio Nelson. For my students, he was the dark, villainous crusader who in 1967 had conquered their country in six fateful days.

Of course, like all my Israeli friends, I kept up on the scandals regarding Ruth and Moshe's son Assi, the most famous scion of the Dayan dynasty. I was an avid fan of his darkly existentialist films, and of his hit sitcom *Be-Tipul* and its HBO version, *In Treatment*. A mass-market tabloid had recently featured Assi, the master of the nihilistic-surrealist vision of Israeli life, naked and sitting like an anchorite on a pillar with his false teeth clutched in one hand.

The other fearless child, the daughter Yael, whose well-deserved fame comes from her championing of human rights—gays, illegal immigrants, and of course Palestinians—is also the high priestess of the family legacy, defender of the brand, and the Dayan child most like her father. Moshe's missing eye, so to speak—Moshe lost one eye during the Second World War. Another Dayan, Moshe's nephew Uzi, built the Separation Wall snaking through the West Bank. I crossed it every morning on the way to work. Other than that, the Dayan name was to me something like the Kennedys, a glittering dynasty generating boundless materials for historians, mythographers, gossip columnists, and urban planners looking for new street names.

I took the bus down. Ruth lives across the street from a power plant, the Dov Hoz Municipal Airport, and a construction site fueled by a building boom. Her apartment building is one in a line of nearly identical blocks. There is nothing in the middle-class and shrub-lined look of the place to suggest that the first wife of a Homeric legend lives upstairs.

She buzzed me in and I took the stairs to her third-floor apartment. The door, with a ceramic, turquoise-colored nameplate in Hebrew and Arabic next to it, was already open, and someone from inside said, "Come in." I stepped across the threshold, and there she was standing in front of me, with thick gray hair and a few strands drooping around her beautiful face. Set deep on the bridge of her nose were horn-rimmed reading glasses. She had on bubble-gum pink lip-gloss, a necklace made of smooth peach pits—Moshe, as I would later learn, made it for her while serving time in a British prison in 1939—and a flowing dress that could have been worn on the ballroom floor of the Titanic. The ring with a Roman coin was on her finger.

"Hi, I'm Ruth," she said holding out her hand and staring at me with pale green eyes. She spoke in perfect English with a slight British accent. When I shook her hand, she stepped forward and I realized she was barefoot.

I stepped inside Ruth's world, utterly dumbfounded. Festooned to the wall next to the door—too large to miss—was a painting of General Dayan in what looked like the pose of a Prussian officer, with the iconic eye-patch replacing the Teutonic monocle. "Oh, Assi did that," Ruth explained with a chuckle. That the son of the chief architect of what most Israelis consider history's most ethical army could create such a caricature was the first sign I was entering a weird and remarkable place.

I wandered around the apartment, which was like a shrine. There were talismans in every nook and cranny. "Excuse the junk," she said to me, gesturing with one arm. Dead for over thirty years, Moshe seemed to cast his long shadow into every corner of the living room. Hanging over a mother-of-pearl cabinet was a bronze and stainless steel replica of his head with an eye-patch. Her other son Udi, a sculptor who wields a blow-torch the way a poet does a pen, made it out of metal from a scrapyard. My eye caught sight of a black-and-white photo above the sofa, a framed photo of two young lovers sitting in grass reading a book of poetry. I had a mental image of the two teenagers rolling around in fields of daisies.

"That's Moshe and me in 1936," Ruth told me. My eye drifted to an oil painting, next to the eye-patch, of mesmerizing sensuality. It was a portrait of Yael, done just after the Six Day War in 1967 when her father conquered the old city of Jerusalem and the West Bank. "She's stunning," I said.

"Well, back then she sure was. A bit wild, too."

Gently leading me by the arm, she took me around the apartment, pointing out framed photographs. One was of her parents in the 1920s looking like anthropologists crouched with Bedouins. She then showed me a photo, the perfect image of harmony, of her three children taken when they were young. "Moshe and I were so happy back then," Ruth said pointing especially at Assi. "It was just after the war in Europe. The kids drove us around the bend, and we were poor farmers, but happy." I still had no idea why she asked me to drop by. "So Mrs. Dayan . . ."

"Call me Ruth. Everyone does."

"Ruth, you said something about a secret."

"Yes, well you cannot tell *that* story," she said raising her voice slightly and smacking her lips, "if you don't have some Levantine spice inside you. A chili pepper or two. You just can't. I've given other writers a crack at it and they failed."

Which seemed like a challenge. "Hmmm. What's the nature of the story?" But before saying any more, Ruth assured me she'd already "checked me out. You're a ghostwriter, right?"

I knew a thing or two about haunting other people's lives, I replied. "Does this secret of yours have something to do with General Dayan?" Was she going to tell me he was still alive, living under a pseudonym in the jungles of South America?

"Oh, him," she uttered under her breath and raised her eyes to the photograph of her poetry-reading lover on the wall. "No, no, no. Everyone already knows his story. I have . . . let's say, a different yarn for you." At this point Ruth came out with one of her phrases that tend to pop up innumerable times in the course of any conversation with her. It was "To cut a long story short," a sure sign that an elaborate tale was to follow.

Ruth pulled out a pack of discount Israeli cigarettes, tapped it until one emerged, and offered me the pack. No thanks, I told her. She lit up and inhaled deeply. "The book I want you to write has been cooking on the back burner for years. With the clock ticking. . . . Do you have any idea how old I am? Ha, talk about living on borrowed time!

"Here, I want to show you something." In front of her, next to a knitting basket, was a large square object covered by a camel hair rug similar to ones Muslims kneel on during the call to prayer. Reaching down, she pulled away the rug: Abracadabra, this is my life! It was a box brimming over with cassette tapes. She went on to explain how for years she had been recording story after story, hundreds of hours worth. *If there was a secret buried somewhere in those tapes*, I thought to myself as she picked them out of the box one by one and piled them on her lap, *it would take an eternity to find*.

While she was fishing through the box, the phone rang and I heard Ruth pipe up, "Oh Raymonda, yes. He's here. Let's talk after he leaves."

The only Raymonda I'd ever heard of was Raymonda Tawil, a militant journalist famous in the 1970s and '80s for using a tape recorder she dubbed her "Kalashnikov" to interview ex-prisoners, grieving mothers, and dissident Israeli officers. (One can imagine Vanessa Redgrave or Jane Fonda playing her part in a movie.) In her glory days she was the most prominent—and hands down sexiest—feminist among the militants, a woman whose intellectual, erotic, rebellious sparks not only attracted people but got others building bombs—she was eventually run out of the West Bank when someone, either an Israeli or a Palestinian, attached a bomb under her Opel sedan. This was before her daughter Suha married the Palestinian leader Yasser Arafat, a man well over twice her age and considered by most Israelis to be a bloodthirsty killer, the Palestinian version of Hitler. But why in hell would the first wife of Dayan be talking to dead Arafat's mother-in-law?

Ruth wanted to inventory the tapes but I was more interested in talking about Raymonda, if indeed we were talking about the same woman. "Raymonda Tawil, was that SHE?"

One of Ruth's quirks is the way she screws open her eyes when she's about to come out with a bombshell. Yes, she nodded, adding that their friendship was the best "secret" in the box, a "dangerous one," too. She turned her attention back to the box and, without looking up, said, "You have to promise not to breathe a word about this to anyone. She tells me she's on some sort of mission." Ruth hesitated, looked up, swiveled her head in my direction, and swept her eyes around the living room, as if she was afraid of snooping ears. "Just don't ask me what it is." She made it sound as if Tawil was on a search for the Holy Grail.

"A mission?"

"Yes, that's right. A mission. She's always on some sort of crusade. She's a dyed-in-the-wool feminist. I have an email."

Ruth read it out loud: "Whatever writer you choose will have to have the patience to go deep in the complicated, perplexing Middle East conflict . . . no, even more. We need someone to dig into the souls of two enemies."

"That's from Raymonda? What does she mean by 'we need'?"

"We've been friends for forty years. She's a very special lady."

"The email says you're enemies."

"We are. We love each other. Enemies can be friends and friends can be enemies in this country."

I was still trying to wrap my mind around her relationship with a "dyed-in-the-wool feminist" and mother-in-law of the Palestinian answer to the one-eyed Moshe, with rumpled combat fatigues and a keffiyeh instead of an eye-patch, when Ruth began talking about the book she wanted me to write. She wanted me, preferably as her ghostwriter "but that's up to you," to dig through her tapes and come up with a book, a book that somehow also featured Raymonda's "mission," whatever it was, and their shared belief that Jews and Arabs can live together without borders and walls and suicide belts and "all that nonsense." Which was the last thing I expected to hear from the widow of the great warrior. "My story . . . our story has plenty of drama, and if you look hard enough," she said kicking the box, "you'll find a murder mystery or two." With that, she crushed her cigarette into an ashtray and looked me over from head to toe as if sizing me up.

"Why?" I asked, meaning "why me?" For half an hour Ruth sang the praises of the various characters she has known in her life, from Ben-Gurion to Leonard Bernstein and Eleanor Roosevelt. According to her, she simply stumbled by chance into the lives of the most extraordinary characters of the twentieth century. The thought never occurred to her that she, too, was a member of this special club.

"And Raymonda?"

You'd think she was talking about Joan of Arc or Gloria Steinem. "You know the magician . . . what the hell's his name . . . David Copperfield? That's what she's like. My God, with her tongue she can go through walls and cut through stone. The *New York Times* . . . or the *Washington Post*, one of the two once printed up a caricature of her as a tigress. 'The lioness came out of the cage.' She was the first Palestinian to talk to us Israelis, to understand us and not let her pain get in the way. Raymonda's the real star of our friendship. I'm just her sidekick, her Sancho Panza," she said with a smile.

Sancho Panza? This would turn Raymonda into a Don Quixote. Now that's a story, I mused: Yasser's mother-in-law on her noble steed swooping down on windmills with the general's widow, on her mule, struggling to keep up.

"Oh, here comes lunch."

Ethel arrived from the kitchen carrying a platter of food. "I hope you're hungry," Ruth said, lighting up another cigarette and blowing out a perfect blue halo of a smoke ring. As she would every time I visited her over the coming years, she wanted to feed me. With each successive trip Ethel piled the dining table with typical Ashkenazi fare with a heretical twist. There was chicken soup with matzo balls, a small plate of chopped liver, some boiled potatoes, and a pork chop smothered in crushed black pepper.

We ate on TV trays so Ruth could continue pawing through the box of tapes while regaling me with highlights of her friendship with Raymonda — how they met in Nablus after the Six Day War; the time Raymonda and Yael, who already knew Arafat, introduced her to the Palestinian leader, and he kissed her three times, right cheek, left cheek, right cheek. "Yasser was so excited, you just can't imagine." What I gleaned from her other stories was that she and Raymonda have a lot in common. "Like two peas in a pod," despite the more than twenty years age difference and that Raymonda wrote about being enemies in the email even though they love one another.

"Time is of the essence. And with these bastards"—I assumed she was talking about right-wing Israeli settlers and Hamas thugs—"driving our two peoples into this killing frenzy, we don't have a moment to lose." She stamped her bare foot on the prayer rug. Ruth, a live wire of energy, was effervescent.

Ruth spent much of her childhood in Imperial London and still prefers reading English to Hebrew. In her library in the back of the apartment, she started rooting through the shelves looking for materials that might help me understand the sort of writing project she had in mind, all the while pointing at books as if they were people standing before us in flesh and blood: she came out with personal anecdotes about Jean Paul Sartre, Simone de Beauvoir, Jackie Kennedy, Yitzhak Rabin, and Albert Schweitzer. "Oh, look at this one." She held up to the light of the lamp the novella *Return to Haifa* by the Palestinian writer Ghassan Kanafani. "I never met him because . . . well, we blew him up."[1]

"You have to try to think of things from their perspective," she was saying, her hands grasping for books. "It wasn't easy for Arabs like Raymonda. To lose everything."

Her eyes were suddenly red. I approached her to give her a peck on the cheek when she set the books on a desk and asked me to follow her to her bedroom. She sat on her bed with stacks of materials and newspaper clippings spread out like tarot cards. "Come here," she commanded, patting the quilt with her hand. "Don't worry—I won't vamp you." To write her book I would have to go through her letters, extracting the gems, she explained. "Who knows? Maybe my kids will chuck the stuff out when I'm dead." I took a deep breath: a dedicated team of researchers would need a year to plow through those letters, mostly in Hebrew, and cherry pick materials from the mountain of cassette tapes.

Ruth held up a fistful of love letters from nineteen-year-old Moshe to her as a love-struck teenager of seventeen. Suddenly she was beaming as she read out some of the letters. "Just listen to this one. I think I know what you think about Moshe. Some sort of John Wayne character, a cowboy with his six-shooter gunning down the natives." Well, think again. "Moshe was a farmer at heart. How else could he have written this?" It was a letter about grafting new shoots in an orchard: "'I remember every one,'" she read from the letter, "'when it was done and when it will blossom, and I feel toward each like a father to a son.'"

"Now isn't that lovely?"

I headed back to Jerusalem and spent most of the night and the next two days reading and taking notes and doing some online research: I learned, for instance, that the Ugandan dictator Idi Amin used to get visitations from God, each time at 3 a.m. sharp, prompting him to fire off telegrams to both Arafat and Dayan. And the Italian journalist and iconoclastic feminist Oriana Fallaci once depicted Arafat's dark sunglasses as a counterpoint to "his archenemy Moshe Dayan's eye-patch."

I ended up making innumerable trips down to Tel Aviv, and Ruth took me on frequent forays back to Nahalal where she and Moshe lived for the first years of marriage. She and I spent so much time together that my snickering friends likened my relationship with this extraordinary woman born the same year as my grandmother to something out of *Harold and Maude*.

I never became her ghostwriter; I was more of a shadow following the lives and friendship of two women who defy everything usually said about the Israeli-Palestinian conflict. Ruth and I carried on a separate line of communication, over email and Skype, with Raymonda. The first time the three of us spoke, they at once began discussing people I had never heard of. "Raymonda," I finally said, interrupting the flow of their stories. "Tell me about your mission. Ruth tells me . . ." I found myself groping for words. "She mentioned something about a mission."

Raymonda threw back her head and burst out in a cackle, blowing a kiss in Ruth's direction. "She's my mission."

"Ruth?"

"Somehow, yes. I'm hers, too, I suppose."

Part I
1917–1956: Of This Tormented Soil

1
"The Happiest Day of My Life"

For most of the family, friends, and guests gathered for the wedding held at the isolated farming village called Nahalal in the fall of 1935, the pair seemed badly mismatched: here was Ruth Schwarz, the daughter of university-educated Jerusalem lawyers, a girl raised with Victorian novels and dance and piano lessons, teaming up with Moshe Dayan, a twenty-year-old farmer, rough around the edges, who looked like a tough Bedouin warrior.

The novelist Arthur Koestler described the area around Nahalal in northern Palestine—a country Jews referred to as *Erez Yisrael*—as "desolate marshes cursed with all the Egyptian plagues." Ruth's parents Rachel and Tzvi, the only ones at the wedding to arrive in a private car, came up in their brand-new Morris "8" with wire wheels and a honeycomb grille.

Travel was arduous and risky in those days. Rachel navigated the car through the dusty paths that passed for roads. Another daughter, nine-year-old Reumah, sat in the back seat, goggle-eyed at the wild countryside. The other passenger was Prussian-born Arthur Ruppin, the head of the Jewish National Fund (JNF), wearing pince-nez glasses and a dark wool suit made by a Berlin tailor.

The only people who weren't surprised at Ruth's choice for a husband were members of the Bedouin el-Mazarib tribe. Many of them armed, they didn't notice the subtleties of class and social differences. For them, all of the Jews were strangers from a far-away world. Nor did they seem like the other conquerors that had been passing through Palestine for

3

centuries. The Jews came with spades, not guns. One of the tribe's young hotheads had recently clubbed Moshe over the head; and, by attending the ceremony, they wanted to show the "Jewish Bedouin" their respect for being strong enough to spring back so quickly from a nasty thrashing.

Under the wedding chuppah stood Ruth dressed like a milkmaid in an embroidered Romanian blouse and a peasant dress a friend had made from a bed sheet. (She had proudly turned down her parents' offer to buy her a proper wedding dress.) Moshe, with the purple knot on his head and a black eye, wore khaki pants, an open-necked shirt, and a sweat-stained cap. The bride and groom, like everyone else that day, were furiously swatting away flies and mosquitos.

The moment the rabbi, who had arrived in the back of an oxen cart from a nearby settlement, pronounced Ruth and Moshe man and wife, the el-Mazarib warriors fired off rounds of bullets into the air, and several musicians, sitting on their haunches, played darbukas. The Jewish guests, including stolid Dr. Ruppin in his beautifully tailored suit and tie, danced traditional Bedouin debkas. In the midst of the merrymaking, while everyone was still dancing and swaying with home-brewed grapefruit wine, Ruth slipped off to the stalls. "I don't think I've ever been as happy as I was at that moment," she would recall nearly eighty years later, "squatting next to the cow, holding its teats. Yes, it was the happiest day of my life."

Before the First World War, Ruth's family had joined a wave of idealists and dreamers from Eastern Europe, who traveled to poor, desiccated Palestine.

Ruth's maternal grandfather Boris came from the Russian village of Kishinev, ruled by a malevolent feudal lord who made a sport of unleashing ferocious dogs from his castle on his Jews. It was on Boris's front porch that the great Hebrew poet Hayyim Nahman Bialik wrote his dirge, "In the City of Slaughter," on the Kishinev pogrom, and what he perceived as a cowering Jewish weakness in the diaspora: "The heirs of Hasmoneans/ who lie in the privies and jakes and pigsties/with trembling knees."

Though Boris was European to the fingertips, he resolved to flee from this ungrateful continent with its "privies and jakes and pigsties." After finishing his studies in chemistry at the Sorbonne in the 1890s, where he attended Marie Curie's lectures, he moved to Palestine in 1903 and opened up a small business producing grease for the Ottoman Hajaz railroad.

Beautiful Rachel, his daughter, met Ruth's father Tzvi at the famed Herzliya high school-gymnasium—where what would become the military, political, and intellectual elite of the Jewish state sat in the same classrooms. In their free time, they were busy discussing how best to create a new society. Rachel and Tzvi, both sixteen-year-old rebels out to overturn social taboos and crusty power structures, committed the unheard of sin of moving in together. It was Rachel's idea, of course.

Ruth came along in 1917. Five years later, the young family headed to London because Rachel and Tzvi enrolled at the London School of Economics, a hotbed of socialist thought, where George Bernard Shaw and Beatrice and Sidney Webb still haunted its corridors.

One of Ruth's strongest memories of Edwardian London was the wedding of the Duke of York in Westminster Abbey, the first public royal wedding in five centuries. Dressed in her Skinners' Girls School uniform and sucking on a purple lollipop, wide-eyed little Ruth sat on the pavement. "I was reading about kings and queens and royalty in my fairy-tale books, and now there they were: men in powdered wigs and ladies in long, flowing gowns, the bells, and horses, and the gilded royal carriages." Her socialist mother, naturally, didn't approve of such "sentimental rubbish," but her little girl went on dreaming of her own prince, with badges and a noble sword at his side.

A mere dozen years later, Ruth married a farmer who could gallop bareback on a horse like an Apache.

At the time of Moshe Dayan's birth in 1915, his parents Shmuel and Dvora lived on the collectivist kibbutz called Degania, the "Wheat of God," close to the Sea of Galilee. As with the Schwarz family, matriarchal dominance characterized the Dayans. Shmuel, not able to endure the backbreaking demands of farming, got work with Dr. Ruppin at the Jewish National Fund whose mission was scouting for land to buy for new Jewish settlements. With her jet-black hair worn in a coronet and covered with a kerchief Russian-style, Dvora was the intellectual of the family: before arriving in Palestine, she studied statistics and sociology in Kiev and in 1910 made a pilgrimage to Tolstoy's estate at Yasnaya Polyana to touch the body of the dead saint. At Degania with her stout constitution, she also did most of the heavy work around the farm.

The family soon moved to a new agricultural commune after the JNF bought 20,000 acres from the Sursuks, a Lebanese Christian family who centuries earlier had gotten it from the Ottoman government. For generations the farmers from the Arab village of Ma'alul, just up the hill, had been working the land, never imagining it could change hands so easily. JNF agents, doing some crude philology, assumed the Arabic "Ma'alul" was a bastardized form of "Nahalal," the Israelite town Joshua had given to the Tribe of Zebulon. Shmuel Dayan and JNF men named the new settlement Nahalal.

Life was harsh in the malarial frontier country known as the Plain of Esdraelon or, in Hebrew, "Emek Israel." Dayan's son Moshe was named after the legendary redeemer who once upon a time led his people from Egyptian captivity; it was also the name of a local Jewish boy murdered by a Bedouin donkey thief. Moshe was one of the first children born on a kibbutz, the ur-kibbutznik, a Zionist Davy Crockett. One Israeli historian would label him the "first born of the sons of redemption." The weekly bath in the Dayan household was in a big copper tub, the water heated over a wood fire outside, and each member took turns in the bathing.

Moshe barely attended school because he was too busy farming. His skin turned dark in the sun while planting, reaping and riding the wagon up the hill to Ma'alul to deliver wheat to the only mill in the region.

Ruth and Moshe's courtship was brief: they met during a summer camp Ruth attended in Nahalal in 1934. Back home in Jerusalem, she couldn't get the handsome Moshe out of her mind—the "first born of the sons of redemption" was the ultimate catch. A year later, she returned to Nahalal for good with a trunk filled with clothes and books. While taking a few walks around a eucalyptus forest, the two young lovers carved their names on a tree—"M. + R." That was the extent of their courtship.

Marrying Ruth and joining the Schwarz household offered Moshe some immediate dividends. While he was prepared to join a work team in the swamps that was, he confessed to his bride, a "real paradise of malaria and tuberculosis," he openly envied her middle-class family in Jerusalem and the perks of city life. Even more enticing was her access to power. The Schwarzes were a lot better connected than the Dayans. Rachel and Tzvi were high school schoolmates with top members of the Zionist leadership in the country. They were also close to the founders of the Haganah, the underground Jewish army.

Rachel Schwarz might have been a socialist, but she couldn't imagine her daughter living in a leaking shack and sharing her life with a penniless and uneducated country bumpkin. She spoke with Harold Laski, the Marxist economist whom she knew from her time at the London School of Economics, and with Chaim Weizmann, the president of the Zionist movement. Laski and Weizmann in turn pulled strings with Cambridge University to offer Moshe a spot. Ruth and Moshe took a fourth-class passage on the SS *Mariette Pasha*, packing a few threadbare clothes into a Bedouin rug of camel hair instead of the proper leather suitcase offered by Ruth's parents. They made a rather "lunatic pair," Ruth recalled, with their grubby sandals and decidedly egalitarian attitudes.

The let's-rough-it attitude only went so far. Rachel and Tzvi subsidized them with regular sums of money, and their upper crust friends helped find them a place to stay. Moshe first had to learn English properly. The two pedaled around the city on old bicycles, with Ruth helping him improve his English.

Moshe hated London, despised the damp climate, and it offended his Bedouin sense of male honor to be dependent on a mere girl to communicate with people he wanted nothing to do with, anyway. His attention was soon back on Palestine, a country suddenly aflame with civil war.

2

The Syrian Prince

Months after the Schwarz-Dayan wedding, in April 1936, at his Montfort Castle on the other side of the Esdraelon Valley from Nahalal, Habib Hawa threw a glittering three-day wedding extravaganza for his sister-in-law. The English called Habib the "Syrian Prince" because of his poise and sense of entitlement, and the fact he lived in a Crusader fortress.

Habib was raised in a wonderful jumble of worlds: on top of the pyramid stood the Ottoman governor and his retinue of officers and belly dancers, there were the patriarchs in Jerusalem, Latin and Greek with their icons and archaic rivalries; next came families like his headed by men traveling back and forth to Alexandria, Damascus, and Beirut on the new railway line, men who carried on long conversations about a better future over the glowing red embers of a nargilla while sipping Lebanese wine. These aristocratic families were served by a bevy of butlers and maids and mistresses. On the bottom of the social rung were peasants sweating in the fields. Bedouins with long flowing desert robes occasionally led their camels through the countryside. Automobiles began to appear on the roads when Habib was a young boy.

Habib was a product of the Ottomans, if only because its decrepitude determined much of his early life.

His grandfather was the governor of Aleppo and his father the honorary British consul. Habib studied at the elite Jesuit St. Joseph School in Lebanon and then Alexandria—when he returned to Palestine on visits, he took a private train. In the Galilee, his family owned 40,000 acres around the family's Montfort Castle, and members of a Druze clan took care of the tobacco fields, the pork farm, and the stables of Arabian horses.

Back in Alexandria he lived the life of a young dandy. He grew a fashionable toothbrush mustache and cavorted with his class peers and the demimondes of the city, lighting the ladies' Dunhill cigarettes using ten-pound notes.

Habib eventually headed off to study law at the Sorbonne and stood out with his olive-colored thin face, his tall and slender frame, his francophone polish and refinement. Following the British capture of Palestine in 1918, he returned to Acre to manage his family's far-flung and feudal string of properties and estates including seventeen villages. Habib, with his own ship for trading in wheat and other commodities, became the chief contractor of the British army in Palestine and Egypt.

Habib reminisced to his daughter Raymonda many years later, after becoming a pauper with a bad limp from an Israeli bullet, how since the days of Richard the Lionheart the country hadn't seen such a grand wedding feast. "I was like King Sarastro in the *Magic Flute!*" There were belly dancers, French chefs, costumes for a ball, a full orchestra brought in from Cairo, and over a hundred guests, including top British officers and Arab notables with herringbone jackets and monographed handkerchiefs.

Raymonda's mother, Habib's wife and the sister of the bride, was the only one at the castle privy to his secret plan. With the brandies and finest whiskeys flowing, he chose the perfect moment to launch a rebellion he hoped would frustrate, once and for all, the Zionist designs on his country and his honor. Under the veneer of the pleasure-seeking grandee, freewheeling, fun-loving Habib was an Arab nationalist with a strong awareness of a thousand years of family history in Palestine, and someone who regarded British rule as a mere stopgap before Arabs could become the masters of their own fate.

The English brought modern administration, indoor plumbing, the rule of law, and helped Arabs build a modern society, and for that he was grateful. What he resolutely opposed was the Zionist plan to erect a tractor-drive modern Jewish state in Palestine, and to do so with British backing.

To get to the castle in their fleet of Fords, Citroëns, Mercedes, and even a few Rolls-Royces, guests traveled along a bumpy country road. Most of the invitees must have been delighted to attend the three-day party because it felt like reentering the romance of the Crusader period. Nowhere in Palestine was there such pomp, nowhere was the food so sumptuous, nowhere the atmosphere more glittering. The only frown in the otherwise perfectly choreographed ceremony was on the face of Habib's sister Sylvie. It had been four years since her younger brother had "dishonored" the family by marrying "the wild villager," and she had yet to forgive him.

The "wild villager," named Christmas and the sister of the bride, wore a Coco Chanel dress, rayon stockings, and a string of pearls. Habib was still very much in love with his wife's lithe beauty, feisty character, and American-bred independence: Christmas came from a family in the Christian village of Kfar Yassif close to Haifa, and was raised in New York. She had decisively New York attitudes about gender, democracy, equality, and the ludicrousness of class snobbery. She would be the source of her daughter's feminism. She and Habib's sister Sylvie avoided one another. In a society in which women were expected to "keep among themselves," Christmas smoked cigarettes with the officers and businessmen, talked politics with some of the invited political leaders, and held her own during debates about the brewing conflict with the Zionists.

On the second day of the wedding party, following yet another bacchanal feast, and after Habib had retired to his chamber for a nap, Christmas saw the signal from the valley. She roused her husband and told him the guerrillas were ready to strike.

Habib dressed in his tuxedo and tails, stopped the thirty-piece orchestra, and asked the British officers to meet the guerrilla leaders he now summoned up from his stables. The meeting was brief and cordial. Without giving away details of precise time and place, Habib let the officers know there would be trouble that evening. The two sides shook hands, the officers left the wedding, and the fighting broke out later that night. Nahalal, the biggest settlement in the north of the country, was the first target. The Plain of Esdraelon has been the pathway of warriors since the Battle of Megiddo in the fifteenth century BCE. There the Greeks battled the Maccabees, and the Jewish armies defied the Romans; Mongols, Mamluks, Salah al-Din, and Allenby all seized the valley because of its immense strategic worth. It was the most natural place for the rebels to begin their attacks.

That night guerrillas shot dead the gardener who had taught Moshe how to graft fruit trees.

3
Night Squad

Meanwhile, in London, Ruth dragged Moshe to the Old Vic Theatre to see Shakespeare's *Julius Caesar*; not understanding a word, he left at intermission. Ruth, on the other hand, sat enraptured at strong, noble, beautiful Julius Caesar, played by John Glenn. She cycled home, the line burning in her ears: "The fault, dear Brutus, is not in our stars, but in ourselves."

The fact that Moshe's parents had named him after a victim of Bedouin violence was a constant reminder that the Jews had but a tenuous hold on their ancient land. Though for Arab nationalists the Zionist appetite for land was a casus belli, the leaders of the Yishuv had no choice other than rapid expansion. With the Nazis in power in Germany, they had to bring as many Jews in from Europe as possible, and this required buying land for the growing population. Arthur Ruppin, alarmed by events in his native Germany, had what he described as a "congenial" chat with the chief Nazi race theorist, the so-called "race pope" Dr. Hans F. K. Günther, a man obsessed with blond hair and long Aryan foreheads. Jews weren't inferior to "Aryans," Dr. Günther assured him; they just had no place in Germany. Ruppin and the Zionist leadership worked hard to transport shiploads of threatened Jews to Palestine.

For Moshe, the need for the Zionists to break the will of the Arab opposition was greatly reinforced by the first reports of the raid on Nahalal. With his teacher killed, and family and friends under attack, being marooned in London threw him into a fury. He began snapping at Ruth over trifles; everything was wrong, the weather, the food, the people, and English language; if she didn't share his feelings about Erez Yisrael, there had to be something wrong with her, too.

Ruth cabled home an SOS, and Ruth's parents immediately sent money for the tickets, and the two were off.

Habib Hawi continued supporting the nationalists as the rebellion spread out and turned more deadly. He moderated his backing with prudence after a British district commissioner was assassinated in the Galilee and the British overreacted by dispatching a group of Arab notables into exile. The leadership of the rebellion shifted away from men such as Habib, university-educated gentlemen, to armed gangs and unlettered men fighting in the name of Islam.

As part of a system of defense against raids, Moshe joined a group from Nahalal to set up a settlement in the hills just above Nahalal, the site mentioned in the Bible. Moshe, Ruth, and their friends lived in the makeshift fortress, continuing working on their farms, hiring themselves out as guards, or planting JNF pine seedlings to transform treeless grazing lands into the King George V Forest.

Ruth and Moshe got a room in a primitive two-room shack with a crude wooden planked floor. Moshe banged together a table and bed from oak logs. The outhouse was located out back, in the direction of a reeking cowshed.

Insurgents took shots at the hut after sundown. Moshe wasn't around much. He had received orders from the Haganah to join the Jewish Auxiliary Force, a British special police unit preventing guerrillas from puncturing holes in an oil pipe and lighting the oil on fire. By the spring of 1937, as commander of a small group, Moshe wore a woolen Turkish tarbush and khakis with sergeant's stripes.

Once again, Ruth's elite background helped Moshe, a mere rural cop, rise above his village origins. Her first teenage boyfriend Zvi, a fellow Jerusalemite, was now a rising star in the Haganah, and with his sense of purpose and ambition, his education in languages and military strategy, and his charisma, many considered Zvi destined to lead the underground organization. One day in 1937 he pulled up to the Dayan hut behind the wheel of a Studebaker loaded down with heavy guns and grenades. In the passenger seat was Orde Charles Wingate. Wingate, wearing a safari hat, was the British army's top man in counter-insurgency operations and someone Moshe would come to consider a genius, the "Lawrence of Judaea."

Wingate, a Scotsman and member of the Plymouth Brethren sect, was also a crackpot noted for tics such as wearing an alarm clock around his wrist and, in a threadbare Palm Beach suit or preferably naked, belting out his favorite Old Testament passages. Winston Churchill's personal physician considered him fit for a lunatic asylum.

"Ruthie," Zvi called from outside the hut. The familiar voice made her knees wobble, and she struggled to catch her breath, as if the oxygen had been suddenly sucked from the room.

She opened the door and led Zvi and the British officer into the house. Was it a mistake not to stay with the gangly Zvi with his china-blue eyes, who wrote her love letters and even a short book written by hand into a school notepad titled "Diary of a Bloated Fool"? Wasn't Zvi brimming over with life, the opposite of brooding, melancholy Moshe? Wasn't he the only one who ever truly loved her? Sure, she and Moshe took trips up to the ruins of a nearby Crusader castle to make love. But Moshe was more businesslike than romantic, his mind never fully turned from the fighting down in the valley.

Zvi gave Ruth an awkward peck on the cheek, and from his furtive stares she sensed his undiminished love. But Zvi wasn't there to rekindle a teenage flame. He drove to Nahalal to recruit Moshe into Wingate's Special Night Squad. Moshe came in from the field behind the hut, greeted the two men, and suggested they step outside to talk. He wasn't certain he could trust Wingate, and instructed Ruth to rifle through his knapsack in search of anything suspicious while the men discussed military affairs.

In the months that followed, Ruth saw less and less of Moshe, as he developed a student-guru relationship with the strange Scotsman. Before carrying out an operation, Wingate recited passages from the Book of Joshua referring to particular tracts of territory, and like a football coach he pepped up his warriors with talks of "You are sons of the Maccabees, the first soldiers of the Jewish army." Following each successful ambush, he stripped naked, munched his raw onions, and buried himself again in the King James Bible.

Moshe picked up from Wingate a fondness for the ancient Israelites. He was especially impressed with Joshua's—and Wingate's—"iron will" and his desire to "carry the fight to the enemy." One letter to Ruth recounts a guerrilla action against eighty Arab insurgents with Wingate at the front, his stout pistol in hand and his bible in his knapsack, and Moshe and seven of his men trailing behind.

Arabs, naturally, regarded the Scotsman and his counter-insurgency methods as criminal. Wingate ordered his commandos to burn down or blow up over one hundred houses in Kfar Yassif, Christmas's ancestral village.

4
The "Cripple"

Ruth was hoping that the birth of their first child in 1939 would keep her man around the hut more, and the name they gave their daughter must have put a wide smile on Wingate's face: "Yael" is the fearless woman in the Bible who dispatched her pagan foe with a tent peg.

But Ruth saw Moshe even less because Mandate authorities, while shooting and bombing Arabs into submission and chasing the mufti out of Jerusalem, had at last admitted that the policy of creating a Jewish homeland against the will of the majority of the population was a lot more trouble than it was worth, especially with war on its way in Europe. The new policy, introduced in 1939 and known as the White Paper, throttled Jewish immigration, severely limited land purchasing, and foresaw a transitional period of ten years during which the British would maintain control, followed by elections for an independent national parliament. The math was obvious: free elections meant Arab domination and the end of the Zionist dream. Habib and his friends clinked glasses of brandy, toasting diplomatic victory.

Ben-Gurion, vowing to fight the White Paper, ordered the Haganah to set up clandestine arms factories and accelerate the pace of illegal immigration of Jews fleeing Nazism. The operation was so clandestine that all Ruth knew was that her rail-thin twenty-four-year-old prince was never around to help change the diapers.

She was jealous of the other women her age who were rushing around in jeeps and learning how to fight. "When you are on a moshav, the birth

16

of a new calf seems the center of the world." Sick of all the neglect, she toyed with the idea of taking the baby and fleeing back to her parent's home in Jerusalem. She changed her mind in October 1939, when Buggy, their boxer bitch, showed up at the shack with a note from Moshe tied to its collar: "Ruth, we have been arrested and taken to Acre . . . I hope it will end well. Kisses to you and Yael."

A month after the Nazi invasion of Poland, British police caught Moshe and a group of others with illegal arms. They were sentenced to ten years of hard labor in the old Ottoman fortress in Acre, a prison populated by rapists, killers, pimps, and highwaymen.

Ruth's indefatigable and selfless devotion was on full display. She turned over every stone to get her man out of prison, including putting on her old cotton wedding dress and trooping over to the British command headquarters at the King David Hotel and pleading his case before the commanding office, a "very nice old gentleman" fated to die in a terror attack by the Jewish group the Irgun. She went as far as writing to King George VI, inspired by childhood storybooks where the hero always has to prostrate himself before his Majesty. Nothing helped.

Over the coming eighteen months Ruth took Yael and traveled from the farm to visit Moshe, his head shaven and wearing a chain-gang uniform without buttons. The English prison warden, a mean-spirited, one-legged man named Captain Grant, wouldn't let them get close enough to touch. There was a long coil of barbed wire, and she held Yael over her head so Moshe could see them. A guard once threatened to shoot at Yael when she tried to crawl through the wire.

Moshe only got to touch Yael once during his time in prison. Ruth's old flame Zvi drove her and Yael to Acre in a 1938 Ford convertible with a heart-shaped grille and fender catwalks. A Sudanese policeman, a physical giant of a man, took pity and lifted up the daughter over to him. For the first time in Ruth's life she noticed tears in Moshe's eyes—he still had both.

Ruth's letters to Moshe are lost; his replies, smuggled out by Jewish workers, survive. "My Ruth," one letter goes, "if only I could pass on to you one thousandth of the love I feel for you both every night . . ." In another, he mused that if freed he could be a truck driver, a security guard, a construction worker, or return to the farm so long as he could have a quiet life with her and Yael. "The day will come and, very soon, you'll be knitting, and I'll be reading and the darling will be crawling on the rug."

After four months in the fortress, Moshe and his fellow Haganah men were moved to a camp and allowed to work in the fields to grow their own food. Conditions improved, as did Ruth's access to Moshe. She was able to bring him things from the farm, including O. Henry's "The Cop and the Anthem" about a hobo in New York by the name of Soapy. The two even managed to see one another alone, in the middle of a field sitting on a pile of crunching and crackling eucalyptus leaves. Mosquitos swarmed where they kissed for the first time in months.

Ruth took a first-aid course in Haifa, and was volunteering in Tel Aviv when Hitler's ally Mussolini ordered his airforce to bomb the city's seaport in July 1940. "Bodies were smashed to a pulp," she wrote to Moshe in one of the letters Zvi airdropped from his Piper Cub plane. "I realized what it is to see small children like Yael without legs or hands or faces." A bombing raid pulverized the house next door to where Ruth and Yael were staying, and Yael was missing. She turned up hours later with torn clothes and shrapnel wounds on her leg.

Dayan's letters to her, written on toilet paper and smuggled from the fortress, continued giving her a glimpse into his life. There is still the occasional confession of longing and love, but politics and the national struggle are dominant. One letter tells her about his wishes of becoming a leader of a determined group of fighters who, within a decade, would emerge as the underdog victors over both the British Empire and the Arabs. "You cannot imagine how much people here love and respect me. Nothing like this has ever happened to me in any company I have been in."

In February 1941, Rommel's armies were threatening Egypt and Palestine, and the British gave Dayan an early release from prison. Ruth thought the family would live happily ever after; with Moshe's days in the underground over, he could now read to little Yael on the rug.[2]

At first Moshe acted as if he were home for good. He ate ample helpings of Ruth's good cooking, the two made love, they talked about spring planting, they laughed. What Ruth didn't know was that the British released him because they badly needed manpower. Rommel's advances in North Africa and the presence of Vichy forces across the border in Lebanon made a new separation inevitable.

Zvi and members of the Haganah's striking force turned up once again at the front door of the Dayan shack with a new assignment for Moshe: it was to take part in a secret operation in Vichy-held territory in Lebanon. Zvi explained to Moshe that the Jewish forces were to join a group of Australians in seizing roads and bridges. The operation began in the northern Galilee. Ruth drove with Moshe to the Lebanese border, and from there the men packed their ammo and headed into French territory. All went as planned until Moshe, in what would become his signature daredevilry, rushed a police post, tossed a hand grenade to take out a machine gunner, and went to survey the landscape for enemy troops. A bullet, fired by a Senegalese sniper, pierced the lens of his binoculars, scattered glass and metal into his right eye cavity, and tore out the side of his face.

It took many hours to evacuate the half-dead Moshe back across the border and drive him to a hospital in Haifa. He never uttered a whimper; he clenched his teeth and endured the pain. Doctors didn't try saving the right eye because there was no eye to save; they couldn't even give him a glass eye due to the absence of bone. The best they could do was to scrape away the burnt tissue, shrapnel, and bone fragments, and hope he wouldn't die of infection. What the sniper's bullet left him with was a lifelong case of severe and recurrent pain, paralyzing headaches and insomnia. Ruth includes a personality disorder to his list of troubles.

She dedicated herself to him and felt strangely content, because at least he was home—no more fighting, no more secret mission, half blind but otherwise intact with two strong arms; and even a man missing one eye could be a fine farmer. For Moshe, his life was over; he felt most alive leading men into battle. What good was an expert in Wingate's counter-insurgency warfare with much of his field of vision cut off? How could such a man lead commandos into battle? He now considered himself useless, washed up.

The shooting had a deleterious effect on his already anti-social leanings: Moshe became even more of a loner, an aloof laconic man who communicated with nods and gestures more than words. Back on the farm, when he heard Ruth was pregnant again, his reaction turned "violent" because it was too late for an abortion. How was a "cripple" supposed to support yet another mouth? The remonstrations were of no use. Their first son, Ehud or "Udi," the "strong warrior" from the Bible, came along in January 1942.

Oddly, Ruth regards the war years as the happiest they ever spent together. Despite the interminable hardships of the place, the small family set down roots, each year working the fields from brown to luminous green. Ruth still had just one desire, that they stay wedded to the wholesomeness of the farm, their lives enriched by the transcendent feeling of sowing and reaping.

She relished sloshing through mud up to her ankles, planting crops, raising Yael and Udi, milking cows, and scooping up manure so that Moshe could plow it back into a garden where he was experimenting with strains of Japanese cauliflower. She loved the haystacks and goats, the boxer bitch Buggy, a new mule nicknamed "Lord," and trips into the hills where she and her farmer husband made love. Living in threadbare but blissful poverty, she and Moshe had their third child. A milk truck drove her to the local hospital for the delivery of their son they named Assaf or "Assi," the leader of King David's choir.

5

A Christmas Tale

A s for Raymonda, she says she was born under an evil omen. The problem began when Habib insisted on naming her after the heroine of Alexander Glazunov's ballet with its hints of Moorish Spain, noble Crusaders, and villainous Saracen knights. He wanted his only daughter to be another Anna Pavlova, his favorite ballerina.

Like many people among his elevated social class, Habib liked to consult the famous Polish-Jewish clairvoyant Wolf Messing: back in Europe both Einstein and Freud tested his powers. The war had just broken out in Europe, and Habib needed advice on investments. In passing, he mentioned to the soothsayer that his wife had just given birth to a girl, and her name was going to be Raymonda.

"Oh, you mustn't use that name!"

"Why not! It has a delightful ring to it." He was tapping his tasseled Italian shoes, and his hands, with diamond rings on his fingers, made a dismissive gesture. He was incredulous that the psychic should so respond to a tale that ends with a feast and dancing at a castle to celebrate the marriage of two lovers. Habib was entranced by ballet and the glittering, sumptuous life of a vanquished era of nobility.

Wolf Messing saw something else. "If you name your daughter Raymonda, catastrophe after catastrophe will befall on you. Blood and killing, divorce, and hatred will never end."

"Nonsense!" said Habib.

21

Raymonda was too young to have much more than dim memories of the war years or the Allied victory celebration in 1945. She naturally knew nothing about the way news of Nazi extermination camps and the world's inability or unwillingness to stop the genocide generated a rage and frustration among Jews that would burn, and keep burning, all the way into Raymonda's clammy cell in the Moskobiya Prison many decades later. Zionist groups ran clandestine factories churning out bombs and bullets in anticipation for the armed struggle for a Jewish state. An international arms operation, with donations to the Blue Boxes spread throughout the Jewish diaspora, smuggled in Lancaster submachine guns and bazookas.

Her first recollections are of the family villa in Acre, where as a five-year-old she loved listening to the waves just below her window beating rhythmically against the walls of the twenty-room mansion. In the garden grew a gigantic cedar whose shadows created dappled, dancing patterns on her clothes and across her face. She wandered from room to room and stared with enchantment at the painted ceiling, the grand piano from Leipzig, the volumes of books bound in satiny Morocco leather lining shelves in her father's library, the oil paintings, Habib's chestnut brown box of cigars.

Across the bay in Haifa, Raymonda could see the warships of the British Royal Navy sending up tall plumes of curling smoke. In the narrow alleys of Acre were solemn religious men with robes and beards and funny-shaped hats—Sheiks, Roman and Greek Orthodox priests, Baha'i, and rabbis. She can still describe with minute detail the iron gate to the church that was sea-blue, chipped and rusting, and decorated with two peacocks, one painted black and the other white; above the gate were interlocking iron-wrought hearts welded together to form a triangle topped with a cross. She remembers the minarets' pencil-shaped tops, too; and the carved, latticed mashrabiya balconies jutting out from the stone walls—because of their tight-fitting wooden slats, pious women could peer out into the street but no one on the street below could catch a peek of them within.

It was a city with the twisting, narrow, crowded aesthetic of the Levant with tall, swaying palms in gardens and church bells ringing out the Angelus.

Her fairy-tale world was about to end.

During the first postwar years Habib continued to travel overseas on business, to Marseille and Cairo. Closer to home he took his motorcar to Haifa and its salons and saloons, leaving Christmas to raise Raymonda and, on trips back to the castle, manage the army of servants and the farmers tending the tobacco fields and pig farm.

Christmas with her bobbed hair gained fame throughout the Galilee for her liberated ways. She loved taking off her Coco Chanel dress, putting on riding britches, slipping a silver sword into a smooth hide sheath and, accompanied by Nubians, riding her stallion through the countryside. That said, as a liberated American woman, Christmas saw Habib's aristocratic world as silly vestiges from the long vanquished world of knights and dueling pistols and the inherited system of privileges, titles, rank, and family name.

The feudal pretensions became even more evident after Habib, drinking heavily at the parties in the salons of Haifa, began sinking into debt. As if the boozing, womanizing, and financial bungling were not enough, his patriarchal need to control, and his unwillingness to stomach his wife's independence, worked like a torpedo that blasted a hole in their marriage.

To shield her from the quarrels, Habib drove Raymonda in his shiny Oldsmobile to his sister Sylvie's mansion on King George Street in Haifa, facing the sea near the port. Sylvie, married to one of the wealthiest tycoons in the city and a woman who considered speaking any languages other than French considerably beneath her dignity, employed two cooks, a valet, and a chauffeur for her silver-gray Daimler. On the baby grand piano in her living room, made of polished mahogany, she played the Chopin she learned at the prestigious girls school Notre Dame de Nazareth on Mount Carmel.

Habib and Christmas divorced in 1947, just as the country plunged back into internecine conflict. It was too much for Christmas: she had come to Palestine from America, a country with civil rights and a degree of equality for women, and here she was a feminist caught in the mentality of the harem. She rebelled by packing her bags and leaving him. She got a job and rented a small apartment in Haifa.

It was considered so scandalous that Habib ripped Raymonda from his estranged wife's arms—she was kicking and screaming and flung her favorite doll to the floor—and whisked her off to a Nazareth convent run by French-speaking sisters from Lebanon and Malta. He instructed the nuns not to permit the mother to visit. Raymonda's two brothers George and Yussuf were sent to a boarding school in Jerusalem. It was only on weekends that Raymonda could return to Haifa to see her divorced parents.

Sylvie felt vindicated by her brother's marriage with a "villager," the half-wild American feminist. In collusion, the two siblings cooked up a story, telling Raymonda that her mother was dead but she shouldn't mourn because Christmas died a martyr's death: the dastardly Zionists blew her up in a terror attack. Raymonda cried and screamed and shook her little child's fist at God for snatching away her mother. Then one day, while standing on her aunt's terrace, she saw Christmas walking up the street from the railway station where she worked as a clerk. At that moment Raymonda believed God had heard her recriminations and, showing mercy, had raised her mother from the dead.

Christmas saw her daughter, opened the gate and ran up the stairs to the terrace. Raymonda leapt into her arms, and through eyes filled with tears of joy she saw Aunt Sylvie scowling down at them from the upstairs balcony.

6
Civil War

Throughout the war Ruth awaited word on the fate of Zvi. He had disappeared during a sea raid on the Lebanese coast. Word never came; Zvi vanished forever, swallowed into the waters off the Lebanese coast.

In December 1946, Ruth and her younger sister Reumah were in a Paris hospital run by nuns. A French surgeon mistakenly thought he could fit Moshe with a glass eye. While in Paris, Reumah met Ezer Weizman, a pilot who looked like a Hollywood war hero with his tight golden curls and crystalline blue eyes. During the war the RAF veteran gained notoriety for loop-the-loop aerial maneuvers and the long list of kills to his name. Hard drinking and backslapping jokes fit into his fighter pilot cockiness. He had flown into Paris on a Piper Cub en route to London to plot with other members of the Irgun the assassination of the British military commander in Palestine.

The notorious playboy in his faded RAF flight jacket wanted to take Reumah with him to London as he continued on his secret mission. She declined because Ruth, with Moshe in excruciating pain after the botched operation, talked her into heading off to a German castle to work with Jewish orphans from Theresienstadt and Bergen-Belson.

Ruth's hopes that Moshe would finally return to the hut on Nahalal, this time forever, never came through. The unfolding events produced a perfect pairing between his personal myopia and need for action. With the British Navy preventing hundreds of thousands of refugees in displaced persons camps from immigrating to Palestine, Ben-Gurion demanded a

Jewish state. There was no more enthusiastic backer than Moshe: The British had to leave, and he believed that in the ensuing battle with the local Arabs, Jews would surely prevail. Egypt, Transjordan, Lebanon and Syria threw down the wild card. Would the scrappy remnants of a people who had just been nearly exterminated find itself in a war with the wider Arab world? How could the Haganah fend off an attack by regular armies with large arsenals of planes and tanks?

Zionist terror against the British met with fierce reprisals. The British tried everything, from sending Irgun fighters to the gallows at the Acre fortress to presenting to both sides a flurry of proposals, resolutions, and expert opinions. But in the end, the bankrupt British Empire lost its will to root out and defeat an utterly determined and ruthless Jewish underground. Fighting victims of Nazism was also a hard policy to defend.

The British set a date: on May 15, 1948, they would go home. Still nominally in charge until then, the British tried to separate the Jews and Arabs with barbed wire.

The UN then voted in support of a partition plan in which Jews, with a third of the population, were to get over half the territory, including the fertile coastal strip. Arabs kept the cities of Jaffa, Tiberius, and Hebron, along with the stony Biblical heartland up in the hills of Judea and Samaria. Jerusalem, symbolically the biggest prize of all, was to remain internationalized.

Back on the farm, Ruth and her fellow farmers danced through the night in celebration of the UN vote; Ruth baked enough cookies for the entire village. Up in the Jewish neighborhoods in Haifa, with their large numbers of refugees from Nazi Europe, people honked horns and set off fireworks.

Habib and his friends listened anxiously to the reports on Radio Cairo. Everyone knew that the partition was a formula for civil war. How could politicians in New York, spouting the language of human rights, simply hand over large swaths of territory, including the Hawa family's lands, to European immigrants? How could the same governments that a couple of years earlier had failed to come to the rescue of Europe's Jews now turn around and "solve" the Jewish problem by ignoring the rights of Arabs? How could Jews who claimed to belong to the democratic West want to impose such an unjust scheme against the will of the Arab majority? But how could the Arabs of Palestine stand up to the world, not to mention the better organized, better armed, far more relentlessly driven Zionists?

Local Arabs vowed to fight, while Arab rulers, the kings, prime ministers, and generals of Syria, Egypt, and Transjordan, promised to come to the rescue by forming the Arab Liberation Army. Leaders issued one pronouncement after the next that must have sounded to Jews like something out of a Nuremberg Party rally or from the lips of Haman the Agagite: Ruth describes the general fear of "Arab armies gathering on all fronts." Hebrew newspapers quoted over and over the Egyptian diplomat and secretary general of the Arab League, Azzam Pasha, in his gruesome prediction of "a war of extermination and a momentous massacre which will be spoken of like the Mongolian massacres and the Crusades." It would be a cakewalk, this war between Arabs, children of Muslim warriors, and a nation of greengrocers and owners of haberdasheries. The only point of dispute among Arab generals, in their starched and pressed military uniforms weighed down with honorary medals, was who would take credit for this glorious work of liberation? The Syrian president bragged to everyone about the secret weapon he had up his sleeve: a nuclear bomb fashioned by a golden-handed Damascus ironsmith.

With such delusional allies, Palestinian Arabs had little chance against a large and trained Jewish militia, along with hospitals, ambulances, and a communications network that gave even isolated outposts the sense of belonging to a broad, intelligent movement. The more avowedly terrorist organizations like the Irgun frequently worked hand in glove with the Haganah.[3]

In January 1948, a group of Haganah men blew up the luxurious Semiramis Hotel, owned by Habib's sister and located in the Arab neighborhood of Katamon, in Jerusalem. The Haganah communiqué spoke of the hotel as an "important meeting place of Arab gangs," making it sound like a dingy din of pirates and not the fancy hotel it was.[4] The Spanish consul was among the two dozen people killed in the blast.

With the Haganah still an illegal underground army, Moshe's actions were a closely held secret, and Ruth had no idea whether he was fighting, and if so, against whom and where. She had three children to protect, and in the evenings she heard the constant din of bullets raining down on Nahalal from the Syrian and Druze guerillas hiding out in the forests around the Arab village of Ma'alul. Syrian fighters shot Eli Ben-Zvi, the dreamy, poetic son of Israel's future second president Yitzhak Ben-Zvi. Ruth had been his scout guide years earlier; his fiancé Pnina lived next door in Nahalal. The wedding cake and cookies were all ready just as the news came of his death. "Pnina sat there holding her wedding gown, alternating between tears and hysterical laughter."

One funeral followed the next. To revenge a massacre near Jerusalem,[5] Arabs slaughtered the son of the Nahalal schoolmaster, a Tolstoyan pacifist, along with thirty-four other students at the Hebrew University. Snipers shot a poet and pianist named Itzhak, also a neighbor of Ruth's. To the mourners at the funeral she read a poem he left behind: "I would like to be/As the echo of the field's breathing,/As the play of light in the empty space/Winged with wings of song/ . . . like everlasting youth."

In March 1948 the local postman, riding a bicycle, delivered a special cable from her uncle to attend his son Yossi's wedding in Haifa. As a little girl Ruth used to go to the Zion movie theater to listen to her uncle play violin for silent movies. At least a dozen times, tapping her bare feet to her uncle's music, she stared up at Rudolf Valentino's dashing smile in *The Sheik*, admiring his kaffiyeh, moon-shaped sword, embroidered vest, camel-hair kaftan, bullet belt, and polished riding boots. The wedding coincided with Reumah's arrival by ship with hundreds of orphans from the German castle.

Just as Ruth was about to leave to Haifa for the wedding, news came that nineteen-year-old cousin Yossi had been knifed to death. He had gone to buy a shirt for the wedding. He caught an Arab taxi in the city, even though he was warned that the cab drivers weren't to be trusted. "No, that's ridiculous. I'm from Haifa, and I know the Arabs." His cocksureness ended him up in a public toilet, his body cut to pieces.

A week after Yossi's murder, Moshe's younger brother Zorik was shot by Druze fighters. Zorik was the most vivacious of the Dayans, a big, blond, handsome man filled with life and humor and love; Ruth felt like his mother or older sister. The body lay rotting in the field for three days, unapproachable because of Druze sharpshooters.

Moshe had to identify Zorik's body. Ruth, driving a car with jerry-rigged armored plates from Nahalal along winding, dangerous roads, met Moshe at a kibbutz near Haifa. Through binoculars, they looked out onto the field alive with red poppies and wild chrysanthemum, and saw Zorik's crumpled body. Zorik's son Uzi, the future architect of the Separation Wall, was just three months old.

Moshe drove his brother's decomposing remains back to his and Ruth's shack in Nahalal, where it was washed and prepared for burial. Ruth meanwhile continued on to the port of Haifa to greet Reumah and the four hundred orphans brought over from Germany. An armored bus picked up the children and distributed them to kibbutzim in the area.

7

Fall of Haifa

Moshe proved to be a tireless and fearless soldier, and his injury was hardly a handicap because, he later quipped, aiming through the scope of a rifle only required one eye. Fighting renewed him, and he was grateful. He had everything to gain—meaning, purpose, power—by rushing headlong into fresh battles. This freed him up to be utterly daring, to excel in the art of improvisation—Wingating it.

In early March 1948, two months before the British withdrew and the impossible partition was supposed to come into effect, Ben-Gurion summoned Moshe and eleven others to the Haganah's secret headquarters in Tel Aviv, a redbrick sock factory dubbed the "Red House," to advise him on the next phase of what the Israelis would call the War of Independence.

Ben-Gurion and his twelve disciples, poring over detailed maps and aerial photographs, discussed improving defense positions against invading armies from the neighboring Arab states. In practice, what they came up with required capturing the cities of Tiberias, Safed, Jaffa, Acre, and Haifa.[6]

A month after the Haganah meeting in the sock factory, Raymonda left the convent in Nazareth and traveled to Haifa to join Christmas. She arrived in the old city near the port just as Jewish forces surrounded the Arab quarters. Food and medicine were no longer getting in; prices skyrocketed; the poor faced starvation. Mortar shells rained down from the

Jewish neighborhoods up on Mount Carmel: Where were the heroic Arab defenders? Where were modern-day Salah al-Dins?

With fighting cutting off access to the Red Cross station where Christmas lived, Raymonda had no other choice but to go to Aunt Sylvie's mansion on King George Street. She wasn't there more than a couple of days when the fighting shifted, and Arab irregulars perched on the balcony of the aunt's house traded fire with the Haganah men on the other side of the street. A mortar attack destroyed the neighbor's mansion along with half of Sylvie's: Raymonda shudders when recalling the shock of the explosion, the sound of shattering stone and glass, the "devilish flames" licking at the white plaster, the "acrid smoke" billowing through the rooms.

The francophone aunt who drank her afternoon tea in Meissner cups snapped out orders for her children and Raymonda to grab whatever they could carry. They jumped into the Daimler, and the driver took them to her other house in the German Colony. From the back seat, Raymonda watched crowds of panicked people, old men, women, and children racing in the direction of the port to get boats out of the city. At the port, people rested on concrete loading docks while others milled around restlessly with the blank, vacant eyes of people who hadn't eaten in a week, stripped of will.

The German Colony seemed safer because Sylvie's Jewish friends in the neighborhood pleaded with her, "Don't leave, don't leave, the fighting is almost over." The Jewish mayor was saying the same thing.

But Operation Danny required an Arab-free city, in particular in the neighborhoods near the port.

The family held out for a few more days until one morning Raymonda went outside to play with her cousin Nicolas in the garden. They looked up and saw a mountain of blue and white corpses stacked in a military truck parked in front of the house. There must have been a hundred bodies of men, women, and children piled on top of one another, eyes open, limbs stiff; swarms of giant black flies buzzed around the bodies, which gave off the sweet, sickening odor of death.

Assaulted by the repulsive sight, Raymonda and Nicolas rushed into the house screaming as if they had seen one of the rings of hell. It was too much: Sylvie raced around the house, grabbing children, clothes, some food, and ordered her driver to take them to the port.

Habib turned up just before the Daimler sped off to the ship. Hearing about the corpses and his sister's decision to flee by ship, he picked Raymonda up and sent her back to the convent in Nazareth with two British officers driving a truck. Jews, he was certain, would never attack a convent. Habib then boarded a ship and left the city by sea. He was the only member of the vast Hawa clan ever to see Haifa again.

Christmas never fled Haifa. She stayed behind as a volunteer with the Red Cross to treat the wounded. The final outbreak of fighting was the Haganah onslaught on April 21. Encircled and starving, Arabs in the city were in no position to put up a fight. The so-called Battle of Haifa lasted a single day.

Passing by Sylvie's mansion on King George Street, on April 22, Christmas saw a Yiddish and Hebrew-speaking mob swarm through the half-destroyed house, carting off clothes, furniture, chandeliers, paintings, boxes of wine and brandy, no doubt the Meissner tea cups—whatever they could carry.

8
Hotel Zion

Several days after the mass flight of Palestinians from Haifa, Ruth sat on the terrace of Hotel Zion overlooking the city. The sun was setting and the swallows were soaring and dipping, flapping and gliding; the ships were mostly gone from the port and gone too was the polyglot hubbub of the streets. Ruth, traumatized at the deaths of Yossi and Zorik, and so many others, stared down into the abandoned city. She was astonished by the silence. The shooting had stopped. Chaos, fear, hunger, and death had driven most Christians, Muslims, and Baha'i away from Haifa. As soon as they were gone, Ben-Gurion ordered Arab properties seized. Which was the reason Ruth was on the balcony of Hotel Zion that bright sunny day.

Moshe's presence in the Haganah sock factory signified favor in the eyes of Ben-Gurion. With Haifa and Acre abandoned, Ben-Gurion sent him in with a clipboard to inventory the war booty.[7] Since he was the one in charge, Moshe must have presided over the dispossession of the Hawa family holdings in the city, the villas and cars and bank accounts, as well as the furniture that hadn't yet been plundered.

Moshe asked no questions and showed no hesitation in carrying out his orders; Ruth was made of different stuff. The following day she left Hotel Zion and accompanied him in combing through the properties. In one house they found an impressive Islamic book collection, there was also a cold omelet on the stove: The family must have left suddenly, with little forewarning. Later, in a factory, she pinched half a sack of sugar. Appalled

33

at herself, that night she couldn't sleep a wink. Had the bag been filled with iron it wouldn't have weighed her down more.

Forty-five kilometers away, Nazareth fell to Israeli forces in July. The fact the Arabs remained in their city was the consequence of one man's conscience: the Israeli officer, an honorable Jewish-Canadian named Ben Dunkelman, who had refused orders to expel the population. Because there were always less scrupulous men, Nazareth was filled with refugees from evacuated villages in the region. Driven out by gunpoint, the villagers of Ma'alul, Nahalal's neighbors across the valley, arrived in Nazareth with their meager belongings packed on the back of donkeys.

Raymonda's convent school, protected under the sun yellow flag of the Vatican and the tricolor of France, became a makeshift home for hundreds of refugees. The girls in the convent lived in the dreadful uncertainty of not knowing what was happening to their families. Fingering their beads, the nuns carried out their prayers, canticles, and litanies, intoning Ave Maria and Gratia Plena. There was a smell of incense. The shadows cast by the burning candles. The rivulets from leaking pipes pooling in spots. The slow ticking of watches. The drone of planes overhead. Girls sobbing.

The sisters of the convent, assuming both Habib and Christmas were dead, transferred Raymonda over to the orphan's section. One of the nuns stroked her hair in a gesture of reassurance. Raymonda went to bed each night with the prayer, Please God, make the fighting stop. The tender mercies of God having resurrected Christmas once, she prayed for her and her father to appear again, arm in arm. At night she woke up clutching for a doll; panting, her heart raced because of elaborate nightmares of shrieking mobs armed with the legs of her aunt's oak dining table hitting Christmas over and over until there was nothing left of her, not even a body.

9
Villa Lea

R uth lived off rumors and shreds of information. In a terrifying pre-
monition after the Battle of Qastal near Jerusalem, she was certain
Moshe had been killed. Panicked phone calls went all the way up to Ben-
Gurion, who finally assured her that her husband had survived the battle,
and was fighting on new fronts.

Near his birthplace of Degania he and a handful of soldiers warded
off a Syrian tank attack with little more than Molotov cocktails and a
few bazookas. Following this success, he pieced together a group of ex-
prisoners and Haganah and Irgun veterans. He and his commando unit
hot-wired abandoned cars and a jeep belonging to the novelist Arthur
Koestler and were in business. There were no formal uniforms, no culture
of saluting and spit-polished boots, just passion, nerve, speed, and shock
tactics.

Moshe unleashed his band against the Arab cities of Lydda and Ramle.
Yitzhak Rabin then showed up with the regular army and expelled the
entire population of both cities.[8]

Ben-Gurion was impressed enough to promote Moshe to colonel and
hand him one of the most important military jobs there was, commander
of the Jerusalem Brigade. This made the farmer-turned-commando, a
half-blind daredevil, into one of the leading military leaders of the triumphant Jewish state.

For Ruth this meant leaving the beloved, muddy simplicity of the
moshav—forever, as it would turn out. The family of five drove in a

command car, with a chicken coop in the back, to Jerusalem on a dirt and rock path carved out of the mountainside to bypass areas—it was called the Burma Road—controlled by the Jordanians. In Jerusalem they moved into the Villa Lea, a large stone mansion with seven bedrooms built by the Greek Orthodox Christian Dr. Nassib Abcarius Bey, for his Jewish wife Lea.[9] Like other Arab properties in the Israeli controlled districts of Jerusalem, the house ended up with the Custodian of Enemy Property. Efficient bureaucrats emptied out abandoned Arab homes and stored the plunder in a warehouse.

It was up to Ruth to fill the villa's two dozen rooms with beds and lamps and curtains. Psychologically, the only way a woman who felt guilty about pinching a bag of sugar could go from warehouse to warehouse, picking out chairs and tables belonging to people probably living in tent camps, was to assume that once the war ended, the rightful owners would return. Dr. Bey would get the mansion back, and the other Arabs would be grateful to the Israelis for protecting their things.

Moshe knew better—there would be no return.

10

Married to the State

One reason Ruth preferred the leaking shack and cowshed over the mansion was that the rambling Villa Lea was far too large for her to manage on her own; she needed a maid, and having hired help rankled her socialist sensibilities. The maid pitched in with the cooking and cleaning, a necessity because the house turned into a sort of flophouse for Moshe's gang of commandos, crowding into the available rooms.[10]

The first major social event was the wedding of her sister to the ex-fighter pilot Ezer Weizman, President Chaim Weizmann's nephew. It was the closest thing Israel had to a royal wedding, vastly different from the rowdy singing, dancing, and firing of rifles during Ruth and Moshe's ceremony.

Ruth had her hands full raising children in a dangerous, divided city. In Yael's eyes the new family home was like a palace fit for princes in glittering pre-revolutionary St. Petersburg she had heard about from Moshe's mother or an enchanted castle in a fairy tale.

The villa doubled as Dayan's military command center. The nine-year-old Yael was dazzled by the revolvers and maps in her uniformed father's office, the boxes of ammo piled high in the hallways, and the boldly striding officers who streamed through the house. The front line with Jordan, with its coils of barbed wire and trenches, was just around the corner. From the top floors, Yael could sit for hours staring off at the walls of the Old City. She once ran downstairs excitedly carrying a still hot bullet from the gun of a Jordanian sniper. Four-year-old Assi, the "little Beelzebub" as he was called, was once found wandering in the booby-trapped and forti-fied No Man's Land.

For the first time since moving to Nahalal as a teenager, Ruth had free time on her hands. As the maid cooked and cleaned, Ruth began meet-ing a friend Betty, a born New Yorker, for morning coffee at Cafe Atara on King George Street. The two had a lot to commiserate about: Betty's husband was the founder of the Mossad, and the spy chief was even more secretive than Moshe.[11] One bit of cheerful news Ruth got from Betty was that her husband had intercepted letters of foreign diplomats praising Ruth's—and the maid's—cooking.

Moshe lived in the same house as Ruth, and she saw him every day. Absorbed in the monumental task of keeping the city safe from attack, Moshe's hard-driving work routine from crack of dawn till late at night reintroduced the terrible loneliness that had plagued Ruth since his underground days. Ben-Gurion's favorite commando was sucked up into the vortex of geopolitics when he negotiated with King Abdullah's top gen-eral Abdullah El-Tell the "Absolute and Sincere Ceasefire." Moshe and Abdullah El-Tell conducted clandestine talks to stabilize the long fortified border and bring a modicum of normalcy to deeply scarred Jerusalem.

Dayan set up Mandelbaum Gate, established on the ruins of a villa built by a Russian-Jewish manufacturer of stockings. The Gate was the Checkpoint Charlie of Jerusalem and for Arabs a symbol of the loss of their country and their forced separation from families, neighbors, and friends.

Ruth tried her best to be a part of his life. One of her attempts to have a toehold in Moshe's world was a spy course organized by Betty's husband; but she flunked because she didn't have what it took to betray people: passing the course meant she would have to spy on the foreign diplomats who praised her cooking.

The children worshipped their increasingly famous father. Yael would later describe her father as a "tribal patriarch," and his world became theirs. There was a more human side to the hero, like peeing in the gar-den behind the villa or cleaning out earwax with the house key.

Yael rambled with her father through the "abandoned" Arab villages surrounding Jerusalem, where they gorged themselves off the fruit from orchards whose owners were vegetating in tent camps. In her child's eyes, rambling through the empty countryside and scampering through haunted ruins was a new Eden. Her brave father was the first Adam, she his mischievous little Eve.

On a different occasion, it was Udi's turn to be dazzled by his father. Moshe took the nine-year-old on a pigeon shoot not far from Gaza, a thin strip of land then under the control of the Egyptians. Moshe liked to bag the birds and take them home for Ruth to cook. By chance the hunt was around Tel el Hesi, which was the first major archeological site to be excavated in Palestine. There was so much rain that year that a part of the slope had been washed away, exposing a clay jar. Moshe pulled it out of its mud and, curious about its provenance, took it to an army colleague and part-time archeologist who dated it back to the Iron Age era of David and Goliath.[12] Moshe was hooked. Over his long career as an amateur archeologist, Moshe assembled a private museum full of ancient treasures.

For a man who never lost his boyish love of discovery, Eretz Yisrael, which in his imagination had been neglected and fallow for millennia by Arabs in their "mud hovels," was the world's most thrilling sandbox. With pick and shovel, he pursued his fetishistic mysticism of pure and authentic Hebrew roots, his tactile encounter with the epoch of the Patriarchs, Judges, and Kings.[13]

He had never been happier. Ruth still missed life on the farm, and whenever she could, she took prominent visitors on a tour of the cowsheds. In his book *Strange Lands* the US Supreme Court Justice William O. Douglas describes one such visit "to a pleasant, fertile spot" owned by the "famous Colonel Moshe Dayan and his attractive and brilliant wife." "Brilliant" was an adjective neither Moshe nor Yael would ever employ in talking about Ruth. Married to the State of Israel, Moshe was too busy to notice that his neglected wife was beginning to blossom in unexpected ways.

11
Ave Maria

Like all the Palestinians who fled to Lebanon, Habib Hawa planned on going back to Haifa the moment the fighting stopped. But he heard reports that soldiers from the Israel Defense Forces (IDF), as the Haganah now called itself, were opening fire at people who tried to return to what was now the State of Israel. Gripped by panic, at once he headed back to find Raymonda, sneaking across the heavily fortified frontier at night. Soldiers spotted him in an olive grove and shot at him, hitting him in the leg. They dragged him half alive to a nearby building for interrogation. He would have bled to death if the officer who questioned him — Bechor-Shalom Sheetrit, the future Israeli minister of police — hadn't been his friend. A decent, humane man, Sheetrit drove him, his clothes drenched with blood, to a hospital; and unlike hundreds of thousands of others, Habib was allowed to return to Haifa.

Others weren't so lucky. Christmas's sister, born in New York and married in the castle, fled to Gaza with her family; there was no return for them. Eighty percent of Palestinian Arabs were gone, and those who remained were kept on a tight leash by the new Israeli government: Arabs needed permission to leave their cities and villages and this prevented Christmas from traveling to Nazareth to see her daughter. She was even more cut off from her two sons George and Yussuf on the Jordanian side of Mandelbaum Gate. When Habib showed up at her front door, half crippled with ragged clothes stained by dust and sweat, she fed him and gave him a place to stay. With a pass provided by his friend Sheetrit, he set out to find Raymonda.

In the bitterly cold, rainy January of 1949, the head nun woke Raymonda with a message that there was someone to see her. Downstairs, in the dark chapel, a man emerged from the shadows, stepped across the light cast by a row of candles, his long shadow bending and angling along the cracks of the stones. She noticed the way he stooped and stared, his face was pale, and a pipe drooped from his lips. He struggled to smoke because his two hands gripped the handles of crutches. Her dashing father, the Syrian Prince, had the long, untrimmed beard of a pauper. She flung herself into his arms. From him, she learned that Christmas had also survived. Her Ave Marias had worked once again: the Virgin had brought her back her parents.

Back in Haifa, stripped of Montfort Castle and his properties and with a bum leg, Habib ended up living in a small apartment with mold on the walls; sometimes he stayed with Christmas. He kept hunger at bay by hustling as an unlicensed lawyer. Habib often quoted Victor Hugo's poem *"La Tristesse d'Olympio"* to describe his life after 1948: *Ma maison me regarde et ne me connaît plus*. He was a stranger in his own home.

Christmas continued working as a social worker in Haifa and throughout the Galilee. She was among a handful of educated Arab women left in the country, so the Zionist women's organization WIZO hired her to work with Arabic-speaking Jewish immigrants from the Maghreb and Yemen. She took the job without hesitation: the war had violently unraveled the elaborate fabric of numerous peoples, and not just Arabs. Vast zinc and corrugated iron settlements sprung up all over the country, in appearance vaguely resembling the tent cities erected by the UN for displaced Arabs. Many of these Jews arrived from isolated areas of the Middle East with worms and disease.

She used to take Raymonda to tent camps where they sat on the ground and listened to the stories of the displaced Palestinian peasants who had nothing, and who risked imprisonment or a bullet by returning to their fields to pick olives. "Do you want to be a snob like your Aunt Sylvie,"

Christmas scolded Raymonda the first time she wrinkled up her nose at the smell of open sewage, "or be with your people?"

Christmas, to drive home the message of shared suffering, took Raymonda as well to Jewish tent camps. One Yemenite woman, looking at her children sitting on the dirt floor among the goats, asked Christmas, "Is this the paradise we have been promised? I want to go back home; I feel like a stranger here."

Christmas thrived in her job with WIZO because, for the first time, she felt valued as a woman: Jewish feminists, bucking the patriarchal traditions of Jewish Orthodoxy, ran the organization. Christmas also volunteered her time with UNRWA, working with refugees in tent camps from now dynamited Arab villages. Ever the free spirit, ever a forceful and tireless opponent of injustice, when she gave an interview to UNRWA officials about the situation in the Arab camps, WIZO fired her.

12
Women of Valor

Dayan was so good at his job in Jerusalem that *Life* magazine wrote glowingly about the "handsome young soldier with the eye patch . . . who is regarded as a possible future prime minister." Ben-Gurion was impressed enough to send him to the Negev where there was a lot more action than in Jerusalem. He became a major general in October 1949, and was the commanding officer of the Southern Front, the most important in Israel as it faced the Egyptians. This was a vast region of desiccated warrens, jackals, venomous snakes, and roaming Bedouins, but also smugglers, a few armed fighters itching for revenge, and thousands of refugees trying to return to their lands.

Dayan loved living in a desert camp, going unshaven for days at a stretch, eating wild game, and boiling his coffee over an open fire. Yael, on an extended visit, experienced him as a "Spartan nomad" at heart, crossing the Negev in his battered army jeep along the old Silk Road, a millennia-old caravan path. In what were the happiest days of her childhood, he introduced her to the ferocious beauty of the desert, the hidden life behind the seemingly barren, desiccated hills: its venomous snakes and scorpions, the desert bushes with thorns as "sharp as spears," the soaring raptors. "His bedtime stories had to do with our ancestors who walked this desert, or very close by, and filled my imagination. Abraham and Isaac, Jacob and his brothers, Moses and the Children of Israel . . . Between slavery in the green pastures of the Nile and the promised land of Canaan lay this desert. Only those who traversed it deserved freedom."[14]

One liberty he took—she said nothing to Ruth—was satisfying his amorous appetites for female recruits.

Moshe was given an important task by Ben-Gurion: to empty much of the desert of Bedouins by herding them into small fenced-off areas, and keeping them there under lock and key. People who had been moving in and out of the Negev since the Iron Age were now deemed "infiltrators." As for the refugees filtering back from across the Gaza border, soldiers under his command loaded them onto trucks and drove them over the border, often with volleys of bullets fired over their heads for good measure, just so they got the message. When they persisted, harsher measures were used: hundreds died each year because of landmines and a "free fire policy."[15]

With a maid running the household and her husband rattling along the ancient Silk Road with his jeep, chasing Bedouins from their ancestral lands, Ruth and Moshe's mother Dvorah began working with Bulgarian Jewish immigrants. The project was called Eshet Hayl, from a Hebrew hymn sung on Friday nights to a "woman of valor."

Unlike the Jewish immigrants from the wilds of the Arabian deserts or the Atlas Mountains, the Bulgarians were well-heeled, urban, educated professionals like many other Central and Eastern European Jews. Directly from the boat, government officials bused them into an isolated region of abandoned Arab villages near Jerusalem.

It was an apocalyptic scene. Armies of rats had eaten all the food left in abandoned houses; fattened, the population exploded. When the food ran out, the vermin began to prowl the countryside. The Bulgarians faced rats who had gnawed through wooden windowsills to get into their homes. The horrified women wanted nothing more than to be back in a city and work in their professions. But they had no money, and no way out.

Ruth discovered during her visits that these displaced immigrants, barricaded inside their homes and lamenting their move from green Europe, possessed handmade lace curtains, tablecloths, intricate embroidery and other needlework made all the more striking by the rats swarming around their homes. Ruth, who had never shown any interest in fashion or design, lit upon the idea of working with handicraft as a way of providing these immigrants with an income. She came up with the idea of them making crude bags from jute sacking and bits of scrap wool. She supplied materials, and the Bulgarians made bags by adding bamboo handles and knitted patterns onto the jute. Ruth then made a deal with the director of WIZO, a friend, to sell the bags through the WIZO shops.

Ruth travelled by bus or hitchhiked on her journeys around Israel. On one occasion Moshe's car zoomed past, but the driver didn't see Ruth with her heavy bags of material. She repressed her first impulse—of crying her eyes out—by gripping her bags and defiantly sticking out her thumb. "Damn him," she said to herself. She loved him fiercely but wasn't going to be crippled by him.

Soon, however, she demanded a car from Moshe, and was able to drive up and down the lengths of the country, from the Negev desert all the way north to the Lebanese border looking for people with handicrafts. She found women from Yugoslavia able to knit; others from Hungary and North Africa who embroidered. With the help of Bezalel Art School in Jerusalem, she organized a training course for new Jewish immigrants from Iran, Libya, Algeria, Romania, and a dozen other countries.

13
The Beauty Contest

Christmas's experiences in the 1950s continued to be bitter, though punctuated by a few triumphant notes. She smuggled a prisoner out of Acre fortress by dressing him in a nurse's uniform and driving him to the Lebanese border, where he scampered undetected over the frontier, to freedom. When Shin Bet agents showed up at her home to interrogate her, she greeted them with a poker face and uncharacteristic falsehood, and convinced them she'd never do such a thing.

Acre, where she lived, was no longer the old prewar town she had known. Its original population had left. After the war, homeless Arab villagers came and occupied some of the abandoned houses. The State of Israel gave away the mansions to Jewish families from Poland and Germany, Iraq, and Tunisia. Such a population mix lent the city a rich polyglot flavor. Each time Raymonda visited Christmas on school holidays, the spices, music, and the Arabic on the street made it seem as if she were living as equals in a shared land. If only someone would do away with the pass laws, the soldiers, the barbed wire, and Mandelbaum Gate. Why shouldn't Jews and Arabs, including her brothers in East Jerusalem, live as equals in the same country?

The few European Jews living in Acre, refined and educated, were her mother's closest friends. "You need to get to know my friend," Christmas told Raymonda during one of her visits back home, introducing her to a strikingly beautiful woman from Germany with a bluish tattoo on her arm: "the woman reminded me of Marlene Dietrich." Josef Mengele had

46

"performed an operation on her so she couldn't have children." Raymonda should never blame the Jewish people as a whole for Arab suffering, her mother told her. European Jews had experienced unimaginable evil.

By 1954, Christmas had a new social work job in Acre. Always energetic and filled with ideals, always prepared to swallow humiliation and loss and move on, she raised money for an ambulance to serve Jews and Arabs alike. When the ambulance arrived, the citizens of Acre decided to celebrate. People unbuttoned their emotions: there was drinking, dancing, singing. In the middle of the carousing and merrymaking, the organizers announced an impromptu beauty contest for girls.

Christmas grabbed her daughter by the hand, whisked her off into the ladies room, smoothed out her tangled hair, put a thick coat of lipstick on her lips, and led her out again and into a row of other girls lined up before judges.

Her mouth gaping open, fourteen-year-old Raymonda stood there, wanting nothing more than to snap her fingers and disappear.

One by one the other girls fell away, until she stood, trembling, next to a Jewish girl. At first, people in the crowd assumed Raymonda, with her chestnut brown hair, was Jewish. As she stood there as a finalist, Raymonda noticed people whispering and pointing. From the scraps of conversation, she heard "she's an Arab." The judges, all Jewish, gave the blue ribbon to the other girl. Raymonda, relieved that the ordeal was over, left the stage and darted back toward Christmas. Bedlam broke out. A clutch of Arabs and a few Jews protested, which elicited a cacophony of catcalls. A Moroccan Jew said in Arabic: "You piece of Arab shit, you can't be prettier than a Jew." A fellow Jew pitched a beer bottle at the man. "You're the piece of shit . . ."

Emotions were stoked even more as an elegiac poem was being read by an Arab, beseeching his "beloved" to come back "home from across the iron border. I am your lover in the Galilee. I am awaiting your return on a white horse. You will ride across the mountains, and no invader will keep you away."

The head judge, grabbing the loudspeaker, vainly appealed for calm. Folding chairs began flying. People ducked under tables from projectiles

thrust in every direction. Fighting broke out—Arabs against Jews, Jews
against Jews—with fists and feet and even teeth, and the brand new ambulance went into service by ferrying the wounded to the local hospital.

After hours of pandemonium, the judges huddled together. A compromise was reached: both girls won. This round of the Arab-Jewish conflict
had been solved.

As a prize, Raymonda got a dark chocolate cake and a bottle of champagne, which she presented to her father. Habib appreciated the gift—it
brought back sweet memories of his dandyish exploits in Cairo. Why
had she participated in such a contest? For him, the whole episode had
been degrading for a member of the Hawa family, his little princess.
"Mother had to assure him I hadn't worn a bikini but was dressed modestly." *Ma maison me regarde et ne me connaît plus*, he sighed.

In the fall of 1954, Raymonda moved from the straight-laced Nazareth
Sisters to a more relaxed convent in Haifa. Most of the girls there were
European Jews. Some had converted during the war to save their lives,
and their families decided to remain within the Catholic fold and continue their Catholic education.

Raymonda and the other girls hated them in their fashionable dresses
under the school uniform. Their families were living in their homes
and neighborhoods. The Jewish State was doing much to help them
integrate while keeping Arabs separate and watched over, their movements regulated by pass laws. "Let the dead bury the dead," the nuns
liked to quote from the Gospel, teaching the girls love and tolerance.
"You have to live, and to live you must love thy neighbors as thyself."
And they were all neighbors now, the sisters taught the girls, Israel was
their shared homeland. The Arab girls learned about Hitler and the
Holocaust. "Slowly, we grew to understand each other. Stronger than
that. We loved each other."

The Jewish girls were more worldly than the Arab Christians; many
already had boyfriends, were aware of their bodies, had a repertoire of dirty
jokes, and were more modern. Raymonda had a secret attraction to their
sexually uninhibited European Jewish culture. These girls never betrayed
an air of arrogant superiority; never did she feel she was a stranger in

"their" state. "Unlike some generals I've encountered over the years, they didn't feel the need to hold my head under the water."

Her dearest friend Dvora was a Holocaust survivor, and it was in the context of such barbarity that she came to understand Dvora's fierce love of Israel. Dvora described a hatred she could not begin to comprehend, and she cried with her. When Raymonda read *The Diary of Anne Frank*, she cried even more when a nun, whose family had also been murdered by the Germans, said to her: "In this world you will see evil people, like Hitler. But Anne Frank refused to build her life on confusion, misery, and death. She believed that people were really good at heart." The only person the nuns taught her to hate—not the Jews, not the Israelis—was the mastermind, Adolf Hitler.

Dvora lived with her family in the house that had once belonged to Raymonda's aunt Sylvie, in the German Colony. Her first visit there was harrowing:

It was a lovely spring morning; the sun was warming up the city after an overnight rain. Two women soldiers stood outside a shop, both chewing gum, a rare luxury in those days. One had a dyed-blonde look and the other was dark; she must have come from Iraq or Iran. The dark soldier said something about a bathing suit to the light one. They were both wearing khaki.

"No way," she said. "Navy blue. That's not my color. It'd look better on you."

"You think so?"

"C'mon, the color brings out your eyes."

She's right, Raymonda said to herself: *The light soldier has the same color eyes as mine. Maybe I too should be wearing navy blue.*

"Shalom," said the light one to Raymonda, as if she knew what she was thinking.

"Shalom," she replied, looking at her and thinking how strange it was to speak the same language. *She must think I am one of them. . . .*

She continued walking. The church bells still sounded, tolling for parishioners now mostly gone. Raymonda ambled through streets filled with Hebrew, French, German, and English, just no Arabic. More female soldiers were standing on the curb, guns slung over their shoulders. They looked friendly: one was smiling at her and said "Shalom." "Shalom," Raymonda said for the second time that morning. The soldier wasn't her enemy. No one needed to tell her that; her smile told her so. *Or does she even know who I am? What I am?*

She continued on a street now renamed Bialik, her favorite Hebrew poet. She was looking for her aunt's old house; it hadn't changed in the slightest. She rang the bell and the door opened. Dvora's mother didn't step aside to let her in, she stood there in the doorway, as if she wasn't sure what to do with her. It was awkward having her there; it made her nervous. Or guilty because she occupied a house filled with Raymonda's aunt's piano, plates, draperies, rugs, her mother-of-pearl Damascus furniture, the French oil paintings of landscapes, the crystal chandelier over the antique oak dining table, the one with the lion's feet. Raymonda noticed the tattoo on her arm. Dvora's mother too was a survivor of the death camps.

Once inside Raymonda couldn't help herself. "YOU ARE THIEVES," she exclaimed, bursting into tears. "This house doesn't belong to you!" Dvora fled into another room. "Listen," her mother, a beautiful blonde woman from Poland, began in a gentle, refined voice not without compassion. "We didn't steal your aunt's house. We had a house in Poland. We lost everything, too. I understand you because we, we are like you." She went on to tell her about gas chambers and the murder of her family.

Dvora's mother, as though she was reading Raymonda's mind, said: "Some day, and hopefully very soon, Arabs will return to their homes, and Jewish refugees would find new homes, and everyone would live together in peace. I would much rather have peace than your aunt's beautiful home."

14
"Maskiteers"

R uth was wrenchingly carving out her independence. She had little choice, being married to a man nearing the pinnacle of the military pyramid. In 1953 Ben-Gurion appointed him chief of staff. With his headquarters in Tel Aviv, Ruth's parents put up the money for him to buy a house in a new neighborhood for top officers named "Zahala." The street was fittingly named after Joab, the commander of King David's army. Moshe put a 500-year-old Turkish cannon in the family's front yard. Ironically, the cannon pointed to the house across the street, which belonged to his young protégé Ariel Sharon.

Ruth insisted on buying her own furniture, while the three children loved playing hide and seek in the backyard filled with Roman sarcophagi, millennia-old gravestones, and Byzantine church pillars Moshe spirited away at night from archeological sites. The country's archeological treasures became their playground.

Ruth and Moshe made a strange couple, and with their three children, they were already the most colorful, and most eccentric, dynasty in Israel. During the day, the generalissimo was building a crack fighting force. He was home every night, for the first time in years, and reading to little Assi lullabies by Nathan Altermann:

> This land. Trodden, just like this, by a wandering sadness,
> Trailing in her thunders, calling her: 'Where art thou?'

Speak to her, tell her of things that are other,
Tell her of fields that are learning to smile.

The dutiful father who tucked little Assi into bed at night was one of
the most brilliant, uncompromising military chiefs of staff in the history
of the business.[16] Dayan didn't care for army protocol or for the pressed
trousers of the parade ground. He showed up to meetings with dusty
sleeves rolled up to his elbows; his boots were caked with mud—even
his eye-patch was dirty. To one soldier raising his arm in a salute, Dayan
tossed him a grapefruit: "Catch!"[17]

The biggest military threat he faced was the Fedayeen guerrillas who
"bore in their hearts the memory of the defeat of the War of Independence
and hoped for a second round," as Moshe Dayan lectured his soldiers.
"Let us not today fling accusation at the murderers," he told mourners at
a funeral after a fatal Fedayeen attack. For years now, they sit in their refugee camps in Gaza, and before their eyes we turn into our homesteads the
land and villages in which they and their forefathers have lived. We are
the generation of colonizers, and without the steel helmet and the gun's
muzzle we cannot plant a tree and build a home."[18]

In March 1953, a group of Fedayeen crossed over the Jordanian frontier and ambushed an Israeli Egged bus in the northern Negev. The guerrillas shot the driver before turning their guns on the passengers, one by
one. All eleven, murdered.

For these guerillas, former farmers surviving off UN rations, they had
nothing to lose. For them, losing their lands was a fate worse than death.
Fighting was the only way to restore their shattered honor. These "men
of sacrifice" or "suicide fighters," so called, were the first foot soldiers of
a guerrilla army Arafat, Raymonda's future son-in-law, would eventually
lead.

To put an end to the killing, the IDF formed a special commando
strike force headed by Ariel "Arik" Sharon. The Unit 101 was a clandestine club of fighters trained in the art of revenge and what in a spirit of
extreme generosity might be called deterrence. The 101 was less of a military unit than an ad hoc strike force. In a grandfatherly nod of approval,

Prime Minister Ben-Gurion dubbed the unit a "hothouse for heroes," and lauded Dayan's "almost insane daring balanced by profound tactical and strategic judgment."

On a typical Friday Moshe and Ruth, along with Reumah and dashing Ezer Weizman and a couple of friends, headed over to a Tel Aviv movie house, and from there it was on to Greek food at the Acropolis and the dance floor at the Dan Hotel. Her preferred spot was Café Kasit, the popular venue for free-spirited actors, poets, swingers, and a colorful menagerie of other avant-garde types. There was Nathan Alterman and his girlfriend, in front of bottles of whiskey. Or, the drink-sodden poet Amos Kenan once was about to punch Moshe in the nose when Ezer wrestled him to the ground. Ruth took up smoking while in the company of Israel's Beatniks.

Several of the people Ruth met in Tel Aviv cafes would later become Raymonda's friends, too. Whenever Ruth wanted to meet the leftist journalist Uri Avnery or Amos Kenan, it was in a parked car, outside of the former 1948 fighter pilot Abie Nathan's hip California Café, next to the Cameri, the best theater in the country. She felt the need to arrange such clandestine tête-à-têtes because Avnery, Kenan, and Nathan were notorious leftists, despised by the Zionist establishment. But they were also the only ones who understood Ruth, her dreams, her efforts at living out her old socialist dreams. They understood she needed to escape a lonely marriage with a relentlessly driven and very damaged man, with shrapnel still lodged in his skull.

In 1953, Golda Meir, then minister of labor, called Ruth into her office. She had heard about all her good work with immigrants and asked her to head up a department for women's work. Ruth agreed at once. A perfect name was given for the new venture: Maskit, which means "picture" from the Psalms. Her coworkers were the "Maskiteers."

Over the coming months, she became the general, leading her troops of Maskiteers, scouring the countryside for craftspeople barely out of the Middle Ages, giving them training, and connecting them with the best avant-garde designers. Ruth was offering these immigrants a future.

One group of craftspeople Ruth and her Maskiteers discovered during their hunt for crafts was a clan of a hundred families from the deserts of Libya that had, up to then, lived in their own man-made caves of Tripolitania, dug twenty-five feet into the sand, as a defense against wild animals and desert marauders.

Perhaps their best find was in an abandoned Arab village near Lydda, settled by an ancient Yemenite-Jewish tribe of master silversmiths from Wadi Bayhan, on the ancient Perfume Road on the southern tip of the Arabian Peninsula. In Arabia, they had been the King of Yemen's personal makers of daggers and swords. In Israel, they lived in squalid tent camps, living off handouts from the Jewish Agency. Even their adobe houses in Yemen were better than their dingy army-surplus tents they shared with chickens and goats. What's more, they had lost what was essential to their lives: their dignity.

Ruth promised to help them develop their craft and market what they made. Some of their jewelry and embroidery ended up in high-end shops on Fifth Avenue in New York City.

Maskit came to be one of the largest employers in the country, by far the largest run by a woman. But in Moshe's blinkered view, Ruth remained the weak, dependent woman who was too often on the verge of tears, a caricature that rubbed off all too easily onto fourteen-year-old Yael. Plainspoken and churlish, Yael had an aristocratic grace, unconquerable true grit, and was as strong as a stallion; she was clearly the leader of the Dayan brood and the repository of Moshe's nationalist dreams. Swelling with pride at being the daughter of a hero, she felt vastly superior to her peers—and to most grown-ups, too.

Everyone tolerated what Ben-Gurion dubbed Yael's "flamboyance" until rumors cropped up that she was spending too much time with Uri Avnery.

One day during one of Moshe's frequent trips abroad an officer from military intelligence called and revealed to Ruth that Yael might have passed on top military secrets to Avnery, secrets on a Commando 101 raid which ended up in Avnery's political tabloid *HaOlam HaZeh*.[19]

The journal was a national sensation because along with the investigative reports attacking Israel's most cherished national myths and illusions, it featured bare-breasted beauties on the back cover.

Ruth naturally defended Yael by informing the man on the telephone that Moshe's daughter, a girl raised on the present prime minister's lap—Ruth's "uncle," Moshe Sharett who had succeeded Ben-Gurion in 1953—would never betray the State of Israel. Never! She slammed down the receiver.

Had Yael, in fact, done such a thing? Instead of confronting Yael directly, Ruth had Ezer do it. Yael was defiant: no, she hadn't passed on secrets. *Keep your suspicions to yourselves!* she thought. Moshe was also suspicious, and the minute he returned from his trip he sent two goons to jump Avnery and break his hands. As for his daughter, he returned home, strode into her room, gave her a warm kiss, and then slapped her so hard she nearly flew across the room, followed by a second flat-handed whack. "I love you very much, but don't take advantage of it."[20]

In ways only psychoanalysis could unravel, these hard and swift slaps drew Yael closer to her father, and further away from Ruth. "No blames," recalls Yael, "no psychology, no question marks as to how we ever reached this gap or rift, and above all, no moralizing. Two slaps . . . and a renewed facade of happiness and unity which supplied a good alibi for both of us," Yael continued. "We both wanted, with different degrees of legitimacy, not to be slaves to the confining dictates of family routine."

Against the background of this father-daughter alliance, Ruth pressed on with her work. Maskit's first public exhibit, at the main Tel Aviv museum in 1954, was a resounding success.

15
A Mission in Life

In 1954, Raymonda began spending more time with her mother during breaks from the convent school. Christmas, delighted to have her back, took her on long tours of their lost life. In Acre, they walked from one mansion to the next. "This used to belong to your Uncle Michel . . . that one over there was your father's cousin . . . the stone villa with the awnings was your father's, that one your great aunt's." Walking to the edge of town, they reached the checkpoint manned by Israeli soldiers, where Arabs had to show their passes before crossing. They turned around and headed back to the center of town.

Arab neighbors furtively tuned into the banned Voice of Palestine from Beirut, broadcasting details on Commando Unit 101's depredations. This was the first time Raymonda heard the names Ariel Sharon and Moshe Dayan. "No matter what these men do to us, we will never give up our rights," said Christmas to her.

By way of Kfar Yassif that summer, she drove Raymonda into the hills near Montfort Castle. They descended into a valley with gnarled olive trees and former tobacco fields now sprouting with JNF pines. Looking up at the castle, Christmas, "her voice trembling," recalls Raymonda, gave a kind of eulogy of the family, a eulogy with an urgent appeal:

> You should never forget this view because it's yours. Never
> mind that it was taken from you and your family. No matter
> where you are, remember: these olive trees are rooted in an

56

eternal land—they are eternal, and so are we Arabs. When
you are older, you must return to the valleys and the forests.
Feel and sense the beauty, take in the fragrance of the lilies,
the perfumes of the wild flowers . . .

The two ended up driving to the village of Rama to visit Father Michel
De Maria, an Italian priest renowned for his piety and, like the Polish-
Jewish Wolf Messing, for his clairvoyance. Jews, Christians, and Muslims
lined up to see him. The chief of police of Tel Aviv sought his help in
solving the case of a serial killer. Dayan consulted him about missing
soldiers. The father's fame went well beyond clairvoyance. In 1948, after
the Israeli military forced the villagers of Rama to leave and pushed them
north toward the Lebanese border, he met with Israeli intelligence officers and negotiated their return to the village. Gentle strength achieved
what Fedayeen bullets never could.

Christmas wanted to ask him about her sons George and Yussuf.

They pulled up to the front of an old stone church topped by a tow-
ering cross, visible for miles, and passed through a wrought iron gate,
into a garden. The pungent scent of jasmine together with the statue of
St. Joseph reminded Raymonda of her convent in Nazareth. She was a
damaged child who had spent much of her early years grappling with
loss and anxiety. But within the walls of the church, she sensed an inef-
fable tranquility; it was like snapping out of a nightmare and finding
herself safe again.

A strikingly tall man with olive-green eyes and a head of thick black
hair approached them. He greeted Christmas by her first name, and then
turned his attention to Raymonda, bowed slightly, and extended his hand.

"This is your first time you're staying with your mother, isn't it?" She
and Christmas looked at one another. How did he know? Raymonda
grabbed his hand and wanted to kiss it, but he pulled away. "No, my
child," he said. "No need for that."

At that point, directing his gaze at Christmas, he said: "I am glad you
brought Raymonda to see me. She has had a very difficult childhood,
being separated from you for so long. It is a dreadful sin to tell a child her

mother is dead. So many people have conspired to make this beautiful child suffer." He turned to Raymonda. "My dear friend, you are protected by the Virgin and by angels and saints. You have no need to fear."

How does he know my name? she wondered. *Or about my aunt's cruelty? Who is this man?*

"Madame Hawa, you too have suffered because of the separation from your children. You are strong, alive, even if your children thought you were dead. They took your children from you, but you have been helping the poor and needy. You are a great woman. A saint."

Christmas began weeping, her hands covering her eyes. "Father," she said, her face still concealed. "Please tell me. How are my sons?"

Father Michel lifted his eyes to a crucifix hanging on the wall as if it were a hypnotist's crystal. Raymonda was spellbound. "George and Yussuf are far away; they are beyond the walls of Jerusalem. Do not cry, Madame, because they are in good hands with honest Catholic priests and nuns on the Mount of Olives." Still with his faced fixed on the crucifix, he described in detail their lives, what they looked like, what they were doing. "Be joyful: they have successful lives ahead of them."

"Shall I see them again?" She too was staring at the statue on the wall.

"You shall, but just for a short time; you will never live with them again. This is your destiny. There will always be a wall between you and them. Walls of wars and bloodshed; dividing you will be oceans and deserts. They will live in strange lands."

There were other people in the room waiting to talk to the priest. The priest said with a tender expression, "Take care of Raymonda. She has a mission in life."

For Christmas, the way his beard quivered and the rustling of his black wool cowl made it seem as if he had betrayed a dark secret, the grim tidings of a prophet.

"Father, a mission? Is she going to be a nun?" Her hands, strong from working, covered her face once again. "I don't want to lose her." Not even to the Church.

"No. Her mission will be outside, in the world. She will encounter many dangers and will need our intercession. I know," he continued with his gaze locked on Christmas, "I know that you have raised Raymonda not to hate. That's her mission—to show many, many others, Jews and Arabs, the same thing. To help restore love in this promised land." He said nothing more about the "mission."

Back in the convent, from the window of her room, Raymonda contemplated what Father Michel De Maria said. She saw in the "mission" a secret treasure buried in her future and which she now had to uncover. This was her quest, her "Holy Grail," as she would say.

16
Tristesse

Occasionally, from beyond the frontier, a priest or a nun smuggled a note from George and Yussuf, hidden inside a prayer book. Over the Christmas break in December 1955, Christmas received a letter from her sons, sent via Europe. The invisible masters in State Security opened it, discovered a photograph, and the next day she lost her job as a social worker. She was a "security risk," an endlessly malleable term that could cover any behavior they didn't like, such as a mother receiving word from a child.[21] Christmas ended up working as a seamstress for a detention center filled with the children of refugees arrested for stealing in Tel Aviv or Haifa. Raymonda watched as her mother's vitality leaked away.

Sitting at her antique Singer sewing machine at the detention center one day, Christmas must have seen the embers of anger radiating from Raymonda's eyes—how dare the Israelis turn you into a menial worker! She took her foot from the pedal. With fatigued yet calm words, Christmas took a long breath and opened her eyes again—they looked suddenly bloodshot. "Listen. The world spins, and everyone gets his turn. We were once the owners of this country, and now we have to work to survive. Don't be bitter—there is no shame in working. People died in the war; whole villages were destroyed; our friends disappeared. Your brothers are gone too . . . These boys here," she pointed her chin to the delinquents. "Can we blame them? They are from the villages that were destroyed: from Bassra, Kuweikat, Kabri. Their families were driven across the border, and only they remained, and now they steal from stores in Tel Aviv or Haifa or get into fights.

"I don't know why we have to suffer. There is one thing I shall never stop clinging to, and nor should you. As women, we are trapped by men in our society, but we have to keep fighting, even if it seems to be a losing battle. And we fight without hating. Hatred is what men do. We win through love."

Raymonda had not forgotten Father Michel's words. But her life's mission of "winning through love" was too much to expect from a teenager who listened to clandestine radio broadcasts from Cairo or Beirut each time she went home to Acre. On Radio Cairo, she followed stories of "glorious" Fedayeen operations and "brutal" IDF retaliation. In Egyptian-controlled Gaza, a 120 mm mortar slammed into a market and killed fifty civilians. Eighty-one Egyptian soldiers died in "Operation Volcano," a revenge operation after Fedayeen shot four Israelis. The radio reports were invariably followed up with nationalistic songs, praise for the heroic martyrs, and a rousing speech by the Egyptian strongman Gamal Abdel Nasser, the son of a village postman who had risen to be the charismatic leader of the Arab world.

Back at the convent school in Haifa in January, the head nun, her face pale and hands shaking, stood in front of the students, grasping a piece of paper. She had just received an order from the military authorities: Jewish children were no longer permitted to study at Christian schools. The Jewish girls, Raymonda's best friends, would have to leave at once. The school itself might have to close, the nun continued, because Jewish students made up most of the student body.[22]

At first there was stunned silence. How was that possible? To be sure, there were pass laws for Arabs, but Jews could go and do as they pleased. How could the government bar them from studying with Arabs? The Jewish girls had become their sisters; for Raymonda they were liberators. How could the state of Israel enforce separation? Something must be done. Maybe the cardinal or even the pope could intervene.

Remonstrations were futile. As the Jewish girls' parents came to pick them up, Raymonda cried as she hadn't since she believed her parents had died in the war.

The school indeed shut its door, and in September 1956 Raymonda moved to St. Joseph's girls' school, on the Street of the Prophets in West Jerusalem, run by French, Irish, Maltese, and Lebanese nuns. In the evenings the girls were cooped up inside the gated compound partly because Yiddish-speaking Hasidim, their neighbors, sometimes spat at Christians, as though at the devil himself. A contraband novel Raymonda read at night was Françoise Sagan's *Bonjour Tristesse*. The novel fascinated her. It was about the life of a sexualized seventeen-year-old Cécile and her playboy father whose life's motto he took from Oscar Wilde: "Sin is the only note of vivid color that persists in the modern world."

Next to the school was a hospital. The Jewish nurses liked to meet their lovers after work, in the hospital parking lot. Boyfriends with Beatnik sideburns and goatees played love songs on the guitar to the buxom nurses. Raymonda and the other girls would switch off the lights and huddle around the windows to catch sight of flirtation turning to lovemaking. "Aflame with desire, we were all curious to discover the secret for ourselves, the forbidden fruit."

Then, overnight, the nurses and their lovers in the parking lot disappeared, mobilized for battle. There was pandemonium in the country: among Jews, there was talk of a second Holocaust, with Nasser cast in the role of Führer. Hebrew newspaper columnists warned of it being minutes before villainous Nasser was strong enough to launch his war of extermination. State propaganda repeated the strongman's rousing and bellicose rhetoric on Radio Cairo against the Jews, typically right after the Egyptian diva Umm Khaltoum's concerts.

The nuns sent the girls home during a general mobilization for war. In Acre, Raymonda saw the French and British warships across the bay, in Haifa. Huddling around at home with her mother and neighbors in Acre, she sang along to patriotic songs on Radio Cairo, and like the other Arabs in town, she fully expected the Egyptians to deliver a mighty and decisive blow against the Israeli military. Adoring Arab throngs called Nasser "Al Rais," the Boss.

Meanwhile, the Iraqi-Jewish next-door neighbors were just as certain Israel would win, and not only win, that they would take Cairo, take Egypt, make a sweep of the entire Arab world. "We are invincible," they said, citing one of Moshe Dayan's cocksure speeches. "The world is with us."

17
Moshe's War

Ruth was always on the prowl for immigrants with skills she could employ in Maskit's growing operation. She heard about George Kashi, a businessman from Baghdad, who had owned a large weaving factory and exported to England cloth for use in Harris tweeds. Arab nationalists, quoting the Arabic edition of *Mein Kampf*, had expelled him and the rest of the ancient Jewish community. Ruth looked high and low for Kashi, tenaciously tracking him down in the most unlikely of places: George, his badly crippled wife, and their twenty-two-year-old son Albert, were living in the dilapidated hut she and Moshe had occupied in the defunct kibbutz of Shimron. This former factory owner and friend to people in high places in Baghdad was a defeated man who drank too much.

She perked up the demoralized man's mood with the idea of reestablishing the factory. The only hitch was he couldn't do it on his own. He wasn't a healthy man. To get the factory off the ground, he needed his son's help. Albert was a master in the weaving business and all the machinery that went along with it. But Albert dreamed of joining the air force, and was doing everything he could to be accepted into the service. He had already done his army service in a tank unit, and George was terrified at the idea of his son going back into harm's way. The idea of reestablishing the family business was the perfect tool to keep him close to home. If he just gave up the ambition of becoming a pilot.

Ruth had been around the military long enough not to be taken in by the legend of its superiority over civilian life. "Albert," she began, "your

64

father needs your help. Just put this talk of the air force to the side for a year or so. Let's get the factory up and running first." He agreed. The family moved out of the hut and into a real apartment in the development town of Migdal Haemek, the Israeli town built on the ruins of the Arab village of Al-Mujdal.

In late October 1956, with war with Egypt imminent, Albert, the master weaver, was called up for duty in the tank unit. Just before he left for the army base Albert met Ruth at the Café California to talk. His father, he explained, was in the hospital, for an operation. Albert pleaded with her not to breathe a word of his army duty, for fear it might cause his father to have a heart attack. "But if I'm not back within four days you'll have to tell him, because he'll have to decide what new work to put in the loom." Albert had come up with an ingenious new fabric, and there was just enough of the cloth in the looms for a few days of work.

That night Ruth steered a US Army jeep in the night, without headlights, to a blackened military airport to pick up Yael, on the final commercial flight before the Israeli-French-English sneak attack began. Seventeen-year-old Yael lived in England working for the *Jewish Observer* and living with H. G. Wells's daughter-in-law.

Once again, Ruth was clueless about her husband's machinations. Her information came from the state-controlled radio. Society ladies gave their gold rings and necklaces to support the war effort. Volunteers dug trenches in public parks; there were blackouts and drills, and people lined up around blocks to give blood.

Moshe executed his plans with the knowledge that his IDF was an unconquerable juggernaut. The slogan "We are invincible" was no hollow boast. What he envisioned was a victory as decisive as Prussia's humiliation of France in 1870.

The Franco-Anglo-Israeli attack began on the warm, clear morning of October 29. The IDF under his command was in fact "invincible." Moshe raced into action. His jeep was hit, and bullets punctured the outer skin of his plane, but nothing slowed down his hopscotching from front to front. He behaved like the Apaches who believed certain war paint protected them from the US Army's Winchesters. Brother-in-law Ezer, the commander of a major air base, coordinated air attacks.

Moshe poetically dubbed his war Operation Kadesh after the spot in the northern Sinai, where legend says the rankled Moses smacked the boulder with his magical rod that brought forth water. The more secular French and British designation for the campaign was "Operation Musketeer." Whatever it was called, it was a masterstroke of total surprise and effectiveness. After dust had settled, Israel's flag flew over vast swaths of Egyptian territory, including a narrow sliver of land known as the Gaza Strip.

To celebrate victory, Dayan took the family to Sarabit al-Khadim, a mountaintop, the site of the Egyptian sanctuary of the XII Dynasty, dedicated to the Goddess Hathor. Moshe commandeered his army helicopters to loot antiquities, including three half-ton 3,500-year-old stelae covered with hieroglyphs. A statue of a bird ended up in the family garden on Joab Street.

In the wake of a brilliant campaign, Ruth's life seemed more glamorous than ever. She was the wife of the conquering hero, deferred to everywhere she went. Even among the newly conquered Arabs in Gaza.

Israeli newspapers almost never mentioned the two hundred thousand Palestinian refugees in Gaza. Politicians avoided the subject, as well. But Ruth knew they were there. The day after returning to Tel Aviv from the family outing to Sinai, she hopped into a US surplus WWII-era army jeep and, with her secretary named Esther, dashed off to Gaza, across the old fortified Israeli-Egyptian border, maneuvering through blasted out tanks.

She drove directly to the mayor's office in Gaza City and, after introducing herself as Mrs. Dayan, asked if he could help her find jewelry makers whose work she thought she could use in Maskit, along with supplies of amber. Gaza had no amber and no jewelry industry, he informed her, just rugs and carpets. The mayor took Ruth to a factory, owned by six brothers, with over a thousand medieval looms and baths filled with deep indigo blue dyes. She was treated with rounds of black sweetened coffee.

Back home in Tel Aviv, she was soon in touch again with the six brothers, asking that they begin working together. They were easy to convince.

Within the brief period of Israeli occupation—by March 1957, President Eisenhower forced the Israelis to give Gaza back to the Egyptians—Ruth put some new life in the Gazans' ancient craft by sending modern designs, better dyes, and new materials to the brothers' factory.

Part II
1957–1970: Two Friends

18
Punished by Love

Israeli soldiers, returning to Migdal Haemek, were at first full of good news. One of Albert's friends claimed that he was savoring the victory, and was still with his unit down in the Sinai. There was some mopping up that needed to be done there. But as days went by, and there was still no word from Albert, worries mounted. Ruth, visiting his father in the hospital, told him about his son's role in the war. At first his parents were relieved when one of Albert's friends assured them he was alive and well, and was heading home soon.

Ruth, sensing something was wrong, set out to find Albert on her own. She headed south in the jeep to find his tank unit. No one there knew anything about his fate. Perhaps, they told her, he might be in a village deeper in the desert where someone supposedly had spotted him. So on they drove. Again, no luck.

Ruth spoke to the army's chief chaplain back in Tel Aviv and learned that a Sergeant Kashi might have died on the first day of the fighting, trapped in his tank and burned to death. There was just no proof. The only bit of identifying evidence on the charred body was an embroidered undershirt. Ruth returned to the Kashi home and asked Albert's mother if she embroidered his shirts. "No," said the mother, trembling. She sensed what was coming and denied the truth if only to live in the illusion for a few more minutes that Albert was still alive.

Ruth was determined to do something not just for the memory of Albert but for all of the young, beautiful boys she had known in her life—Zorik and Zvi and so many others crowding Israel's military cemeteries. She set her designers to work on turning fabric, created by Albert, into the most stunning line of dresses and blazers she would present to the fashion world in the United States.

She was in the bar of the Dan Hotel, meeting with her designers, when an Italian journalist buttonholed her and asked her, "Is it true you are divorcing General Dayan?"

"Divorce? What are you talking about?" The fashion designers, clearly feeling awkward, got up and left Ruth alone with the journalist.

"Well, everyone's talking about it. Word is that you're divorcing your husband."

"Why on heaven would I do that?"

"Mrs. Dayan, because of his affair, of course." This was the first time Ruth heard about his tryst with Rachel. For months, people had seen Moshe arm in arm with a stewardess he had met on a Rome-Tel Aviv flight. He was known to have had flings already, with young, old, big, and small. He fell in love with Rachel.

As Ruth heard more details from the journalist, she felt faint. She had experienced many deaths in her life, just nothing so devastating, so debilitating. It finally forced her to admit that the farmer she married was no longer there. The kibbutznik she loved, and still did, would never have deceived her so publicly, as if her feelings were unimportant.

Back home, Ruth confronted him with details she had managed to glean from the Italian journalist, and without a hint of guilt, with the same sangfroid with which he took enemy fire, he said, "Yes, you are right. I have met someone else. And I won't stop seeing her. It's up to you. You're the mother of my children, and we've had a good life together. We still do. I won't ask for a divorce, but if you want one, I won't stand in your way."

The indifference struck her just as hard as the affair itself. Questions exploded like fireworks in her mind. Why was he being so cruel? Did he want to punish her for loving him? She didn't want to leave him—divorcing the minister of defense, and a war hero to boot, was bound to be spread all over the newspapers, his tawdry behavior exposed. It would hurt the children. Yael especially, with her newfound European sophistication and her constant quoting from Françoise Sagan's *Bonjour Tristesse*, would blame her for dragging the family through the mud. She was a forty-year-old, working eighteen-hour days, and wasn't about to start over with someone else. Ruth decided to tolerate the affair.

While she continued feeding Moshe his favorite cookies and cornflakes, she went into a period of mourning and of hoping for a return of the Moshe, the farmer she had married.

19
Mandelbaum Gate

Days following the end of the 1956 war, word reached Raymonda that her cousin, the daughter of Christmas's sister, died in a playground in front of a church in Gaza, killed by a stray IDF bullet. Far more chilling rumors circulated among the girls at the convent about a massacre in the village of Kafr Qasim, inside Israeli territory, near the border with the Jordanian West Bank. The victims were like Raymonda: though citizens, they were considered a danger to state security.

The first time Raymonda thought of crossing through Mandelbaum Gate on the one-way journey to King Hussein's Trans-Jordan, irrevocably surrendering her right to return home, was just before the holiday break in December 1956. Christmas got a pass and paid a visit to Jerusalem. They stood on the roof of the Pontifical Notre Dame Hotel, looking out toward the Old City and at the seam of barbed wire that was cutting her off from her brothers. Christmas talked to Raymonda about the natural freedom she had as a woman growing up in New York — "and then I came to this country, still in the Middle Ages." Her words were reinforced by the barbed wire down below, as if the shackles she was expected to wear as an Arab woman, and the geopolitical scars below, were of the same order of magnitude, driven by the same male will for power and domination.

Christmas's face darkened: it was wrenching to be so close to her sons George and Yussuf and yet hermetically cut off. She offered a prayer, asking the Virgin to tear down the walls and blast open Mandelbaum Gate.

Raymonda, too, looking down at the slithering seam dividing Jerusalem, felt the ghastly injustice of separating people. The Jewish friends she had made in Haifa were not responsible, nor were the adults protesting against the government, nor the average Israelis she met on the streets of Haifa or Acre every day. Female soldiers chewing gum and talking about bathing suits hadn't committed the crime. But someone had.

State Security strictly forbade Arabs to have contact with anyone on the other side. The Jordanians were just as draconian. But since she lived in Israel, the leaders whose names she knew from the radio—Dayan, Sharon, and their ilk—came to personify the chilling logic behind separation. In her inner court of law, she tried and convicted Sharon and Dayan for innumerable crimes, including severing her ties to her Jewish friends.

She would also come to blame these leaders a month later at the Interior Ministry office in Haifa, when she witnessed a soldier, spittle from chewing tobacco running into the black stubble on his chin, savagely kick an Arab man on the ground, over and over, in his side.

The main reason she chose to leave to Jordan was Habib. She was his only daughter and, with George and Yussuf for so many years on the other side of the border, the only child he felt he knew. This penniless aristocrat, the prince who lived in a rented room and hustled as an unlicensed lawyer, carried with him the pride of his heritage, along with old-world snobbery and class prejudices. Raymonda, tall and beautiful, attracted whistles from men, Arabs and Jews. He had no doubt that soon she would yield to someone's amorous attention. He just wanted to make sure it wasn't someone beneath him. A commoner. If the Hawa family was to claw its way back from catastrophic loss and penury, she had to find the right match. Impeccably dressed—he had enough money to do that, at least—his hair gray, walking with a walking stick because of the bum leg, he asked her to join her brothers.

"What we have here," he exclaimed, referring to the Arabs who remained in Israel, "is not your society." The families he considered socially acceptable, and still rich, were in East Jerusalem, Amman, Beirut, or somewhere else. "I will not permit you to marry a villager!" He was like the legendary Kingfisher whose kingdom, the family's aristocratic honor and wealth, could be healed by Raymonda crossing over to the other side. She had to leave her mother and her friends behind, and join George and Yussuf in Amman.

By agreeing to be an instrument in Hawa family honor, would she be abandoning her mother? Was her father trying to separate her, once again, from Christmas and her influence? What about the "mission" Father Michel De Maria spoke about? How could she fight against the hatred poisoning the Holy Land by leaving it?

She vacillated. Her "mission" was clearly to stay. She contemplated asking Father Michel but was afraid he would counsel her to defy her father, something she couldn't do. By crossing the border she would never again wander the valleys of the Galilee with her mother, never again would she see her Jewish friends in Haifa. She might as well have stepped into a rocket ship with no way back to earth. The Jewish mayor of Acre, a friend of her mother's, urged her to stay. "Raymonda, leaving your *imma*, your mamma, is wrong. You mustn't leave."

Habib's influence was stronger.

In March 1957, Christmas drove her to Mandelbaum Gate. The Israeli officer who led her across the border permitted them one last tearful hug, and he took her to his Jordanian colleague on the other side. It was a hot spring day when she left the Jordanian border station, shaped like an oversized doghouse, and stepped into the heat. Her brother George was standing a few meters away. She hadn't seen him since she was eight years old: he was tall and had a dashing pencil mustache, along with Habib's noble pose, with a straightened back and fixed, direct gaze. She paused for a moment before rushing into his arms. It was as if she were at the edge of a cliff, bending over to see the bottom and seeing nothing. Her heart was racing, unsure whether she should continue. Was the mayor right? Would she ever see her mother again? But it was too late. The Israeli border authorities held her passport, and they wouldn't give it back, even if she begged and implored.

George too was crying because, craning his head, he was unable to see Christmas, who had already been ordered away from the border. As he tried to catch sight of her, the Jordanian soldier pointed to a woman in the distance. "You see that shadow? That is your mother."

20
Under the Shekhina's Wing

George and Raymonda embraced. He led her to a decrepit taxi that, hissing and braying like an old mule, drove down to the Jordan Valley and up again to Amman. It didn't take long for her to figure out that her brothers expected her, following Arab tradition, to be modest and know her place in society: to submit blindly to their will, and all for her own good, George never ceased assuring her, because Jordan was such a conservative society. "You should never leave the house alone; we are not in Israel; we are in an Arab country."

The first evening in Amman, George took her to a villa in a compound for top military officers. Instead of going to sit with the other women, she drifted over to the room with the cigars and cognac, lured by animated conversation.

When George tried to shoo her away—"go back with the women"—the Jordanian army's chief of staff, Field Marshal Sadek al Shareh, intervened. "My dear friend," he turned to George, "why are you sending away such a lovely lady?" The field marshal had an important question for Raymonda: he asked her if she knew Father Michel. Indirectly he had recently communicated with the clairvoyant priest about missing Jordanian pilots. Father Michel received photos of the missing men and, in a vision, saw their frozen bodies on a mountainside in central Turkey.

By sharing her own story of Father Michel, the debutante attracted the admiration of the men in the room. Too much so for George's tastes, and back at home, he slapped her across the cheek. "You are not going to become like our mother! Do you hear me! You are going to be respectable."

In Amman, there was no easy escape from George's control. Muslim zealots were known to fling acid at westernized Arab women immodestly showing their kneecaps. Most of the people on the street were men with kaffiyehs and women with hijabs.

The social circles her brothers belonged to can best be compared to White Russian barons and dukes, in Paris in the 1920s, with their genteel ways, their nostalgia, and their delusions of returning to their old way of life. These faded men of impeccable manners met for drinks and cigars in their clubs and, when George let go of his leash, they grilled her with questions about Israel and the Jews, and what was happening to their former lands and villages and cities, in what was now the Jewish state.

Marooned in a masculine culture, Raymonda no longer had a mentor—no Christmas with her feminism and humanistic values, no nuns, no Father Michel, no worldly Jewish friends. The only guides she had left were books. If only to escape from the tyrannies of life in Amman, she married an affluent Oxford-educated banker named Daoud: he called on the family three times before submitting his marriage request. Following the wedding and a European honeymoon during which she couldn't stop crying, he whisked her off to the provincial northern town of Irbid, in antiquity a Roman settlement famous for its wine and its shrines to Dionysus. Only ruins remained of those happy, bacchanal days. Daoud founded the Ottoman Bank in the town, and at night, while he was reading the paper or talking business with friends, his teenaged bride reread volumes of Simone de Beauvoir and Françoise Sagan. In secret, under the covers, she scribbled lines in her diary about feeling trapped by a stultifying Arab patriarchy and longing for the "free-and-easy existence" she had had in Israel. The poetry of Hayim Bialik came back.

> Wind blew, light drew them all.
> New songs revive their mornings.
> Only I, small bird, am forsaken
> under the Shekhina's wing.

Alone. I remain alone.
The Shekhina's broken wing
trembled over my head.

The closest she could get to returning home to Acre was the West Bank. She needed two years of cajoling before Daoud agreed to move to the Palestinian city of Nablus, the ancient Roman Neapolis. Raymonda liked to head up to a sacred mountain outside the city, where the Samaritans believe Abraham had nearly sacrificed Isaac. From there, she could see the Mediterranean coast in the distance.

Who was she? A Jordanian? Never. A Palestinian? Yes, but what was Palestine but lines on an old map. Was she an Israeli? Yes and no. She no longer had citizenship in the country, even if by sensibility she was a product of the mongrel Jewish-Arab, Hebrew-Arabic culture of Haifa and Acre. Her only links to the country were Israeli radio broadcasts and reports from the rare travelers crossing the fortified borders.

Raymonda gave birth to her first child, Diana, in 1958, in the St. Joseph's Hospital run by French nuns in Jordanian-controlled Jerusalem. Through the window, she could see Mandelbaum Gate and the Israeli flags flapping blue and white on the building beyond no man's land. A nun smuggled a note to Christmas telling her of the birth. The same nun told her of Raymonda's next child, Jubran, in 1960. It wasn't until the end of 1961, with the birth of Leila, that Christmas was permitted to visit Raymonda and meet her brood of grandchildren.

The Israelis were now permitting Christians to cross the border on Christmas Eve, and so Christmas used the eponymous holiday as her chance to see the new baby. Flinging herself in her mother's arms, she sobbed on her shoulder out of joy but also out of a melancholy awareness that the visit of a few hours would end all too soon. Christmas was only forty-seven, still beautiful despite her hardships.

Later at the party, she noticed in her mother's lively hazel eyes a flicker of indignation. Its source wasn't the division of Jerusalem, or the surly Israeli and Jordanian border guards; Raymonda's behavior was causing it. During a reception for businessmen and notables, she had withdrawn to be with the other women like a dutiful Arab wife. "Why don't you sit with the men?" Christmas, as fiery and free as ever, scolded her for *mauvaise foi.* "If you don't claim your rights, you'll be doomed to eternal submission!" She paused and continued. "I gave you independence. When you were a teenager, you went everywhere—to Tel Aviv, to Haifa. And now—this? Why are you allowing them to turn you back into . . . into an Arab wife?"

Shivering, Raymonda was too ashamed to respond. She wanted to rush into a washroom and burst into tears. She drove with Daoud back to Nablus, a disillusioned mother of four, having failed her mother and betrayed her "mission." The idea of finding true love, that impetus for crossing over Mandelbaum Gate in the first place, seemed like a cruel joke.

21
New Face in the Mirror

"Until we extend the circle of our compassion to all living things, we will not, ourselves, find Peace."

—Albert Schweitzer

Bottling up the pain of betrayal, Ruth poured her energies into Maskit. By 1960, Moshe had retired from the military and began pursuing more private hobbies. Along with digging up Maccabee coins and oil lamps and marble torsos, there was Rachel and a bevy of other lovers. One distraught lover rang up Ruth to complain that Moshe was cheating on her with a fourth woman. The mother of a different mistress, who was Yael's age, placed a tape recorder under her daughter's bed hoping for blackmail material.

Among Jews in Israel, growing prosperity meant that few Jews wanted to work in handicraft. With her brief experience in Gaza working with the six brothers, Ruth decided to venture into Arab villages inside Israel, starting with the women of Umm al-Fahm, at the time a two-mule town, because there was no industry and the Arabs, given the military regime controlling their movements, couldn't freely seek work elsewhere.

Ruth charged into town with a Romanian-trained technician and an expert on looms named Mandel Vasseli. Mandel, having only read about Fedayeen in the tabloids but having no direct experience with Arabs, was

82

a bigot filled to the brim with every stock cliché current at the time: Arabs as violent, lazy, anti-Semitic, inveterate thieves and liars. But since he loved rugs, he agreed to set up a workshop in the village. Ruth was the perfect matchmaker, and Mandel ended up adoring the women who worked the looms, and they reciprocated the affection. Mandel and the women of Umm al-Fahm produced the most exquisite creations, including a rug that wound up in the lobby of the Tel Aviv Hilton; another, the "Agam" rug named after the artist who designed it, decorated the presidential mansion around the corner from Villa Lea in Jerusalem.

Maskit still had no money in the bank, and the only way to get some was to drum up business abroad: in those days few Israelis could afford high fashion. Teddy Kollek, the mayor of Jerusalem, an old friend of Ruth's and the general director of Ben-Gurion's office, promised to help. He knew the biggest names in American Jewry, including Stanley Marcus, head of a retailer for high-end Neiman Marcus. Marcus agreed to organize an exhibition of Maskit's latest fashion line. But at the last minute, due to the faltering health of the manager—he had terminal cancer—Marcus backed out. Undaunted, Kollek put Ruth up in a suite, at the Plaza Hotel in Manhattan, and set up a meeting with Barney Balaban, the legendary president of Paramount Pictures. Balaban began his career as a messenger boy at a cold storage company to become one of the most powerful and feared moguls in Hollywood. Kollek knew that he was a close friend of Andrew Goodman, the head of the Fifth Avenue department store Bergdorf-Goodman.

Kollek and Ruth stood in Balaban's office when he made the call to Goodman. "Not interested," exclaimed Goodman in a loud growl over a speakerphone. He gave money to Israel, loved the country, kept a picture of Herzl in his wallet; he just wasn't going to do business with Israelis. In his view, they had nothing of value to offer his company. Israeli fashion? It sounded like an oxymoron. What did Mrs. Dayan expect him to do? Introduce khaki shorts into the summer catalog? Balaban was so unrelenting that just to get him off the phone, Goodman fobbed him off by agreeing to at least send one of his buyers up the street to the Plaza to meet Ruth.

The buyer took one look at the Maskit dresses, stripped to her panties, and began trying things on. She fell in such instant love with the clothes that a few months later she helped put together a fashion show, organized to sell Israeli bonds, in which Lauren Bacall and Shelley Winters stood next to Ruth on the stage, in front of two thousand fashion aficionados in Miami, to watch top models present coats and dresses.

Ruth told the story of Albert and how he was burned to death in his tank. You could hear a pin drop. Rabbi Abba Hillel Silver, an American-Jewish legend in the audience, told Ruth he had never heard such a poignant address. That night the fashion show raised $16 million in bonds, a whopping $100 million in today's dollars.

Lonely, desperate Raymonda got her first glimpse into the secrets of the Dayan family when in one sitting she devoured Yael's roman à clef *New Face in the Mirror* (1959), one of the most successful novels to arise out of the *Bonjour Tristesse* craze. Someone smuggled the banned book into Jordan, and it ended up with Raymonda. She couldn't put it down until she'd read through it twice. Sitting in straight-laced Nablus, a town without the basics of cosmopolitan life—no university, no theater or concert hall, the only cafes inhabited by men smoking hookah and playing cards—the Yael she imagined was a Françoise Sagan in khaki, a proud, emancipated woman; and each time she picked up the book she was reminded of the freedom she had had in Haifa. That Yael was the daughter of Moshe Dayan didn't matter. It was Yael's courage to defy the norms of society that made her into a kind of alter ego.

Prudish Israeli critics, taking umbrage at Yael's brazen sexuality, accused her of "undressing on Jaffa Street." She wrote the book in English, and American readers snapped it up. A *Life* magazine photographer, fated to die in the Six Day War, captured Yael in a photo titled "La Femme Fatale." Dressed in an IDF uniform and posing beneath a set of skull and crossbones, her eyes are cast into a corner, and her mouth is opened slightly as if reciting a poem by Arthur Rimbaud. In another photo she stares right into the camera, the skull hovering over her head like a macabre nimbus, her military shirt unbuttoned. In the same series, she is in Paris smoking a cigarette with a silver filter, reading a book in French.

In one scene in the novel, which begs for Freudian exegesis, the female protagonist, a soldier, lies in bed with two long guns. "I could feel them through my pajamas, where I could warm them and get used to them." Upon waking, she is holding the weapons in her hands "so tightly that they hurt . . . I thought it easier to believe in Father's hardness than in his love for me, so I ignored the love . . . And you, Mother, it was easy to believe you to be weak and in need of me." Yael knew about her father's womanizing; she also knew that her mother was employing more people than any of the large companies in Israel. Still, the mother character comes off as an emotional wreck alternating between fits of hysteria and racing off to assist the next band of helpless immigrants: just the kind of woman Yael was determined not to be.

Shortly after the novel appeared, a scandal broke out surrounding one of Moshe's mistresses, and in his political-erotic tabloid Uri Avnery covered the story in all its pornographic details. Ruth, lips pressed tight in a grim stoicism, refused to answer the swarms of journalists that followed her. Yael's response to the lurid revelations wasn't to judge her father morally or question the way he fled behind what she described as a "solid shell of superior indifference"; it was his taste in mistresses that she found "appalling." If she was critical of anyone, it was of Ruth, as if it were she who was at fault that Moshe went off, looking for someone else.

Eleven-year-old Assi told Ruth to "leave the bastard." From that point onward, Ruth and Assi formed a coalition against the competing alignment of Yael and Moshe.

22
Reverence for Life

1960 was a turning point for the most famous dynasty in Israel. Ruth and Moshe were living separate lives, joined by a common roof and not much else. Twenty-one-year-old Yael moved in with the Greek-Cyprian director Michael Cacoyannis. She did the public relations for his film *Electra*, suitably based on the ancient Greek myth of matricide. In many circles, her book made her more famous than her father. "I dress up—it can be Pucci or Gucci or Ricci; I give an interview to *Elle* or *Vogue* . . . I answer fan mail and phone calls. I go out, dinner or a club, or theater . . . with writers, artists, publishers, film people, or just rich people who like to be surrounded by artists."

Ruth and Assi took a ship to Athens to visit Yael, and the three drove her sleek-bodied Citroën DS to Delphi. It was there that Assi decided to embark on an acting career. The oracle came from friends of Yael's who had him act out a sex scene, and he did it so well that they declared him to be the future Brando.

Not long afterward, Ruth set off on an adventure. After years of putting on a brave face, enduring humiliations with fatalistic dignity, she needed to fly the coop. To escape, Ruth's South African friend Clara Urquhart, a staunch opponent of apartheid, took her into what most people considered the heart of darkness to meet the Nobel Prize laureate for peace, Albert Schweitzer.

As a world-famous doctor, scholar, organist, and humanitarian, with his fifty years of working in the jungle along with his campaign against nuclear bombs, Schweitzer had a number of zealous disciples; and of these, few were more zealous than Clara, who journeyed to the shores of the Ogowe River each year to volunteer.

The regulars of Cafe California predicted Ruth would get to Schweitzer's humanistic redoubt and stay for good. If she couldn't do much to change Moshe or get back to Gaza to help the refugees, she could give her empathetic love to the Africans.

Ruth and Clara took a rattletrap prop plane—a "flying sardine can"—to the capital of Gabon, and from the landing strip it was by dugout canoe. A handful of half-naked oarsmen loaded them and their luggage into the canoe, and with accompanying songs began to paddle upstream through steaming jungle. The exotic sounds from the jungle and the oppressive stickiness in the air made Ruth imagine herself as Katherine Hepburn's character in the *African Queen*.

As they approached Lambaréné, she noticed a huddle of people dressed in white waiting for them at the landing. "Welcome," said Dr. Schweitzer, who had a shock of white hair and a jackdaw perched on his shoulder. "We have been waiting for you and I am glad you are here." Frail, tiny Clara disappeared into the old man's embraces while Ruth got a polite handshake and a gentlemanly bow.

Among the first things she noticed about Schweitzer's compound was the rotting stench that pervaded everything, and the cultic behavior of some of his followers. With the stultifying heat and afternoon downpours, the living, dying, decomposing vegetation, and the merciless struggle for existence—part of the compound was a leper colony—she realized that only the hardiest and most idealistic of followers, or the looniest, could hack it. One doctor walked around with a monkey in his pocket, and a nurse shared her shack with a wildcat. Outside Ruth's hut, and next to the TB ward, sat a witch doctor casting evil spells against Schweitzer and his team for taking away his business. A highlight of the trip for Ruth was a Nativity play put on by the denizens of the Leper Village. The Grand Docteur built the village with the money he got from his Nobel Prize.

Ruth spent most of her time working in the orphanage with abandoned babies. (According to the local beliefs at the time, identical twins brought bad luck and were pitched into the forest.) Her bed was a narrow army cot, she read at night with a kerosene lamp, and the shower—it was in back of the dining hall and hung from a rope—was a big bucket with nail holes on the bottom. She went to sleep accompanied by cicadas and bullfrogs, and sometimes tom-toms.

She also did her best not to be lured in by the doctor—she had learned her lesson about being sucked into the orbit of a strong man's charisma. The weeks she spent in the primeval wilderness gave Ruth ample time to observe Schweitzer from up close, quirks and all. She likened the nightly dinner scene around the table to the tea party the mad-hatter gave in *Alice in Wonderland*, with Schweitzer in the role of the mad-hatter. While he went native in some things—his opposition to flush toilets, for instance— when he sat down for a plate of crocodile fillets prepared in the German sauerbraten tradition, he spread a freshly laundered linen napkin on his lap, and carved the fillet on Alsatian china. Following the meal, everyone gathered in a room decorated with a cuckoo clock to sing Lutheran hymns. He played Bach toccatas on a warped, out-of-tune organ.

Another of his quirks was a pantheistic nature worship he called "reverence for life." Ruth saw him nearly swat a new arrival, Maria Preminger, for killing a mosquito as it was sucking her blood. (Her husband Otto had just come out with the movie *The Exodus*.) "There are two means of refuge from the miseries of life," he announced. "Music and cats." His greatest spiritual breakthrough in life wasn't healing people or playing Bach's fugues. It was watching hippos in the Ogowe River, caring for their young.

Odd though he undoubtedly was—with amazement she watched him tiptoeing to avoid stepping on bugs—he was immensely kind. Schweitzer racked up a wall full of degrees in philosophy, theology, and medicine and nevertheless decided to give up the good life of a professor in Wilhelmine, Germany, and headed to the rainforest to serve people that self-defined civilized Europeans dismissed as poor savages, the precise opposite approach to life of Moshe's ego-driven will-to-power and worship of money. The secular saint was a counter figure to Moshe. Here was a charismatic genius using his powers to preserve life, at all cost.

The leftist bohemians at California Café weren't far off the mark with their prediction that Ruth would stay. She thought about it mostly because the human closeness and Spartan dedication brought back memories of her days on the farm, and it reinforced her aversion to materialism, and the mad scramble for wealth that was already then making inroads into Israeli society. An additional factor that tempted her into staying was the reigning pacifism of the hospital. No one there, and especially not Schweitzer, deferred to her as the wife of the general.

Shortly after Ruth's return to Israel, she received a letter from a woman she had met at Schweitzer's hospital camp. The woman told her about a deadly epidemic racing through the orphanage, and she expressed her gratitude to her new friend for her "gentleness of spirit, purity of heart, modesty of soul." Ruth was able to care for the children because she too understood "suffering."[23]

23
A Man Problem

Ruth and Moshe still took trips abroad together, often under false names and with a squadron of bodyguards. On Joab Street, she hosted foreign dignitaries passing through. Ruth took one guest, Eleanor Roosevelt, to meet the Yemenite Jews. She also invited Sartre and Simone de Beauvoir for lunch. She wasn't so impressed with him, a "funny-looking little man with those thick glasses that made him look like a turtle." Simone de Beauvoir was something else. She got a signed copy of *The Second Sex* out of the visit.

In the years leading up to the Six Day War in 1967, Yael the jet-setter ran around in the liveliest circles in Europe. Her parents visited her on the island of Crete where Michael Cacoyannis was filming his masterpiece *Zorba the Greek*. Besides drinking ouzo with Anthony Quinn, she wrote her next novel, *Death Had Two Sons*, a romanticized contrast between the life experiences of a vital, virile kibbutznik and his father, a Holocaust survivor wasting away of cancer.

If Moshe was the ur-kibbutznik, the "first born of redemption," Assi was the pot-smoking anti-hero. Yonatan Geffen, Moshe's nephew, moved in with the Dayan family following his mother Aviva's suicide and his father's abandonment. Yonatan and Assi became inseparable. It was an attachment Moshe wasn't crazy about because they sat around at home, got high whenever they could, read Freud, Nietzsche, and Schopenhauer, and, inspired by Arthur Rimbaud, the two wrote existentialist poetry to the loud accompaniment of Dylan's protest ballads. The quiet sanctuary of the home in Zahala was interrupted by loud howls of "The Times They Are A-Changin'," Dylan's legendary album boiling over with rage at racism, poverty, and war. Moshe was beginning to think that Assi was a good-for-nothing when his youngest child made no bones about his hatred of the military. In basic training, he went AWOL and wound up in the stockades for thirty days.

Over on the other side of the fortified border, intellectuals were up in arms to hear about Sartre and Simone de Beauvoir's visit to Israel. Raymonda felt especially betrayed, as if the two had stood her up on a date.

She was finally catching up to Yael in her reading. Bored and desperate, feeling suffocated by chauvinistic Arab society and caged in by her own home and a conservative husband, she soaked up every book foreigners brought over the border to King Hussein's desert kingdom. Her mother's example of American-style liberation coupled with summer trips to Beirut, an open, free city considered the Paris of the Middle East, gave the restless wife the courage to wiggle free of tradition by rebelling against her expected role as docile wife and mother. If she couldn't return home to Acre and couldn't fulfill her "mission," at least she could breathe some life into Nablus's stultifying patriarchy.

The impetus came through reading Henrik Ibsen's *A Doll's House* and seeing herself in the character of Nora, the pretty, pampered, and enslaved child-wife who, in a journey of self-discovery and out of rebellion against male domination, left her husband and children. While Raymonda wasn't about to do that, what she did was enough to become a center of scandal. People questioned her respectability for driving a car on her own: in those days, the West Bank was almost like puritanical Saudi Arabia, and she was the first woman to do it. And she liked driving fast.

She raised far more eyebrows among the Nablus elite, and approbation from Daoud, by inviting an eighty-player jazz ensemble from Indiana to perform in the city. Nablus was split between pro and anti jazz factions. Opponents didn't like the idea of so many Americans, all nicely dressed boys in suits and dark narrow ties like the Beatles on the *Ed Sullivan Show*, descending on their well-ordered, conservative town. The fact a housewife could play the impresario for such a large and unprecedented event got the rumor mill going that she was a CIA spy.

Daoud took a lot of ribbing about her madcap idea. Ignoring the sniping and his spirited but futile approbation of her "shameless behavior," she took on the role of a Parisian salon hostess during the Age of Voltaire by opening up her home as a gathering place, or refuge, for the local intelligentsia and members of foreign consulates from East Jerusalem, where the denizens of the salon discussed Nasser and feminism and other seditious subjects. She read and translated long, dramatic passages from *Madame Bovary* and *A Doll's House* to a room filled with people uncomfortably shifting in their chairs.

Friends of her banker husband ramped up the pressure on him to bring her to heel when she starting writing articles in the liberal newspaper *Jerusalem Star*, articles sprinkled liberally with citations from *The Second Sex*: "Just as in America there is no Negro problem, but rather a white problem; just as anti-Semitism is not a Jewish problem, it is our problem; so the woman problem has always been a man problem."

She ignored Daoud's remonstrations and demands that she act like the other respectable wives in town. She had given him her youth and now three children, and she wasn't going to sacrifice her dreams.

Far more of a problem for Raymonda than Daoud was King Hussein. In his British officer's uniform and wearing a kaffiah, the monarch brooked no dissent. Bedouin soldiers, with canine loyalty, conducted house searches in Nablus, looking for "subversive" materials by communists, Nasserites, and Palestinian nationalists. She hid two dangerous books in a safe spot: *Madame Bovary* and *The Second Sex*. She had practically memorized them by now, with each fresh reading prompting long diary entries about the panicked sensation of being strangled and her desperate search for love and freedom. Wiping away the tears, she burned her beloved volume of Bialik in the garden. Yael's book ended up in the safe hands of a visiting diplomat's wife.

In 1963, Raymonda was back at Mandelbaum Gate for her annual Christmas meeting with her mother. There she stood, pregnant with her fourth child, waiting for what seemed like hours. Where was she?

Had something happened? A Catholic priest approached Raymonda and laid a gentle hand on her shoulder, "Your dear mother has passed away." Chronic stress had broken Christmas down, and she died of a heart attack at the age of forty-eight. The priest, seeing the anguish on her face, said, "You look like the sad Madonna. The tragedy of the Palestinians is imprinted on your face." This time, unlike the rumors of her death she had heard as a child, she knew her mother was gone, that she would never see her again. Feelings of shame for having followed her father's desires and leaving her mother returned. The only thing that pulled her from a crippling depression was the new child growing inside.

Months later she was in labor and Daoud drove her to Jerusalem in their Buick Electra with fins. It was dark, rainy, and cold. The contractions were becoming stronger and stronger, and with each curve they took through the two-lane mountain roads of northern Palestine, Raymonda gripped the car seat and moaned. Faster! She was afraid of delivering the baby in the front seat. Daoud picked up the speed. "Why do I always give in to your idiotic whims?" he asked her, exasperated. "Why do you insist on having the child in Jerusalem? Don't we have hospitals in Nablus? Of course we do. Why can't you be like everyone else?"

But she wasn't like the others. Jerusalem was the symbol of a city where, like Acre, Jews, Christians, and Arabs once lived together in tangled, Crusader-era quarters. Because of that and because of the nuns from Raymonda's old school on the Street of the Prophets, she had to give birth in Jerusalem.

Suha was born in the French hospital on Mount Scopus. Friends brought large silver platters of Nablus's famous cheese dish covered with almonds, pine nuts, and pistachios. The French nuns decorated her room with exquisite embroidered pillows. "I looked at my beautiful child and felt overwhelmed by God's precious gift. From out of the window I saw the rising sun to the east brightening the walls of Jerusalem into a light pink. In my three previous births a French nun had smuggled a letter from Mother across Mandelbaum Gate. Now there was nothing."

The next year, in 1964, Habib got permission from the Israeli and Jordanian authorities to spend a week with Raymonda in Nablus. He was already suffering from the cancer that would kill him. After a week, an ambulance took the Syrian prince back to the border, and from there he wound up in a hospital in Tel Aviv where he died alone and was buried in a mausoleum in the ancestral family cemetery in Acre.

24

The Women's Strike

In 1966 Yael was finishing up *Dust*, her latest novel about an immigrant town situated in what she portrays as barren wilderness and built by young, starry-eyed pioneers under the thrall of Zionist "dreams that are thousands of years old."

Though she never made it back to the shores of the Ogowe River—Schweitzer died in 1965—Ruth followed Clara's clandestine work for the African National Congress (ANC) in South Africa.[24] She also kept up her frenetic schedule with Maskit, working mainly with Arab women and flying back and forth to Europe and America for fashion shows. On one longer trip to Asia on behalf of Maskit, she flew into Saigon on a last-ditch effort to breathe life into her marriage. Moshe's book on the 1956 war was so good that an Israeli newspaper commissioned him to trudge off to the jungles to report on the American war in Vietnam. One of the iconic images from the trip comes from *Time*. The spread it did describes Moshe as "knee-deep in mud" and "pushing doggedly ahead into Vietcong territory . . . moving like a worm in hot ashes."

Without telling him, Ruth packed a small gun, the kind that the saloon owners carry in the Westerns, threw her things in a bag, and headed out to find him.

Saigon was in the middle of war. Already in the airport Ruth saw only soldiers, and she could hear the sound of bombs from the incessant Vietcong attacks. The driver who took her to a run-down hotel on the outskirts of town, where the electricity had been cut off by a recent guerrilla attack, told her to keep the window of the car open in case some-one tossed in a grenade. Just pick it up, he instructed her, and lob it back. "Be quickie, quickie, or we deadie, deadie!" The same driver told her she wouldn't be able to visit the villages where much of the best handicraft came from because they were under Vietcong control. The rebels would kill him if he drove her there, and take her hostage.

From the hotel, Ruth sent a message to the American top man General Westmoreland's office asking them to pass on the news to Moshe that she was in town. Within a couple hours, Moshe turned up in an armored jeep.

"What the hell are you doing here?"

"I've come to see you," she replied. "Why else would I be here? Are you happy?"

"A little. Well, yes." And he was. The two had the last romantic evening of their marriage. They went to a Chinese restaurant, where they laughed and drank, and then at the club they danced the fox trot, all the while bombs were exploding outside, the rattle of gunfire rose above the wailing sounds of horns and trumpets of the orchestra.

The next day he returned to the jungle, and Ruth spent two days in Saigon listening to the tragic tales of Vietnamese prostitutes in the bars, serving the American boys.

In early 1967, Raymonda was reading Sartre's *Nausea* and *No Exit* about a crippling, profound ennui. She had a lot of time on her hands for con-traband books because the king had imposed a strict curfew on Nablus, with orders to open fire on anyone moving around at night without per-mission. She had to mothball her literary salon.

Brute suppression was the palace's response to a popular protest move-ment against the government for its weak-kneed response to an Israeli raid on a West Bank village. Operating from Jordanian refugee camps, Arafat's guerrillas snuck into Israeli territory and killed three soldiers with a bomb. The Jordanian government, fearful of Israeli reprisals, offered to use bloodhounds to hunt down the men responsible. The king sent a neighborly letter of condolence to the Israeli government.

Chief of Staff Rabin ignored Jordanian entreaties and unleashed six hundred soldiers, backed by tanks, across the Jordanian border. They targeted the village of Samua. While the villagers had had nothing to do with Fatah, meting out justice was not the purpose of "Operation Shredder." The scores of civilians killed or wounded and the homes blown up by sappers delivered the message that Israel was invincible.

As soon as word reached Nablus, people poured into the streets chanting, "Yesterday it was Samua, tomorrow it could be Jenin or Nablus." The monarchy's loyal herdsmen, Bedouin nomads resentful of better-educated and wealthier Palestinians, beat demonstrators with rifle butts, flayed them with their camel whips and fired live rounds into crowds. Hundreds of demonstrators ended up in El Jafar, the dreaded desert concentration camp. The regime slapped a strict curfew on everyone else.

On one occasion Raymonda was at home in the bathroom, brushing her teeth, and she looked up to find a soldier outside the window. He kept the rifle raised and drew a bead on her chest. She let out a scream, and the soldier scurried off.

With her neighbor Sahar Khalifeh, a friend and novelist from the Women's Union, Raymonda sped into action.[25] In one of her contraband feminist books she read about the women in ancient Greece who had called a sex strike to put an end to war. In a variation on the theme, and with politically active men sitting in prison or otherwise muzzled, she and partners in the Women's Union sent word to hundreds of women, and the following day they marched to the governor's mansion with their demands. To the soldiers, too dumbfounded to open fire, the women chanted at the top of their lungs, "Arms for self-defense! An end to the brutality of the army! An end to the curfew! Release the imprisoned intellectuals and political leaders!"

A few days later the government suspended the curfew, while keeping the regime's repressive apparatus in place. The king, fearful of overthrow by restless Palestinians who made up half the population of his kingdom, learned one fatal lesson: next time the Israelis start shooting, he had to respond with at least a symbolic show of resistance.

25
Six Days

"Then God looked over all he had made, and he saw that
it was very good! And evening passed and morning came,
marking the sixth day."

—Genesis 1:31

It was in an atmosphere of clampdown and the muzzling of dissent that
over the radio Raymonda listened to Nasser stirring up the Cairo mob
with heartrending addresses. "Our basic objective will be the destruction
of Israel," Nasser said, emboldened by fresh shipments of Soviet weap-
onry. "The Arab people want to fight."

The more histrionic the rants, the louder he beat the war drums, the
more bloodcurdling the threats, the more Raymonda suspected that the
man nicknamed Al Rais—"The Boss"—had no intention of taking on
American-backed Sparta. From Sartre and her mother, she developed a
disdain of inauthenticity, so evident in the play-acting of Arab leaders.
Nasser was posturing.

During the days leading up to a war that would change the lives of
Israelis and Palestinians for decades, most Israelis weren't nearly as per-
spicuous as Raymonda and felt like outgunned underdogs facing a dastardly maniac. Newspapers and radio commentators made references to
the *Führer* and described how mustachioed Nasser had hired ex-Nazi
rocket scientists to execute his evil plots. From the press came deafening

drumbeats to get Dayan back at the helm of the military. For most Israelis he was like the masked hero coming to the rescue of the innocent victim, tied to the railroad tracks.

Ruth felt the same way. Moshe might have been a womanizing rascal but his love for the State of Israel was unquestioned.

The wave of national hysteria pressured Prime Minister Levi-Eshkol to hand over the Ministry of Defense to Dayan. The old team was back: Moshe, Rabin, Ezer Weizman, and Arik Sharon. Weizman, elated to have his brother-in-law in charge, talked about "leadership walking on two legs and having one eye." Ezer provided him with a detailed plan to destroy the Egyptian air force with a preemptive raid.

The morning of the sneak attack, on June 5, Moshe had toast and cornflakes with Ruth followed by coffee and croissants with his mistress Rachel. His mood was "fantastically optimistic," Rachel said later, and not least, because a fortuneteller he consulted assured him that the war would end in glory.

According to Israeli plan, the US-supplied Phantom and French-supplied Mirage jets, dipping and diving over the Egyptian desert, decimated the Egyptian air force.

In the West Bank, the seething discontent of King Hussein's subjects, barely contained by his camel-mounted soldiers, was the reason he opened fire once news reached him of the Israelis' attack against the Egyptians. His feeble efforts led to the Israeli military juggernaut's conquest of what was left of Palestine.

The following day, June 6, brought to Raymonda's mind the Jewish fortuneteller who had warned Habib against giving her the name "Raymonda." Instead of celebrating her birthday with American-style frosted cake, candles, and balloons as her children had planned, she listened to sporadic BBC reports of Israeli advances on Jerusalem. Nablus was graveyard still. Radio broadcasts from Cairo spoke of an assault by "enemies and cowards," and other verbal exercises in self-deception. King Hussein feebly pleaded for Palestinians to "kill the infidel wherever you find them, with your arms, hands, nails, and teeth if necessary."

Switching stations to Israeli radio, Raymonda heard a husky male voice, like that of a sports announcer, proclaiming, "We have taken Ramallah, Jenin, Tulkarm, and Kalkilya. Our troops are now approaching Nablus. The enemy forces are surrendering."

The Tawil family lived in Nablus in the greenest corner of Palestine, and throughout the day before the fall of Nablus they sat in the basement because troops from the Israeli position were firing a hailstorm of bullets at the side of the house. On the other side of the valley, above a copse of pines, Weizman's jets launched rockets at a company of tanks belonging to the Jordanian army fleeing from the hopeless fighting in the north. Within minutes the tanks were split open like tin cans, their turrets blown open, their cannons facing random directions.

When Raymonda headed upstairs to grab water and food, what she saw out the window—bodies littering the orchards—brought flashbacks of 1948. Down in the valley were thousands of refugees streaming out from the city of Kalkilya. Pushing wheelbarrows, dully, ploddingly, the people were dressed in whatever they could grab before running, as if the devil himself were at their heels. Society ladies, flinging away their high heels, hobbled barefoot.

She threw on a pair of sneakers and, waving a white bath towel in her hand, dashed out of the house until she reached a group of women, children, and a few old men. One woman, bleeding from shrapnel wounds in the kidney, collapsed in front of her. "What's happening?" They told her that Israeli leaders had ordered their evacuation, and the Israeli army was systematically destroying the town, using tanks and dynamite. "We were forced to leave." A dozen voices rose at once. "The soldiers—they brought everyone to the mosque and ordered us to get out of the town. Even when we left, they shot at us."

The refugees were in desperate need of food and water. She and Daoud did what they could, which wasn't much; there were hundreds, thousands, and more arriving by the hour. As dusk approached, she and her neighbor Sahar Khalifeh drove along deserted roads to the St. Luke's Evangelical Hospital in Nablus to see if they could send anyone to tend to the wounded. Nablus hadn't yet been conquered, and the king's soldiers manning the checkpoints let the two women pass. It was getting late; the sun dipped down behind the bare brown hills. There was dust in the air, and a strange smell, a portent of the horror that was to strike later that night.

The chief surgeon at the hospital was screaming, "What do you mean help you? I can't operate here in the hospital." Wounded people from Kalkilya filled the corridors. "I need plasma; all my supplies are bad because of the electricity." Power outages cut the juice for hours at a time, and the hospital lacked enough diesel fuel to run the generators. Some of the wounded were Egyptian and Iraqi officers. Raymonda went home to get hand-tailored business suits from Daoud's closet and gave them to the wounded officers so they could be smuggled out before the Israeli army showed up to arrest them.

"Hey, where the hell are my suits?" Daoud later wanted to know.

"Well, with some luck they're on their way to Cairo."

The next day, instructions from the mayor of Nablus for citizens to hang white sheets from their balconies removed all doubt: Palestinians had lost the city before putting up a fight. It was dead quiet as Sahar and Raymonda jumped back in the car and returned to Nablus to find the director of social work in Nablus at home in his house slippers. They pushed the reluctant man into the back seat of the car like in a hijacking, painted a crude red cross on the hood, and headed directly to the provisional headquarters of the Israeli military. They dodged roadblocks, whizzed past wrecks of jeeps, burned out and still smoking, and dodged bodies on the street, most of them civilians. Bullet casings littered the ground.

Then suddenly, there they were, Israeli women in uniforms. They were foreign invaders, and as such, Raymonda had to oppose them, even though she had more in common with them than the docile wives of Nablus. The IDF women, crackling with health, were less like invaders than a group of idealized women in a fashion ad.

The director of social work assumed the soldiers would either shoot or arrest them. "You don't know these people," snapped Raymonda. "I do; believe me, we'll get through." Given her education in Haifa, she was one of a handful of Palestinians who could distinguish between soldiers following orders and their invisible, all-powerful leaders giving them. The only Israeli leader whose face she could conjure up was piratical Dayan's. Soldiers hadn't initiated the destruction of Kalkilya: that much she was certain of. Soldiers hadn't ordered napalm dropped on peasants' fields.[26] Generals did.

Speaking Hebrew, she dazzled a clutch of male soldiers who let them pass all the way to the command post. The men, their caps canted at rakish angles, whistled and shouted at Raymonda and Sahar, *Ezeh chatichot!* What babes! The director of social work, too faint to move, remained silent.

"Raymonda!" She stared in disbelief. There in front of her was one of her Jewish neighbors from Acre, an Iraqi. They had played hide-and-go-seek together as children.

"What the devil are you doing here?"

"I should ask you the same question," she rejoined after they hugged one another, all to the astonishment of Sahar and the other soldiers. "We are going to Damascus, Raymonda," he said with a boyish excitement in Arabic. "We're on our way to Syria. We're gonna kick the shit out of them!" She had family in Damascus, and to hear her childhood friend boast about "kicking the shit" out of the Syrians and attacking Damascus, the jewel of the Arab world, horrified her just as much as the senseless destruction she had seen that day. She turned cold. "Instead of giving him a slap, I brushed past him." The next day in the Golan he died when he stepped on a land mine.

One of the older officers asked Raymonda where she learned Hebrew, and she told him her story. He turned out to be an old schoolmate of Habib's. "In honor of your father," he said in a refined literary Arabic, "I will help you," he said. He took the three to the director of the Israeli Red Cross, but when they asked him to transfer plasma to St. Luke's, the director, sworn to the Red Cross's motto "with humanity, toward peace," barked out some vulgarities and called Arabs "primitives." "Yeah sure, you attack us, you want to drive us into the sea, and now you come to us for blood! Go to hell!"

Raymonda wanted to lunge at him with her polished fingernails. "You Israelis are the ones who cut the electricity to the hospital. You ruin our blood supply and then call us primitive!"

Habib's old friend intervened and demanded that the Israeli Red Cross transfer blood to the hospital. He then introduced Raymonda to an extraordinary man, Dayan's military governor for the West Bank, a veteran kibbutznik and scholar named Zvi Elpeleg.[27]

She told Colonel Elpeleg about the refugees from Kalkilya, and at first he didn't believe her. "Then come to my home this evening and meet them," she replied. He did. The sight of hundreds of people camped out in fields, hungry, thirsty, evicted from their homes, shocked him into sending jeeps and tanks to deliver milk and bread to the refugees, and to evacuate the wounded to St. Luke's. Raymonda struck up a conversation with one of the soldiers, an immigrant from Morocco who spoke French and expressed boundless bitterness at what he had witnessed during the fighting, things that went against what he called the "democracy and humanity of the Jewish people." He lifted up his assault rifle with a look of almost deranged horror. "You must believe me, madam, I didn't use the rifle. I saw soldiers shoot down children, but I didn't. *Croyez-moi, Madame.*" The cruelty he had witnessed wasn't Jewish. "What's happening to this country?" he continued with a string of curses. "The land of our ancestors, the land of the prophets. Like Dayan, the great prophet!"

Raymonda translated as some of the refugees asked the French-speaking soldier if they could return to their homes. "Ask Moshe Dayan if you have a place to go to. Kalkilya no longer exists! Finished!"[28]

26
The Dayan-asty

"Dayan is wearing Jerusalem like a new pair of shoes."
—Halim Isber Barakat, *Days of Dust*

The closest Ruth got to the fighting was when an Iraqi Russian-supplied Tupolev bombed a neighborhood close to Nahalal, wounding twenty-one and killing a distant member of the Dayan clan. Ezer phoned her to assure her that Zorik's son Uzi, serving in the paratroopers, was safe and sound in the freshly conquered Sinai.

In a matter of a few short weeks Dayan catapulted from being a washed-up retired general gluing together Iron Age pottery shards to being featured on the front cover of the June 16 edition of *Time* with the banner headline "How Israel Won The War." An English tabloid voted him the fifth sexiest man on earth, and fashion models in London, Paris, and Tokyo took to sporting eye-patches.

Most people associated him as the leader of the daring Jewish underdogs, a modern David that knocked out the villain in as few days as God conjured up the cosmos. The iconic picture of Moshe marching to the liberated Western Wall in the Old City reinforced the message that the Jewish people were finally in control of their own past, present, and future. The listless years of retirement made him receptive to myth-mongering, and standing in the narrow passageway between a wall built by King Herod, the Wailing Wall, and the Maghrebi Muslim quarter, the oldest in the city—Arafat had spent four years there as a child—he surveyed the scene. Some of his soldiers wept openly just by touching the legendary stones that once belonged to the Second Temple. Moshe waxed poetic on Jewish history: "How many times did the Jewish people have such a victory? Not since King David and Alexander Yannai." From between the Herodian stones he plucked a flower for his mistress Rachel.

Assi, a soldier in the paratroopers, sat out the war in the north close to the Lebanese border, playing chess. Udi, a six-year veteran of the Navy Frogs, landed in the stockade because he commandeered an army jeep and roamed around the freshly conquered Golan Heights. Lieutenant Yael, the most Alpha among the lot, was a correspondent in the Negev and Sinai deserts, the main theaters of war. At one point she found herself in a ruined enemy outpost, and despite the fact that Daddy was far off, she sensed his ubiquitous presence, more powerful than ever. "His face was with me, his strong, stable gaze, his calm, composed confidence, brain ticking away like a radar searching for options in a circular movement."

Yael shared a helicopter ride with General Sharon, then a husky, manly, handsome warrior she addressed as Arik instead of "sir" because she had grown up across the street from him. Staring down at the West Bank, Sharon turned and exclaimed gleefully with a little boy's wide-eyed enthusiasm and his "diabolically brilliant military brain: This is all ours now." In a different chopper ride over the conquered Sinai, with her father and Uncle Ezer this time, she looked down at corpses floating in the Suez Canal. "It must be unbearable," she heard her father say, "to be part of a defeated army."

Not even on the film set of *Zorba the Greek* did Yael feel so alive, so exhilarated, so transformed, as if she belonged to a nation of righteous heroes.

She loved the thrill of danger and the "wonderful sense of comradeship." During the fighting, she wished it "would never end. I never again wanted to return to my old life and face the glamor of a writer's world."[29]

And it was an easy mood to fall into when you consider that a mere twenty-two years had passed since the Nazis had killed most of European Jewry: now she was in a helicopter hovering over the mythic Judea and

Samaria, the land of David and Solomon and the Maccabees, and her father was the new Joshua blowing his horn and causing the walls—the barbed wire—to tumble that had separated Jews from their ancient past.

Ruth shared the euphoria of victory, though for different reasons. Her hometown of Jerusalem was unified again, and everyone was celebrating, Arabs and Jews. On her first trip back to the city, the same day Moshe opened up Mandelbaum Gate, she noticed the way Arabs greeted Jews with the tomatoes they wanted to sell, or the way they hurried off to Jaffa Street in West Jerusalem to find a job or buy a radio at half the Jordanian price. Peddlers offered to sell her "Friendship" pencils made in Communist China. It was like a miracle. The ethnic hatred that had torn the city apart in 1947 and '48 was nowhere to be seen. She didn't notice a single act of violence, barely even a harsh word.

She obviously wasn't looking hard enough.

Unshackled and overjoyed at living again in a land dimly similar to what she knew in her youth, Ruth was soon tooling around the Palestinian lands freely in her Saab coupe. In Bethlehem she wandered around the streets alone looking for friends from before 1948.

Another of her first trips was to Gaza to reestablish contact with the six brothers she met in 1956. While there, she visited a school in a refugee camp to deliver toys donated by Abie Nathan, the owner of the California Café. Nathan had always felt guilty about the role he played in driving peasants from the Hawa family village in 1948. The teacher, originally from Jaffa and missing a leg due to the fighting in 1948, had festooned a banner from the cracked wall of the classroom: "We Shall Return!"

27
Open Bridges

Shortly after the war ended, a Fiat with yellow Israeli plates drove up to the Tawil house, and an elegantly dressed man got out, approached the front door, and disappeared inside. The man was a relative of Raymonda's from her mother's village of Kfar Yassif in the Galilee. No one in Nablus knew him, and his was the first Israeli civilian car to venture into that part of the West Bank. Raymonda's behavior had for years fed the rumor mill, mainly that she was a CIA spy. Now people suspected the stranger of being a Mossad agent and Raymonda of being a collaborator. That night someone slipped a note under the front door. It was her first of many death threats.

Suspicion was for many Palestinians an automatic response to defeat, in particular when Dayan, the man at the helm of the victorious military machine, proclaimed to the international press, days after the war, that there was "no more Palestine," that that chapter in world history was "finished," that "Judea and Samaria" were "part of our land, to be settled, not abandoned," and that Jews were "returning to the cradle of our people, to the inheritance of the Patriarchs, the land of the Judges and the fortress of the Kingdom of the House of David."

And yet the fact that one of Raymonda's cousins could so easily drive across the old fortified border was a sign that Moshe's was no ordinary military regime. With the same speed and determination the veteran commando had used in conducting warfare, he gave orders to clear away the barbed wire and land mines separating Palestinians like Raymonda and

Daoud from their former homes in Haifa, Jaffa, Ramle, and other cities and towns and villages. Everyone, it seemed, was "returning."

In public, his policy for the occupied territories and the million Arabs living there, including hundreds of thousands of refugees from 1948, was referred to as the "Open Bridge." Dayan told General Zvi Elpeleg, the man he sent to govern the West Bank, that the Israeli army had no business running the schools, courts, and garbage collection services for Arabs, and he should stay out of people's hair as much as possible. Elpeleg, the antithesis of the pompous colonial administrator, agreed. The military governor of Nablus, General Givoli, another fine officer of great ability, received the same instructions: Let Palestinians plant their crops, raise their kids, work in Israeli supermarkets—they can even hop an Egged bus for an afternoon at the beach. The "Open Bridge," Dayan knew, was a temporary measure and would only delay the inevitable clash. Because the disarray among local Arabs couldn't last forever, because people don't forget the pain of conquest and loss, because Israelis would have to push through with their "work against the wishes of the Arabs . . . we are doomed to live in a constant state of war with the Arabs, and there is no escape from sacrifice and bloodshed."[30]

With Moshe's often-paralyzing headaches, his one eye that made reading difficult, his spotty written English, and his impatience with sitting at a desk, he relied on Yael for much of his writing. "We will leave [the Palestinians] alone," she declared to the *Daily Telegraph*, "as long as they don't co-operate with saboteurs." The article dangles the prize of "self-determination" in front of well-behaved Arabs.

What Dayan confided to his inner circle of commanders, men such as his pal Arik, was the way amicable relations with local Arabs was a tactic in the struggle over land and resources. He envisioned streams of Jewish settlers populating East Jerusalem and the hills above Jenin, Ramallah, Bethlehem, Hebron, and Nablus.[31] With this long-term strategy, Moshe took decisive steps in inventorying the land, conducting censuses, sending in water and agricultural experts, and laying the bureaucratic foundation for what within a decade would become the settlement movement. Already in 1968 the IDF set up the first militarized moshav along the Jordan Valley.

28
The Return

Weeks after the war concluded, the social event of the year took place in the archeological garden of the Dayan family home. Assi and his bride-to-be had made their wedding plans before the war. Soon after the war, Yael showed up and announced that she, too, wanted to get in on the action and proposed a double wedding. Ruth liked the idea; she just wanted to know something about the bridegroom, General Dov Sion, a man she had never heard of. Moshe knew him because Dov, nearly twice Yael's age, was Sharon's chief of staff. Yael met him a month earlier when he was part of the Israeli drive toward the Suez. Their decision was as quick as the war: "No time for preliminaries," she later told a reporter with a military cadence to her voice, "no time for the slow evolvement of emotions. Life at the front line is concentrated, and you see the good and bad in people at once."

The wedding party threw the spotlight on the goldfish bowl that from the outside seemed to be the most glittering, the most beautiful, most powerful family in the country, all to the accompaniment of a Greek band. Sharon was Dov's best man.

Two thousand guests streamed through the family garden that day, including Ezer and Reumah, Danny Kay, and Ben-Gurion, who "beamed with delight"; even the mayor of Nablus got an invitation. In a photo, Yael leans against a looted bronze door with an ancient Koranic verse etched into the surface. She is wearing a dress made from woven gold fabric from

Albert, the master weaver. From the expression on her face, life couldn't have been better.

Ruth, too, seemed to bask in the glory of her husband's fame. She appeared on the *David Frost Show*, alongside Kentucky Fried Chicken's Colonel Sanders and the movie star Shelley Winters. But none of that interested her, not the television interviews, not the huddle of photographers following her every move, not the exaggerated assessments of Moshe's military brilliance.

Crossing the old border back into the Palestinian lands felt like a furlough from prison. She was back in the unified land of her youth.

Having been an avid reader of Avnery's magazine as a teenager, and a serious student of Yael Dayan's fiction and nonfiction, no one in the West Bank knew more about Moshe Dayan than Raymonda. Days after the war she was in Jerusalem to watch the man in action.

Rumors circulating around Nablus were that the Israelis, led by a messianic rabbi, wanted to take over the mosque and erect the second temple.[32] Muslims and Christians crowded into the old city to see what the conquerors would do. Dayan allayed people's fears by handing over control of the Temple Mount, the site just above Herod's wall, to the Muslim authorities. Though he invited the disappointed rabbi to his kids' wedding, he wasn't going to permit him to incite a religious war between Jews and the Islamic world.

If Dayan showed rare wisdom there, what he did instead was probably the greatest single atrocity committed in Jerusalem since the Crusades. The one-eyed man whose deeds and misdeeds Raymonda had heard about since she was a teenager ordered the expulsion of everyone from the Maghrebi Muslim quarter. The quarter, built shortly after Salah ha-Din drove the Crusaders from Jerusalem, backed up to the Al Aqsa Mosque. Why would Dayan expel several hundred people from their homes?

The rumbling sounds from a fleet of bulldozers crashing through ancient buildings were the first sign of something horrible. Raymonda heard screams of an old woman buried alive under the rubble of her five-hundred-year-old home; held back by a line of soldiers, there was nothing she could do. Eventually, the screams stopped. Raymonda's impotence to save the woman added to the already considerable list of traumas haunting her sleep at night.

The following day, her first foray back through Mandelbaum Gate, was like a hallucinatory dream. Passing unobstructed, she crossed into the new city of Jerusalem and headed to Jaffa Street. The city was throbbing with the life of a nation celebrating its triumph by drinking, dancing, singing the "ha-Tikva." Bare-chested men were kissing women in braless tank tops. What a paradox, she thought, to be under the heels of a free society, a society with a bawdy irreverence in which a worker can tell off a prime minister without disappearing into a dungeon like in the various Arab states. With the colossal destruction she had seen in Jerusalem, she wanted to despise the Israelis—but the lesson she learned from nuns as a young girl was still operative: that the frolicking, freedom-loving Israeli masses were not responsible for the decisions of Moshe Dayan.

She wandered the streets until arriving at a bookstore where she picked up a volume banned in the Hashemite Kingdom, *The Wretched of the Earth*, by the revolutionary enemy of French colonialism, Frantz Fanon. She can't count how many times over the years she read aloud from the preface, written by Sartre, which captured her psychological analysis of most men in power: "This imperious being, crazed by his absolute power and by the fear of losing it, no longer remembers clearly that he was once a man." There was another line that she'd repeat to herself hundreds of times over the coming years, especially during shouting bouts with Daoud and in Shin-Bet interrogation sessions in prison: "We only become what we are by the radical and deep-seated refusal of that which others have made of us."

She returned to Nablus with another book, Yael's *Dust*.

The next week, Raymonda made her way to Acre and to the house where Habib was born and where he lived before it was taken from him in 1948. It was hot by the time she arrived in her Buick with white Jordanian plates. The fronds of the palm trees on the street in front of the parking lot were limp and drooping, idle fishing boats crowded the oily water of the port, and she wandered into the Crusader streets besieged by memories, now and then looking at the names on the iron gates in front of the houses, trying to imagine what it must be like to live in someone else's home, never knowing when a refugee like her might show up with a rusting old key.

On the far end of a square, planted with petunias, was a monument to Jewish war heroes. The language on the plaque was of "liberation," as though, like Rapunzel locked in a tower, Acre had been cruelly held by interloping Arabs, and with millennia of patience waited until the brave Hebrew-speaking liberators arrived to rescue her.

Raymonda plodded onward in the humid heat, along walls Napoleon failed to breach, and she continued, damp with sweat, to Habib's old house with a thick oak door. She stood and knocked, prepared to meet the Jewish inhabitants: *Maybe they'll allow me to climb to the second floor where my bedroom used to be*, she thought. She'd smile; she'd be sweet as pie and make no accusations, no reproaches. Who can blame the new occupants for wanting a palace free of charge? They might be just like Dvora's mother, willing to hand the booty back to the dispossessed and live in peace, Arabs and Jews.

She rubbed her palm along the smooth carved balustrade. Looking up at the house, she imagined Christmas, before the divorce, still young and vital, leaning out the window and smiling down on her. Raymonda knocked again and heard nothing. She began pounding, and still no one opened the door. A wave of images flooded her mind: The servants used to tap lightly on her bedroom door before dinner, and she would put down her children's book: one was Jean de la Fontinelle's *Alphabet*, with an elephant on the front cover holding the letter "A" in its trunk. Back to the present, she sat on the steps rubbing her scraped fist and crying. Through the tears she could see the slender pipe in Habib's hand, the way he balanced it on his palm, proudly inspecting it because he loved its rich mahogany color, and the way the dark brown turned black closer to the cracked volcanic rim.

She cried about her decision to leave her parents behind, and the way both had died behind the once impenetrable border.

Spilling out from a bus behind her were tourists dressed in the simple, unadorned, rough and tumble style of working-class Israelis. All the men wore identical looking white shirts with the buttons open to show the golden Stars of David looped around their necks. Someone jiggled with the lock on the other side of the villa door; the bolt made a mechanical noise, and the door swung open. It was only then that she realized that her childhood home had been turned into a museum of the bygone gilded "Jewish life" in Acre. It wasn't enough to steal the villa; the Israelis also stole her memories, her identity, her past. She followed the tourists like a phantom, silent and with her internal time bomb ticking away. On the whole, everything remained as it was, frozen in time: the spacious rooms furnished in the French style of the 1930s, chandeliers and mirrors with gilded golden frames of carved wooden flowers, the mirror itself spotted with age.

The room was dark with blinds closed against the sun, and the dim light from the lamps gave the rooms with the high ceiling a chiaroscuro effect. The strips of light coming through the blinds cast luminous laser-beam lines on all the tourists who passed close to the large windows facing the sea.

The tour guide explained that the mansion had once upon a time belonged to an eminent Jewish family, and he pointed out the piano, the library with gilded volumes of French literature in red morocco, the oil paintings on the wall, the long tapestries from ceiling to floor, the marble floor, the intricate plaster work, the billiard room, the delicate stone masonry. Ezeh Yoffi, they said like a chorus: "Wow!"

Raymonda was reminded of her visit to her aunt's former house, in the German Colony. THIS IS ALL A LIE, she wanted to scream at the top of her voice. If there were any justice, the piano on which an uncle played Franz Liszt, the furniture, the books would revert back to their rightful owners. Daoud could meet his banker friends in the study, each of the five children would have their own rooms, and her salon, the grandest in the land, would welcome Jews and Arabs alike.

Raymonda felt too dizzy for the words she wanted to shout to come out. She just nodded attentively for a while longer, before leaving the house, never to return. She headed to a seaside restaurant on the ancient fishing port, in use since the Phoenicians and now too toxic for anything besides jellyfish. Under the shade of a scruffy Cyprus pine, and with the brine from the sea mixing with the smell of French fries coming out from the kitchen, she cracked open *Dust* and began reading.

Halfway through the book, Raymonda found herself smoking a pack of cigarettes and fuming because of the way Yael uses stick figures to describe Palestine as an empty land—"empty" in the same way as the family villa in Acre was "Jewish." The novel felt like an affront. As a nineteen-year-old, Raymonda had devoured *New Face in the Mirror* in emotional identification, spiced with a teenage desire for Yael's independence, talent, and fame. *Dust* she read as a conquered subject under the heel of her father.

29
The Emperor

Yael settled into a quiet life with an older military man; soon enough, she was pregnant and spent the coming months writing a book about her father's victory, a victory made inevitable, she fervently believed, because defeat would have meant extermination by Arabs who refused to accept the Jewish people's historical right to Eretz Yisrael. In the series of newspaper articles she wrote in the world press, she continued in her role as her father's unofficial press agent.

The mantle of international stardom started shifting over to Assi, who was now on a film set in Europe working on John Huston's *A Walk with Love and Death*, about two young lovers adrift in medieval Europe during the Hundred Years War. The film set out to deliver the peacenik message of "make love, not war."

Huston invited Ruth to his castle in Ireland, and from there, she headed to Paris, because the American director Jules Dassin, son of a Russian-Jewish barber and victim of the anti-communist purges in Hollywood, had chosen Assi to be his lead actor, alongside Melina Mercouri, Dassin's wife, for the film *Promise at Dawn*.[33]

Yael was also in Paris because her husband the ex-general was appointed Israel's military attaché in Paris. An eccentric viscount, considering it a matter of prestige to be seen with Ruth, and especially the general's glamorous daughter, gave Ruth a lion cub to pass on to Moshe. What else do you give a man with an empire under his heels? The cub's name was Gamine, French for "naughty child." It would later be renamed Ruthie.

The conquered Palestinians, seeing the general with his lioness he called Ruthie in the passenger seat of his jeep, nicknamed Dayan the "Emperor." Never much of an office man, Moshe spent most of his time meeting with his generals and Palestinian notables and farmers, as well as warning the population against giving aid to a nettlesome guerrilla movement called Fatah and its leader, Yasser Arafat.

Attacks continued. Yael, explaining the postwar situation to the world, described in a newspaper article how the "war ended and the terrorists took over." "Daily life," she wrote from Paris in 1968, was characterized by someone "blown up by a mine," "a tractor is shot at, a school bus, two dead, three dead, two civilians, five soldiers, three mines, mortar fire on kibbutzim."

In spring 1968, Dayan finally drew up plans to hunt down and kill Arafat after a mine planted by guerrillas blew up a school bus. On the eve of the raid, Moshe heard rumors of Israelite treasures in a cave, and dashed off for a private dig. And then the cave collapsed, burying him up to his eye-patch. What he missed while encased in a body cast was the first full-fledged battle with Arafat's Fatah movement.

Israeli commandos backed up by tanks crossed the Jordanian border, but instead of being able to act with impunity, as they were used to, King Hussein ordered his soldiers to fight, side by side, with Arafat's Fedayeen. The ensuing Battle of "Karameh"—*karameh* is Arabic for "dignity"—cost dozens of Arafat's fighters along with a number of IDF soldiers; one of Ruth's relatives got shot through the neck. But when Israeli units retreated back over the Jordan River, Arafat was still alive to proclaim victory. His kaffiyeh, dark wrap-around shades, handlebar mustache, and open shirt underneath crumpled military fatigues turned him into the romantic face of Palestinian resistance. *Time* plastered his face on the front cover of the magazine, with the headline: "The Fedayeen Leader."

What made Arafat even more of a legend were rumors that cropped up, shortly after the battle, that he was in the West Bank.

Nursed back to health by faithful Ruth, the accident left Dayan with a twitch in his remaining eye, a speech impediment, a partly lame hand, and even more of an addiction to painkillers. Looking a bit like Captain

Ahab, with a bandaged hand instead of a wooden leg, and surely rankled that the hitherto obscure Arafat had also made it to the cover of *Time*, Dayan set to work. The IDF quickly rounded up a thousand Fatah activists and nearly cornered their cunning leader.

Disguised as a normal family man with wife and child, Arafat sauntered up to an Israeli checkpoint hand in hand with his supposed wife, and slipped away. He was now forming cells by traveling around the West Bank under different aliases: Abu Ammar (which comes from the Arabic verb "to build"), Abu Mohammed, the Doctor, Dr. Husseini, Abdul Rauf, and half a dozen more. Meanwhile, he drove a white VW Bug around the West Bank, with bombs hidden under a baby carriage.

30

In the Bosom of My Country

"All I ask
Is to remain in the bosom of my country
As soil,
Grass,
A flower."

—Fadwa Toqan

Daoud sat at home in Nablus because the Amman-based Ottoman Bank he had been heading up in Nablus shut its doors due to the conquest. He stayed on a nominal salary, without a bank to run.

He was also slack-jawed at the way his wife, with five children to raise, thrived in the relative freedom of a society liberated from the Jordanian secret service, and where the Shin Bet had not yet built up its own repressive apparatus. Raymonda breathed new life into the Arab Women's Union. She also got her reading salon up and running again, and was pouring through fiction, politics, history, whatever she got her hands on. With friends from the salon, Raymonda trooped over to Zion Cinema, in West Jerusalem, to see Assi wearing leotards in A Walk with Love and Death. The movie went over much better than Dust because not only did the general's son Assi look like Brando in A Streetcar Named Desire, not only had he preferred playing chess to fighting during the war, but in a sharp poke in his father's one good eye he used Uri Avnery's girlie magazine as a platform to call for a total withdrawal of every square inch of territory his father had just conquered. Knowing his father too well, Assi assumed that behind his estranged father's nationalist grandstanding, greed and theft were surely motivating his actions in the Palestinian lands.

The Tawil home was also the main meeting place in Nablus for nationalist writers, journalists, and intellectuals wishing to discuss openly the guerrilla attacks carried out by Arafat and his men coming across the Jordan River.

No one knew much about the mysterious rebel able to bedevil the mighty IDF. Arafat was short with cocoa brown eyes and big, sweeping, sometimes comic gestures. Unless he had to put on a disguise to escape a deadly trap, he never smoked and was a teetotaling workaholic. A nervous man, always fidgeting with things—a cheap plastic pen, a tennis ball, a pair of jacks—for relaxation, he watched reruns of *Tom and Jerry* and *Looney Tunes* on a television set up in an underground bunker. As for his lifestyle, the man with the olive-green field uniform and Smith & Wesson .38 in his holster owned next to nothing. His emerging myth was of a man wandering with his intrepid band of guerrillas through deserts and cold mountains in search of his lost homeland.

Months after Karameh, Arafat's Fedayeen ambushed an Israeli patrol, with deadly effectiveness. Dayan sent into Nablus large numbers of troops, beefed up security and checkpoints, and a manhunt proceeded. A squadron of tanks moved into the city and fired randomly into houses and businesses to intimidate the civilian population. Shooting continued unabated, through the night.

Raymonda was in the kitchen pulling chicken and rice leftovers from the fridge when the explosions began. Startled, she dropped the glass dish on the floor, and little Suha scrambled under the table.

This was just a taste of what would happen, once rumors came to Moshe's attention that Arafat, the mastermind of the guerrilla war, was holed up somewhere in the warrens of the medieval Kasbah. The next day generalissimo Dayan, now viewing Arafat as his nemesis, arrived to direct the manhunt. Going well beyond the old Commando 101 method, Dayan threatened to raze the entire city of Nablus "to the ground" if the citizens of the city didn't hand him over. He applied pressure by slapping on a three-day, twenty-four-hour curfew. Tanks took up position in Raymonda's neighborhood; most evenings two or three were parked under their windows, their cannons pointing out into the valley. After thirty-six hours of curfew, the Tawil family of seven was living off water and boxes of crackers. On the final day loudspeakers, festooned to jeeps, bellowed out the following in broken Arabic:

> Attention people of Nablus, dignitaries, and his Excellency Mayor Hamdi Kenaan. Orders from General Dayan. Whoever among you offers aid or comfort, food or shelter, to a terrorist will have his house destroyed; his family will be homeless, and he will be arrested and deported across the Jordan. The General has declared that whoever does not abide with these rules will pay the consequences.

Dayan told the mayor: "I will destroy this town stone by stone." True to his word, his soldiers shot up the place, for a second day in a row. The shelling and gunfire came so close to the Tawil home that Raymonda was sure a shell from a tank was going to blast a hole in a wall and bring the roof down on their heads.

Arafat scrambled off to a new hideout, and for a growing number of Palestinians the hope for liberation survived.

As a woman who still dreamed of going home to Acre, what struck a chord with Raymonda, as she followed his various feats and learned more about "Fatah," was his proclaimed vision for a secular, democratic state encompassing Israel and the occupied territories. What she read into the slogan was that Arabs and Jews alike would live as equals. Through Arafat would she be able to fulfill the "mission" she received as a little girl, had betrayed by leaving to Jordan, but was now able to pursue as a sort of feminist redemption? The Fatah revolution could breathe a fresh, progressive spirit into the patriarchal and tribal power structure that governed Palestinian society. Raymonda took note that some of Arafat's best commandos were women.

1927, London, Ruth with her parents, Rachel and Zvi, and her one-year-old sister, Reumah.

Ruth in London, 1921.

Ruth and Moshe, 1936, Nahalal.

Raymonda's parents, Habib and Christmas, and her
two brothers, George and Yussuf, 1944.

Raymonda's first communion, April 1948, in Haifa.
The photo was taken shortly before the family fled Haifa.

Ruth with Yemenite immigrants, Negev, 1954.

Ruth and her children (from left: Assi, Udi, and Yael). Taken in 1955 in Tel Aviv.

Ruth and Yael in Tel Aviv, 1956.

Moshe and Ruth on ship to Capri, 1956.

Raymonda in Haifa, 1957.

Raymonda and Daoud's wedding in Amman, Jordan, 1957.

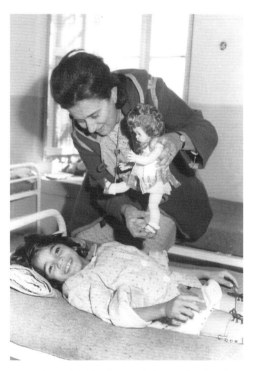

Ruth at a Nablus hospital, December 1970
(this was the same day she met Raymonda).

Raymonda with Uri Avnery in a demonstration in front of the Knesset, 1974.

Uri Avnery

Raymonda at her home in Nablus, under house arrest, 1976.

Raymonda in the Palestinian Press Office in Jerusalem, 1979.

Raymonda on a walk to visit her family's former Montfort Castle, 1978, and reading from her book in Tel Aviv, 1979.

Raymonda with her daughter Diana and Arafat, taken during Arafat's visit to Paris, 1989.

Ruth with President Ezer Weizman, 1993 in Jerusalem.

Photo with Ahmad Tibi, Suha Arafat, Arafat, Daoud, Raymonda, and Mahmoud Darwish taken at the Hotel Meurice in Paris, when Daoud was sick, in 1994.

Raymonda and Arafat in Gaza, 2000.

Ruth at home in Tel Aviv, 2014.

With her mind and heart, Raymonda sided with Arafat, even if some of the local Fatah men, not nearly as progressive as she had hoped, bristled at her willingness to invite Israelis, and men to boot, into her home. This was more than taboo; she was trampling on Arab male honor. With her iconoclastic ways, Raymonda found herself straddling an invisible line. Fresh rumors of her being a spy cropped up, and yet another threatening letter ended up under the door. Written with crude, ungrammatical Arabic she could barely decipher, the letter blasted her for "collaboration" with the enemy. The letter was signed "Fatah."

Fatah's next "operation" was a bomb in the Hebrew University Library in Jerusalem that killed two students. The heads of a Nablus terror cell sent in Miriam Shakhshir, a teenager from an elite Nablus family, the sort of girl who in the past would have been a docile bride for a local oligarch, to carry out the bombing. They must have chosen her because the seventeen-year-old had a head of thick blond hair, large turquoise eyes, and the light complexion of an Ashkenazi from Tel Aviv.

Miriam was arrested, sentenced to life in prison (plus thirty years), and, more importantly for Raymonda, emerged as a symbol among Palestinians for a new sort of woman. Ambivalent about the act itself—killing innocent people was hard to square with the nuns' and Father Michel's message of "love thy enemy"—Miriam's spirit put the fighting spirit back into the Arab Women's Union, not least because as a female militant she was a rebel against an Arab tradition which reserved fighting, especially for matters of honor, for men.

The Israeli response was brutal: some thirty women were arrested, most of them teenagers or women in their early twenties. The military authorities, obviously fearing Miriam copycats, arrested the head of the union. Dayan issued orders to blow up the homes of the women under arrest. Twenty homes were slated for sappers and bulldozers.

One building marked for destruction was a villa in the center of town belonging to a notable family. The mansion was even grander than Habib's in Acre with thirty rooms, exquisite mother-of-pearl furnishings, mosaics, and room after room furnished with Louis XIV tables and chairs.

Before the demolition squad reached the villa, Raymonda leaped back into action by secretly planning a sit-down strike in front of the municipal town hall. And to ensure the protesters wouldn't be clubbed and dispersed, she began phoning Israeli and international journalists and camera teams. She called Uri Avnery, and he promised to be there. He brought with him Amos Kenan, an erstwhile Irgun fighter. Another leftist who accompanied Avnery to the demonstration was Abie Nathan, the owner of California Café and the former '48 pilot. Abie then invited one of his most regular lunchtime guests, Ruth, to join them. She wanted to, but in the end demurred because she knew what kind of reaction it would elicit from her husband.

31
This Is Not a Democracy!

The protest went off as planned, and seven hundred women took part, joined by Uri, Amos, and Abie and a busload of other Israelis. As they marched, they encountered soldiers with batons and translucent riot shields and dark helmets. Awaiting Dayan's order, the soldiers stood ready. "If you do not disperse, we shall shoot," an officer screeched into a megaphone while giving the signal for his men to attack. Steering away from the Israelis, the soldiers flung themselves at the women, clubs swinging like scythes; some fell to the ground, and soldiers kicked them with steel-toed boots. Just as Raymonda reached down to help an elderly woman who had fainted, she felt the sharp pain of torn flesh. A bludgeon had struck her on the back of the head.

"Bitch!" she heard a soldier snarl out in Brooklyn English, as he took another swing, and then threatened to arrest her—she was on the ground staring up at him—because she called him, in the colloquial English she picked up from her mother, a "jackass."

Dayan and his men probably would have considered the protest of little consequence had Avnery not returned to Israel with photographs and graphic description of the club-wielding soldiers in *HaOlam HaZeh*.

The next day, Avnery was dragged from the Knesset because of his fiery speech, warning against the blowing up of Palestinian houses. "You are going to leave a scar in the heart of every person in Nablus," he shouted while being shoved out the door.

The violent break-up of the demonstration, Raymonda told people back in Nablus, was just like Karameh: brute force failed to break the will of those seeking their freedom. "It was Dayan who lost, not us."[34] The cycle of guerrilla "operations," Dayan's iron fist, and Raymonda's activism continued.

The Shin Bet arrested a group of five girls from bourgeois families on suspicion of terrorism. One had tried to plant a bomb in an Israeli supermarket. Once again, the collective punishment Dayan meted out was to blow up the old mansions belonging to their families.

Raymonda rallied public opinion against the home demolition orders, this time firing a telegram off to Dayan. No answer. She got the media involved, *Time* magazine, no less. She organized another sit-down strike in front of the office of the military governor.

The Israeli military governor of Nablus, General Givoli, called her into his office and asked her with alarm, "What the hell are you doing by trying to go against General Dayan?" He was speaking with uncharacteristic emotion. Givoli shifted his attention from the pin on Raymonda's coat lapel "Self-Determination for Palestine" to her file. "Mrs. Tawil, you are playing with fire. This is really no joke." He cleared his throat and looked up from the paperwork. Raymonda noticed a copy of Avnery's magazine on the desk.

The general's mild manner encouraged her to open up to him. "But in Israel as a girl that's what I learned: people go to the streets to protest injustice by the government. That's what Israelis do. It's democracy!"

He took off his glasses and set them on her file. "My dear Raymonda, let me offer you a friendly piece of advice. You are not a little girl in Haifa, and you're no longer an Israeli citizen. Israel is a democracy, true, but in case you haven't noticed, what we have in the West Bank, my dear lady, what we have here is NOT a democracy! It's a military occupation. Shall I spell it out for you? O-c-c-u-p-a-t-i-o-n. Unless you understand the difference, I foresee some big problems for you up ahead." He ordered her to stop working with Avnery, Nathan, and Kenan.

Nervous, she drummed her fingers on one knee. The general began tapping his fingers on the desktop as well before finally spelling out what his boss Moshe Dayan had in mind: "Next time we will take measures against you," he said without a trace of hostility, like he was a doctor telling her to take her meds. He stood up and accompanied her to the door.

"General Givoli, I have a question for you. You are a humanist, I believe. How can you order your men to beat a group of unarmed women?"

He hesitated, as if unsure how to respond. "The order," he finally said with a hint of bitterness, "came from Minister of Defense Dayan."

Part III
1970–1995: Dialogue

32
St. Luke's Hospital

Raymonda's friendship with the Israelis made her a better authority on the dark side of Israeli military history than Ruth could ever be. Long conversations with Avnery taught her about the immensity of the Palestinian disaster. How through the 1950s Blue-Box donations paid for a fleet of tractors and tons of dynamite to destroy Arab villages, over four hundred in all. She read back issues of *HaOlam HaZeh* and came to view Avnery as more than just a muckraking journalist; he was a gendarmerie or an entire battalion. Some people in power didn't take kindly to such criticism. Over the years of its existence, the magazine's editorial offices and printing facilities were mysteriously bombed several times.

From Amos Kenan, she learned details about the 1948 massacre at Deir Yassin—because the avant-garde poet had taken part in it. He was also there for Dayan's conquest of Ramle and Lod, and described how he slammed the butt of his Sten gun on the doors to houses, "Yalla! Get out! Go to King Abdullah!" Soldiers herded the inhabitants into fields, ringed with barbed wire.

Kenan spoke to Raymonda the way a penitent would a priest. At first he had a hard time looking at her, because she reminded him of what he and his pals had done at Deir Yassin and Ramle: "I am worse than any name you can throw my way," he confessed during their first conversation at her home, "worse that a filthy beast, a monster, an assassin, a killer. For twenty years now, my hands have been sticky from your people's blood."[35]

129

By 1970, the Tawil family home was a constant buzz of activity, and long suffering Daoud's patience was wearing thin, because of the stream of people in the house crowding into their home. Their living room was one of the few places in the West Bank where they could discuss the occupation—and other taboo topics, such as feminism. General Givoli dropped by every week or so. The open atmosphere there helped him understand what the Palestinians wanted and needed.

A woman from the family whose villa Dayan had ordered dynamited visited Raymonda. She could find no one else to talk to about a terrible crime. At her job as a social worker, at an Israeli prison in Kalkilya, she worked with a teenaged girl, a victim of incest and in prison for infanticide. The girl was hysterical. She pleaded with her Israeli captors to keep her in prison; if they released her, the family would kill her to preserve its "honor." The social worker was shivering, as she spoke with Raymonda. "I begged the prison authorities, too, but they said they had to follow the rules."

Raymonda found herself in the paradoxical position of asking the Israelis to keep a Palestinian girl in prison. She talked to General Givoli, but even he couldn't prevent prison officials from setting her free. The woman's family murdered her shortly after her release.

Dayan's top general in Nablus, Givoli, at Raymonda's encouragement, began sitting for hours with the five girls in prison, on terrorism charges, trying to find out what motivated them. Why had they turned to laying bombs? What had they hoped to accomplish? It didn't take long for him to realize just how similar their idealism was to his own when he was a youth, a generation earlier, fighting against the British. He began to worry about the health of these bright girls. They would waste away with nothing to do.

Givoli thought about Ruth and Maskit. Perhaps his boss's wife could teach the girls a craft? He knew Ruth would use every opportunity to hop in her Saab and return to the landscape of her youth.

Just as he suspected, Ruth jumped at the idea. Her plan was to deliver toys on behalf of Abie Nathan to wounded children—collateral damage during an IDF operation—at St. Luke's hospital in Nablus, before continuing to the prison.

The minute Ruth entered the front door of the hospital with General Givoli at her side, a huddle of police officers hovered around her like drones around the queen bee. She tried to brush them off, but couldn't. There she was, impossible to miss, wearing a cotton-candy-colored dress and holding an armload of toys, in the company of the general, surrounded by armed men.

Palestinians were whispering and pointing, craning their necks to see her. Raymonda, there in the hospital that afternoon, watched the way Ruth moved through the ward. She had read about her in *New Face in the Mirror*. In real life she made quite a different impression, stronger, quicker, an empathetic twinkle in her eyes.

The minute Ruth got close enough for her to smell her jasmine perfume, Raymonda, in her high heels, taller than most of the soldiers and speaking in the Hebrew she had learned from her childhood friends in Haifa, let her have a piece of her mind. Since hearing radio reports of the massacres in the 1950s, Moshe Dayan had been for her an evil Cyclops. She struck back at his wife. "How dare you come in here pretending to care for children! Do you know what your husband is doing to us?"

Ruth admired the Amazon's spunk but waived off the charges. "I don't believe we've met," she began, holding a Barbie in her hand. "But you should know"—she was shaking the doll in Raymonda's direction, the glass eyes blinking with each movement of her arm—"I married a farmer and NOT a general. Don't blame me for all this . . . this horror." Raymonda watched as tears formed in Ruth's eyes. Her jaws were clenched.

She handed Ruth a tissue but stuck to her guns. "Well, this farmer boy of yours is making our lives hell. Your husband is giving orders to shoot children, and you bring toys! Get out of Palestine!"

"For God's sake, I am NOT Moshe Dayan." The police must have thought Raymonda was going to drive her nails into Ruth. They stood between the two, their thick arms folded like bouncers outside a nightclub.

Raymonda didn't have to say another word. The scene in the ward was straight out of a painting by Hieronymus Bosch: bandaged up children moved her more than anything Raymonda could have said. At first, she stood dumbstruck. "We should have stayed on the damned moshav," she finally muttered to herself, shaking her head.

Ignoring her bodyguards, she turned to the families in the same ward and asked them, in broken Arabic, if there was anything she could do besides handing out toys. Ruth spent so much time listening to the women that she had no time to see the imprisoned girls.

She headed back to Tel Aviv and, by the time she got back home, Moshe was already in his pajamas watching his favorite Egyptian soap opera. He was obsessed with these shows. At first, he barely said a word to her. Ruth headed into the kitchen to prepare dinner for him. She reemerged carrying an omelet and set it down on the table—his single eye watched her every move. "Moshe," she said, "I'm off to the theater in Jaffa. There's a play by some Palestinians . . ."

Moshe had been telling the world that Palestine was "finished" and here was Ruth talking about "Palestinians." He snapped, "WHAT IN HELL WERE YOU DOING SEEING THOSE TERRORISTS IN NABLUS!"

Moshe touched his nose with his trigger finger, and she turned to face him. "Listen to me," and now he aimed the finger at her, as he launched into his tirade, "You should know I put them in prison where they belong." His eye twitched. "You must stop undermining my authority!" He was shaking his hands, as he might around a throat. "I forbid you to continue. DO YOU HEAR ME?" Even in his pajamas, Moshe had all the qualities of a Biblical leader: in turns visionary and despotic, wise and foolhardy, charismatic and cynical, generous and miserly.

But his powers had long ago ceased to intimidate Ruth. Though she hadn't even gone to the prison to visit the girls, the verbal assault over what seemed like a trifle was what stunned her. For three years, she had been meeting Arabs all over the West Bank and Gaza. Why should this be different? He had always encouraged her efforts at helping Palestinians. So what was so awful about handing out toys to children his men had wounded, or setting up a training course for girls in prison?

His sneering, barking demands were too much; blood rising to a boil, she couldn't hold her feelings back. She went into the kitchen to get the general a glass of scotch. Coming out with the drink, she said, as cool as a cucumber, "Moshe, I want a divorce."

Moshe was taken aback. "Do you mean what you're saying? Are you sure?" Yes, she assured him.

"You must be kidding." The man who took on the entire Arab world had for years been afraid to end a marriage he had betrayed a thousand times.

"No, Moshe, I've never been more serious." She had thought about divorce often but because she still loved him, and because Yael expected her to keep up the façade, she endured. The daughter expected her mother to put up with what Yael would call his "avarice, indiscriminate womanizing, loss of idealism and megalomania." Besides, what woman walks out on the hero at the height of his fame?

"I'm finished with you, Moshe." With those words, she left for the play.

During her absence, Moshe phoned up Yael, his chief ally in the family, in Paris. The next phone call was to his lawyer and asked him to draw up the paperwork.

Ruth left the house with a suitcase of clothes, some books, and an eggshell with the entire Book of Ruth inscribed on it by a former convict of the Russian gulag. She would eventually get half the value of the house, but in the meantime she moved in with Assi in an apartment in the old city of Jaffa, overlooking the Mediterranean. Moshe owned the apartment and charged market rates. To him.

The divorce was finalized in December 1971, and Dayan quickly married his mistress Rachel. Scandal-mongering journalists were after Ruth for a scoop, and she finally unbuttoned her soul. "It just wasn't worth it anymore," she told a *Time* reporter. "It was like living in chains. If I were still his wife, there would be six guards here. Now I can drive my car to the Gaza Strip or wherever I want."

Ruth cut off all contact with Moshe, though she would never stop loving him. One night she had a dream in which his antiquities collection came to life like Isaiah's fields of bones. Stele, goddesses, and heaps of shards, swirling in the air as if in a whirlwind, formed a city with turreted walls and towers—and no people. It looked like a depopulated Jerusalem, and was called the City of Moshe.

33
Honor Killing

In February 1970 Assi was enough of an international star to be invited to London to audition for the role of the communist Perchik in the movie version of *Fiddler on the Roof*. During a stopover at the Munich airport, while walking to the El Al 707 with the pilot and an actress heading for the same audition, he saw Arabs running toward them. "What are they doing?" he turned and asked the pilot. "Assi, not all Arabs are terrorists," the pilot jested, which was his way of telling Assi not to be so paranoid. But the men, Marxist rivals to Arafat's Fatah movement, kept racing pell-mell toward them and began shooting and tossing bombs. A bullet hit the leg of the actress. One passenger was killed, eleven wounded. Assi got off unscathed, but his international acting career took a fatal hit because American newspapers spun the attack as an assassination attempt against him. Signing on the son of Moshe Dayan during the high-water point of international Palestinian terror was too much an insurance risk for the producers. Paul Michael Glaser ended up landing the role of Perchik.

Months after the attempted hijacking, Ruth got a call from her sister Reumah. She had to rush to a military hospital in Tel Aviv. She and Ezer's only child, Saul, was in critical condition. While serving on the front line in the Israeli-occupied Sinai, an Egyptian sniper shot him in the head. Doctors weren't sure he would survive. At the hospital Ezer, the cocky, hard-drinking, always joking architect of the Six Day War, sat in the corridor with his face in his hands. From the movements of his shoulders,

Ruth knew he was crying. Was the conquest of the Sinai and West Bank worth Saul's life? Ezer was asking himself the same question that night.

On the way back to Assi's apartment in Jaffa, Ruth stared up at the sky. It was a clear evening and the star Sirius twinkled bright. Her mind turned to her first love Zvi and the torpedo that probably sent him and his men to the bottom of the sea. All the territory in the world couldn't compensate Ruth for the lives she'd seen ruined or destroyed because of war.

Ruth, to keep her mind off Moshe and now Saul, turned much of her attention to the Palestinians. Abie Nathan asked her to deliver toys to the death-defying nuns at the "La Crèche" convent who were operating an "underground railroad." The sisters furtively searched garbage dumps for babies abandoned by their unmarried mothers; families saw in them "seeds of the devil." Often, pregnant woman fled to the convent from fathers and brothers who, as in some dark fetish, felt they had to butcher them to redeem family honor. The women gave birth behind the safety of convent walls. Working with Israeli and European women's groups, the nuns helped some of the women escape with their children across the Green Line into Israel.

Having been raised by nuns, Raymonda was well acquainted with the brave "La Crèche" sisters' dangerous rescue work. She never delivered armloads of toys on behalf of Abie Nathan; instead she set her hopes on a social revolution to rid Arab society of honor killing, the way any plague is dealt with—by isolating and eradicating it. Society's structures had to change; women had to be freed from the tyranny of male honor.

In 1970, everything seemed possible. In the West, the anti-war movement was at its height. The colonial powers were leaving Africa and Asia. Why shouldn't people of good will, Arabs and Jews, be able to join forces for the sake of freedom? Arafat's guerrillas, never strong enough to drive the IDF back over the 1967 border, at least reminded the Israeli people of the high price of oppression.

Raymonda underestimated Dayan's determination to annihilate Arafat and his men. He threatened Jordanian King Hussein with massive retribution unless he reined in Fedayeen groups.[36] In September 1971, the king and his generals moved to expel Arafat and his militants from the country. The Palestinians fought back and very nearly pushed the country into a civil war. Arafat had to be smuggled across the border to Lebanon, while in Jordan the king's loyal soldiers massacred thousands of Palestinians. The center of resistance shifted from Jordan to Lebanon.

34
Umm al-Mu'in

Whenever Ruth drove through Nablus, on her peripatetic travels for Maskit in the West Bank, she dropped by Raymonda's, where more often than not she found Daoud scowling at a household full of hungry and thirsty longhaired activists, foreign reporters, and mothers carrying pictures of sons, and sometimes daughters, who had been swallowed up into Israeli prisons.

Feminists, too, found safe refuge in the Tawil home. In patriarchal Nablus, there was no more avid reader of *Ms.* magazine or of the ideas of Gloria Steinem and Letty Cottin Pogrebin, its two cofounders, than Raymonda. The way she brandished Steinem's call for revolution against oppressive systems of race and sex—against dividing "human beings into superior and inferior groups, and into the cheap labor on which this system still depends"—attracted the attention of Palestinian and Israeli feminists, new mouths to feed for Daoud and fresh material for scandal in Nablus.

At one point, in a jammed Nablus public hall, and with a purple face, he shrieked threats of divorce if she didn't stop her dangerous activism. That she drove this otherwise stolid, even-keeled banker to blow his top in public was yet another cause for his brooding resentment mixed with awe. To Ruth, who developed a deep fondness for Daoud, he confided that he put up with her "dangerous theatrics" because she was his life's "greatest fortune."

Daoud tried to seduce his beautiful wife into a more bourgeois lifestyle by taking her on regular vacations to Beirut, the Paris of the Middle East because of its grand shopping avenues, its cafes and beaches.

It was during these holidays that Raymonda became acquainted with some of the revolutionaries she hoped would liberate Palestine while freeing Palestinians from hidebound traditions. She met Bassam Abu Sharif, a young journalist and recent graduate of the American University living in Beirut, who was a member of the Marxist group PFLP (Popular Front for the Liberation of Palestine). While unaware of Sharif's involvement in hijacking airliners, she knew he was a militant, sworn to the armed struggle. Raymonda gave him his first lesson on Israeli leftists—that working with them was the best way to battle the Israeli army. She was thinking about her "mission." If Israelis were allies, you obviously weren't going to kick them out of the country. Jews and Palestinians had to live together.

Back home foreign journalists were so impressed with Raymonda's shrewd political analysis, and news she brought back from Beirut, that they hired her to provide copy for news organizations, including Agence France Presse. The Israeli left-wing journal *New Outlook* was another of her venues.[37] At gatherings of the *New Outlook* crowd, she met people such as the German-Jewish Marxist Herbert Marcuse, author of *Eros and Civilization*. She brought her children in on a conversation of "polymorphous sexuality."

Far more potentially perilous, with Uri Avnery and his band of journalists Raymonda was driving around the West Bank in a car with Israeli plates, brandishing a tape recorder she nicknamed her "Kalashnikov," and hunting for stories of atrocities. She realized she was treading on thin ice with the IDF; her disguises included multiple wigs she picked up at Anton's, an expensive wig shop in Beirut, and an assortment of designer Italian sunglasses to match.

The changes she saw all around her reminded Raymonda of the Galilee in the 1950s: seizure of land, mass settlement, and breaking up Palestinian society into cantons. Reaching out to Israelis and internationals became an imperative. In her journalism, she wrote about Dayan's policy of seducing Palestinians with used washing machines and construction jobs on Jewish settlements around Jerusalem.

Her budding career in journalism and feminist firebrand earned her the nom de guerre *Al-Muminun*, Mother of Believers, the name of the Prophet's wife.

35

"Wrath of God"

Bassam Abu Sharif, the young journalist Raymonda had met in Beirut, would eventually come around to her cosmopolitan humanism. In the meantime, he was a full-time terrorist, specializing in hijacking planes. A different cell of terrorists carried out a massacre against eleven Israeli athletes during summer Olympics in Munich in 1972.

In the wake of the Munich killings, Dayan and Prime Minister Golda Meir launched "Operation Wrath of God" to cripple the international command structure of Palestinian nationalist groups, chiefly, Fatah. Most of those targeted weren't hijackers or guerrillas; they were writers who fought with words.

Wael Zwaiter, a friend Raymonda knew well from her days in Nablus, was a poet and translator living in Rome. Zwaiter was opposed to political violence, which didn't prevent two Mossad agents from firing their .22 caliber Beretta pistols eleven times into his head and chest, each bullet in memory of the victims of the Munich Massacre he had had nothing to do with.

Fatah's representative in Paris, Mahmoud Al Hamshari, likewise a literary and peaceful man, died when his booby-trapped telephone exploded in his face. (In *Munich* Steven Spielberg casts him as Saddam.) The man Raymonda's oldest daughter Diana would marry, Ibrahim Souss, took over the post of PLO representative from him.[38]

Raymonda was in Beirut in 1972, when the Mossad targeted the playwright and secretary of the General Union of Palestinian Writers and

Journalists, Ghassan Kanafani, "the commando who never fired a gun." In early July, he sat on his balcony, sipping cup after cup of Arabic coffee. That morning he and his sister were reminiscing about their childhood in Acre before their expulsion in 1948. With a caffeine buzz, he got dressed for work and headed out of the house to drive to his office at the Writer's Union. The Israeli car bomb was so powerful that it blew his body into a valley close to the house. Rushing downstairs, Anni stood paralyzed. In front of her was her husband's left leg. Their daughter Laila cried again and again: "Baba, Baba . . ."

Raymonda attended the funeral, and two weeks later she was at the bedside of Bassam Abu Sharif. On July 25, 1972, when he opened Che Guevara's *Memoirs* the bomb hidden inside mutilated his hands and Omar Shariff good looks.

Raymonda was also in Beirut the following April when Ehud Barak, the future Israeli prime minister, masquerading as a woman in a summer dress, sauntering along, arm in arm with what looked like her lover, broke into a PLO man's apartment, and in front of his wife and children, shot him. It was Kamal Nasser, a Christian poet Raymonda knew, read, and adored—he'd had ink rather than blood on his hands.[39]

After she had got word of the killing, she rang up Ruth in Tel Aviv. "You know what that husband of yours did! He . . . he killed . . . O my God . . . he killed my friend! How cowardly to gun down people . . . people in front of their families." Kamal Nasser was the best example of a nationalist choosing peaceful means of resistance. "How could Dayan do such a thing?"

"What do you think I can do about it, Raymonda?" Ruth had a sharp edge to her voice. "You think I'm God and can resurrect him?" Raymonda was angling for a public statement, but Ruth demurred. Maybe the dead man really was a terrorist. Ruth wasn't about to defend people planting bombs and firing on Israeli school buses.

To protest Kamal Nasser's death, thousands of students and other Palestinians converged on the village church in Bir Zeit, to attend a memorial service. Raymonda wrote a petition signed by a dozen politicians, writers, and intellectuals, declaring that the PLO was the sole representative of the Palestinian people. Raymonda sent the petition to local and international newspapers—and fired off a personal copy to Moshe Dayan. The petition caused such a commotion in the Israeli press that Dayan admitted publically for the first time that most Palestinians backed Arafat and not King Hussein of Jordan.[40] Few Israelis wanted to admit that they had an anti-colonial war of liberation on their hands. A Vietnam.

The more people the Mossad eliminated, the worse violent opposition to Israeli rule grew. Bitter disputes within the ranks of Fatah broke out over balancing human lives with the desire for revenge for 1948 and 1967. There were those who agreed with Raymonda that hijackings and bombings and rivers of blood would never bring the IDF to its knees. More peaceful, political means, ultimately resulting in direct negotiations with the Israelis, were needed. Arafat eventually came around to the view.

The "rejectionists," led by a psychotic killer by the name of Abu Nidal, considered any hint of compromise with the "Zionist entity," including mentioning the State of Israel, or having anything to do with Israelis, no matter how left-wing they were, treason. Treason deserving of death.[41] Abu Nidal, a man who would later try to kill Raymonda, and even Arafat, was like Raymonda a scion of one of the wealthiest families in Palestine. Unlike her, though, his mission in life was revenge, not love. He bragged about being the "evil spirit lurking around only at night causing . . . nightmares."

36
L'pozez Akol (Blow Up Everything)

"I will tell you a story
A story that lived in the dreams of people
A story that comes out of the world of tents . . .
It is a story of people who were misled
Who were thrown in the mazes of years
But they defied and stood
Disrobed and united
And went to light, from the tents
The revolution of return
in the world of darkness."

— Kamal Nasser

In spring 1973, following Kamal Nasser's funeral, Ruth sat in the front row, as Raymonda told a roomful of Israelis, at a *New Outlook* conference in Tel Aviv, that so long as people in the West Bank and Gaza lived under the jackboots of a military oppression, and security forces continued arresting, expelling, or otherwise silencing the best and brightest Palestinian writers, Tel Aviv's freewheeling ways couldn't last. Raymonda, all smiles, surveyed the audience. "One day," she said, "we'll come out of the sky with rockets and guns, we'll fall from the clouds like bombs."

"Like bombs," she repeated. She was wearing a long, tight-fitting satin dress with a slit up the side; her hair dyed raven black. From the stage,

Raymonda hammed it up, showing the swell of her breast. "We will destroy Tel Aviv! If you don't listen to us, let's just blow up everything. L'pozez akol."

Her words flowed uncontrolled, uncontrollable, like lava, spilling, spewing, bubbling out.

Ruth applauded. She knew Raymonda was telling Israelis a bitter truth; a woman a few rows back, however, bawled out, "Get out of Israel, you terrorist, and never come back." Matti Peled, one of the more humane generals serving in the West Bank, went up to the stage, took the microphone, and said about Raymonda: "She is coming to us with beautiful eyes but then all of a sudden bullets and missiles are firing out from her rosy lips. We Israelis can only ignore her at our own peril." Ruth applauded again.

Raymonda more or less repeated her warning in early 1973 on CBS television when she told the Israeli journalist, Amos Elon, that to snap Israelis out of the inebriation of the Six Day War, they had to be "hit over the head."

With Olympian delusion, Dayan persisted in his multi-prong strategy of eliminating militants, buying off local Palestinians with jobs while settling the territories he had conquered with Jews. His cocksureness reached such a height that in early 1973, he gave secret instructions to Sharon to chase away three thousand Bedouin families from a part of the Sinai Moshe wanted for Israeli settlement.[42] He and his next-door neighbor Arik cooked up an ambitious program to introduce two million settlers into the West Bank. Who could stop him? The Arabs? A joke going around has a general saying to Dayan. A fellow general pipes up, "How about invading another Arab country?" "Not a bad idea," Dayan slaps his thigh in merriment. "But what would we do in the afternoon?"

With Ruth no longer around to act as the emotional bridge, the relationship between the general and his children grew more and more distant; months would often go by without his children having any contact with him. Even Yael found it hard to reconnect with her father. Now that she had her own children, what bothered her most was his cavalier indifference to his family. "Father . . . would rather not have had children."[43]

Now left to his own devices, without Ruth, he fell victim to "shallow, expensive personal grooming." In his new look he sported cashmere sweaters and Dunhill suits, a favorite of Agent 007 in the James Bond movies. Moshe, the first born of redemption, was also the first of a now common Israeli type: the millionaire ex-general.

The egocentric father put Ruth's role as mother in a fresh light. Though Yael still couldn't resist taking a jab at Ruth's "martyr complex," she was coming to realize how Ruth, "poor and too generous," was the only person who kept the family together. "Mother flooded us with gifts from the nothing she had, and Father charged us for everything."

In October 1973, Ruth was with Yael's former boyfriend Michael Cacoyannis exploring the Sinai for his film *The Story of Jacob and Joseph*. It was a lackluster production, but for Ruth the filming brought her back to the happy days of *Zorba the Greek*, drinking ouzo with Anthony Quinn on the Island of Crete. Maskit's artisans did all the costumes and jewelry for the movie.

Ruth was back in Jaffa when she got a phone call from someone from the Ministry of Defense. Egyptian and Syrian forces had opened hostilities. Israel was under attack!

The Arab onslaught on Yom Kippur left the IDF flatfooted. Once the Egyptians broke through heavily fortified Israeli lines, Dayan cracked up and feared that the "Third Temple"—the State of Israel—was in mortal danger. Golda wasn't quite so panicked, though she asked for pills from a doctor friend "to kill myself so I won't fall into the hands of the Arabs."[44]

The Soviets and Americans stepped in to stop the fighting, but for the Israelis something had snapped. It was the national id—Raymonda heard the sound all the way in Nablus. Moshe's patina of superman rubbed off. One Israeli government official, referring to his failures, said, "In another army, this man should have gone into another room, found a pistol, and we should have heard a shot."

Yael blamed the "treacherous" Arabs for the debacle, while Assi let the world know what he thought about his father, and the army, with the cult film he directed, *Halfon Hill Doesn't Answer*. The Israeli equivalent to *M*A*S*H*, it was the first satire on Israel's sacred cow, the IDF, and is widely considered the best Israeli comedy ever made. The film features a conman, a fat cook, and a horny commander of a base in the Sinai.[45] Assi's other 1973 film, *Invitation to Murder*, is about a serial killer on the loose in Tel Aviv.

Ruth refused to come out in public against her ex. But she did bring a bottle of cognac to support an IDF reserve officer who pitched his tent outside Golda's office on a vigil to get Dayan to resign for mistakes that had cost three thousand Israeli lives.[46]

Dayan continued his fight against Palestinian nationalists as a way for him and Golda to win back some of their tarnished credibility. "There will be no safe haven for you any longer," Golda was now threatening Fatah leaders. "Our long hands, extended in vengeance, will find you and kill you."

Raymonda was testing Israeli patience with her war dispatches that ended up in the international press, in particular her claim that in the West Bank during the fighting, IDF soldiers had abandoned their weapons and fled helter-skelter back to Israel across the old Green Line.[47]

37
Mission Renewed

A bie Nathan became a pacifist during the 1948 war out of a sense of shame: from the cockpit window of a Dakota plane, he dropped bombs on villages where members of Raymonda's family lived and owned vast properties. Two days after the bombings he took a truck to see the damage. Wandering through the ruins, he saw burned bodies scattered everywhere, acts of "destruction, wreckage and death" caused by him and those who sent him. Now, twenty years later, no Israeli was more critical of his country's occupation of Palestine. To liberate Israelis from themselves, with support from the Jesuits and John Lennon, he bought and equipped a ship he turned into the pirate station "Peace Radio."

Ruth was one of his first guests. The leaking barge was steered just beyond Israeli territorial waters and from there beamed out a message of peace to Beirut, Cairo, Amman, and to Israel and the Occupied Territories. Young Israelis, reeling from the war debacle, wanted angry anti-war protest songs—"21st Century Schizoid Man," "The Grave," and "People, Let's Stop the War."

It was probably the first time the Arab masses heard "Rocky Raccoon," "Mr. Tambourine Man," and "Puff, the Magic Dragon." When they weren't dancing to The Beatles and The Doors, the Tawil children were regular contributors to Nathan's call-in talk ham radio shows. The show *Ma La'asot* (What to do?) was the only uncensored forum for Jews and Arabs to debate the past and present, and dream about a better future.

In early 1974 Ruth began traveling the world on behalf of Maskit and the World Craft Council, a UNESCO-backed organization.[48] The long missives she wrote to her children describe a state of mind, shifting between loneliness and excitement, and sometimes a sardonic humor such as her depiction of a visit to Ethiopian Emperor Haile Selassie, the self-proclaimed "Might of the Trinity" and "direct-descendent-of-King-Solomon-and-the-Queen-of-Sheba." Not long afterward, he was toppled in a military coup, executed, and buried beneath a latrine in the Imperial Palace.

Whenever she returned to Israel, Ruth always visited the West Bank to check in on her Palestinian "Maskiteers" making rugs and embroidery. The orphans in Bethlehem couldn't wait to see her pull up in her Saab. It meant more toys. Her and Raymonda's friendship grew through regular conversations over tea in Nablus, Ramallah, or East Jerusalem. The two women had a lot to talk about—women's issues, children, jobs, various permits from the military authorities, and occasionally politics: Raymonda would bring up a list of atrocities she claimed were committed by the IDF.

Raymonda accused Moshe of complicity in the disappearance of the young American-educated journalist, Joe Nasser. The two women had yet another of their standard quarrels in which Raymonda hurled her hurt and vitriol against Dayan, by way of his ex-wife, who stamped her foot exclaiming, I AM NOT MOSHE DAYAN.

Nasser, from a prominent Christian family, was the editor of the Fatah-aligned newspaper *Al Fajr* ("The Dawn"). In a series of articles, he insinuated that Dayan was the ultimate dark force behind the assassination of Fatah leaders in Beirut. He got himself into much deeper trouble by pointing an accusing finger at a prominent Hebron sheik for helping General Dayan get the land for the Jewish settlement Kiryat Arba. A biting caricature in *Al Fajr* showed the sheik with a dusty shoe on his turban, a bruising insult.[49]

After Nasser vanished, rumors made the rounds that the sheik's goons had abducted him.

It was then that Father Michel De Maria came to Raymonda's mind. Twenty years had passed since her first meeting with him, where he had told her the importance of her life's mission. Now, with a picture of Joe in her purse, she set off back to the village of Rama.

The village church jolted her back in time. She felt the same sensation she had as a child, that sense of holiness in the small chapel illuminated by candles that lit up the altar and made the icons glow. The old man, buckled over, his noble face shot through with wrinkles, grabbed her hands with a firm grip and prevented her from dropping to her knees in a sign of respect.

Raymonda didn't need to tell him about the death of her parents, about her life in Jordan and the West Bank; he seemed to know everything. He caught her off guard when he asked about her "activities"—what was she doing with her life? He didn't have to use the word "mission." She knew what he was asking. The old priest followed her account of her activism, her disguises, her "Kalashnikov" with a mildly disapproving expression, as if to say No, Raymonda, your mission is elsewhere. "Raymonda, what is poisoning this land is not a lack of news; it is a lack of love."

Nothing had changed. The message was the same.

Without betraying how much his words gave her a tight pain in the chest, and without mentioning Nasser, Raymonda pulled the photograph of Joe from her purse and handed it to Father Michel. "I'd like to know if this man is alive." He took the picture and disappeared into a room on the second floor of the stone building. Returning half an hour later, he told her that Nasser was still alive. He was being held in a cave in the mountains outside of Hebron.

Raymonda returned to Father Michel the following week hoping for more details, but someone had in the meantime discussed the matter with him, and he was clearly nervous. He only agreed to see her after long pleading. "Raymonda, you need to be careful," he said.

"Father, just tell me how we can find my friend."

He turned his back and faced the wall. He lifted his chin, a quick gesture, to free his neck from his clerical collar. "They moved him. He's at the Moskobiya," the former Russian monastery-turned-Israeli prison in Jerusalem.

Proof of Father Michel's vision came the next day in the form of a threatening telephone call from the police chief at the Moskobiya warning her that by getting involved in the investigation into Nasser's disappearance, she was "endangering the security of Israel," a "very dangerous" mistake. VERY DANGEROUS, he repeated with a raised voice to make sure it sank in. The final word Raymonda heard from Father Michel about Nasser was that he no longer "saw" him. Nasser had been "hit on the head." His body was never found.

Raymonda's name was now being widely mentioned in the Israeli press as a nettlesome troublemaker. This was when Colonel Yigal Carmon, a Shin Bet agent, began tracking her movements. Her activism, and the uncomfortable facts she kept dredging up, kept the well-mannered, industrious Carmon busy.

In spring 1974, the French-Jewish writer Marek Halter and his wife Clare rang Raymonda up with an intriguing suggestion they believed was more disruptive to the Israeli occupation than hijackers. As a child, Marek had escaped from the Warsaw Ghetto and, before becoming a novelist in Paris, he studied pantomime under Marcel Marceau. Clare ran a leftist Parisian literary review. The two convinced Raymonda to jump on a plane and head for the United States, which for Palestinian activists seemed like one continent-sized lobby of support for Israel. They wanted her to stand before audiences, Jewish and non-Jewish, and present the Palestinian case; and, with some luck, she might manage to loosen the stranglehold that Israeli propaganda had on the American mind.[50]

Daoud hit the roof. He was resigned to the life surrounded by scandal and rumors—how many times had he heard that his young wife was a CIA agent? But going on her own to America went too far. No! No! No! He would NEVER allow it. In the end, of course, he acquiesced—and he went with her.

In the air over New York Harbor in May, Raymonda felt the familiar sense of anticipation visitors have the first time they crane their necks to see the Statue of Liberty. It was a stirring experience to see the big, brawny police with silver badges in JFK airport—and to feel no fear of arrest.

She and Daoud ended up staying in a hotel on a derelict street in Manhattan. Choked with yellow smog most of the time, those were the days of New York City's collapse. It barely registered: she felt like flying through avenues filled with muggers and perverts and panhandling drunks—but no soldiers. She was free.

She gave a dozen speeches from the East Coast to the West. Inevitably, someone in the audience would ask her to renounce terrorism. She skirted the issue: no Palestinian nationalist could afford to come out against the "operations," even if in private she knew violence almost always boomeranged. In a related line of questions, she was asked what she thought about Arafat; pro-Israeli Americans considered him a scruffy desperado, no different from Fidel Castro and other Enemies of Freedom. IDF soldiers were the noble cowboys with Winchesters; Palestinians little more than bloodthirsty savages.

She wasn't a member of the Fatah, she told audiences, but where she agreed with Arafat was his call for a "secular, democratic state for Muslims, Christians, and Jews." She would add: "Don't believe what you hear about us, that we are anti-Semitic killers. We are like the Jews. We Palestinians are the Jews of the Arab world."

And for this she got smeared with every name in the book: anti-Semite, Nazi, the pretty face of a bloodthirsty cabal. One woman with bluish hair and kidney-red lipstick rose from her chair and was a lot more hyperbolic even than the Israeli at the *New Outlook* conference: "You come here with your smooth voice and your refined manner, pretending to be humane—but we know who you are! Your people are terrorists, hijackers, murderers! I HATE YOU."

Instead of dishing out hatred in return, Raymonda turned to her, asked for her name—it was Debby. "Debby," she began with a soft voice, speaking into a microphone, "I was raised by nuns from Europe who taught me to love the Jewish girls in my school in Israel. The nuns' love and serenity, their great silence before birth and death, their devotion to humanity and to its great prophets, to the suffering Mother and Child on the Via

Dolorosa: this remains for me a source of power and hope, a mystical hope one can almost say, which is accessible only to those who have lost everything."

Most American Jews were more willing to set aside shopworn prejudices and listen. On the West Coast, in San Francisco, an anarchist anti-war radio station invited her to talk about a political solution to the Israeli-Palestinian tragedy, and her dream of a return to her childhood home of Acre.

The next day, a Friday evening, she visited a synagogue in Los Angeles, with a pipe organ and a pervasive atmosphere of affluence and security. She soaked up the spirit of the place and was mesmerized by the singing and the liturgy and a prayer from the Baal Shem Tov, a prayer that took her back to the nuns in Haifa, and to the primacy of love: "When senseless hatred reigns on earth, and men hide their faces from one another, then heaven is forced to hide its face; but when love comes to rule the earth and men reveal their faces to one another, then the splendor of God will be revealed."

Back on the East Coast, in Washington, DC, on May 15, she was met with a very different atmosphere. She was in a cab when she first heard a radio report of the slaughter of Israeli schoolchildren in Ma'alot, in northern Israel. Fedayeen fighters had taken over a school. Dayan ordered his soldiers to storm the school, and in the ensuing firefight two dozen children died, mostly by Palestinian fire. This put Raymonda physically in danger; members of the Jewish Defense League threatened to kill her "in reprisal for Ma'alot." And in the first speech she gave after the killing, at a Quaker building in Philadelphia, she didn't explicitly condemn the terrorists. Instead, she quoted Sartre's bon mot, that terrorism is a "terrible weapon but the oppressed poor have no others," which predictably spawned catcalls from the audience, "Terrorists . . . maniacs." Midway through the evening the head of the center walked onstage with his arms up. "We just got a call from the police. They have received a warning that if Raymonda Tawil appears at the public meeting tonight, she will be executed." The Quakers, famous pacifists, canceled the event.

38

"Guns and Olive Branches"

The first time Raymonda met her future son-in-law, Arafat, was just after he gave his "Guns and Olive Branches" speech in front of the UN General Assembly in October 1974. Over his military fatigues, he wore a badly fitting cream-colored blazer of thrift store quality and bright tennis shoes. Topping off the outfit was a long checkered white and black keffiyeh. His chin was shaved, more or less, leaving his signature handlebar mustache over his thick upper lip. Arafat slipped off his dark sunglasses and read, in his seductively musical Arabic, the greatest speech of his life. He spoke of the Palestinian yearning for "self-determination" and their desire to "pour all our resources into the mainstream of human civilization. Only then will our Jerusalem resume its historic role as a peaceful shrine for all religions."

> I appeal to you to enable our people to establish national,
> independent sovereignty over its own land. Today, I have
> come bearing an olive branch and a freedom fighter's gun.
> Do not let the olive branch fall from my hand. I repeat: do
> not let the olive branch fall from my hand.

In the West Bank on the day of the speech, students poured out from schools to celebrate. The state of Israel had started with a UN General Assembly vote in 1947; the Palestinians were now using the same forum to kick off their own political revolution. Dayan ordered his soldiers to

153

break up demonstrations. When Raymonda's daughter Diana waved a Palestinian flag, they knocked her down and dragged her by the hair.

Raymonda, back in the West Bank, was accompanying a *New York Times* correspondent to a demonstration when whipping around a corner came a military jeep. Soldiers pointing Uzis forced her into the back of the jeep. The military authorities didn't want foreign journalists to see the hooping and dancing and general euphoria among Palestinians, or the tear gas canisters fired by soldiers in response. In custody, a Shin Bet interrogator let her know she was once again skating on thin ice. "You are singing the praises of that terrorist bastard at the UN, and now you're telling The *New York Times* that Palestinians support him. Well, we're not going to allow you to distort the truth." But one of her admiring generals ordered her release.[51]

For Christmas 1974, Raymonda and her family headed to Beirut. Her first encounter with Arafat took place when one of his advisors, convinced that having a feminist on board might help improve Fatah's public image as unshaven thugs, sent her a message inviting her to the organization's underground headquarters, in the Fakhani district, largely inhabited by Palestinian refugees.

Dozens of men from Force 17, Arafat's personal army of bodyguards, rushed her through the streets. It was well past midnight when they arrived at an unmarked building surrounded by a cinderblock wall with broken pieces of Fanta bottles and pickle jars on top. Arafat's small office was stuffed to the rafters with papers and books and gifts still in their wrappers from supporters; leaning against one wall was a Kalashnikov.

A Fatah man introduced her as a "militant and a feminist." Arafat nodded. Raymonda knew about his daredevilry, his skill at surviving assassins, his vision and ability to unify a fractious Palestinian people. What surprised her was the hypnotic charisma radiating from his half-smile and bulbous eyes. The man's physical vitality was bursting out of his military surplus jacket. His warmth, the frenetic movements of his hands, the drum-roll of his words, conjured up the image of a selfless militant: from Nasser he picked up the knack of alternating between the buoyancy of street language, and the cadence of classical Arabic—one of Arafat's favorite Koranic verses was "The mountain cannot be shaken by the wind."

He seemed equally impressed with her. "You know, I know all about you," he said while stirring honey into his glass of black tea. "You're a daring militant. *Ahlan wa Sahlan.* Welcome."

39
Neve Shalom

"We are a thorn in their throat."

—Mahmoud Darwish

By 1974, Ruth and Raymonda were a well-known pair, racing around Israel and the West Bank, usually in Raymonda's sleek new Citroën SM. The two were an odd couple: Ruth didn't care about style, while for Raymonda it was always important, both out of the natural pride of a francophone and because she was determined to defy the occupiers as a beautiful woman. "I should never wear mustard yellow," she once found herself musing, approaching a company of soldiers. "Next time I'll put on the brandy-colored blazer. Much better." Without fail, she always attracted the amorous, curious eyes of men.

The most public event they did together, with lots of snapping cameras, was a tree planting in the "Peace Forest" of Neve Shalom, the Arab-Jewish village founded by the Jewish-born Dominican monk, Bruno Hussar.

This wasn't a simple photo op: for Raymonda, the setting alone made it dangerous. Neve Shalom is close to the "Canada Forest," which spreads a gentle carpet of pine needles over the ruins of three villages depopulated on Dayan's order in 1967.[52] Abu Nidal and ilk frequently turned their guns on Palestinians engaging in "dialogue" with Israelis. Raymonda had to be cautious.

Bruno, a friend of Father Michel's, was a remarkable man. Having converted to Catholicism for philosophical reasons in the 1930s—as an engineering student in France he had been studying the nature of human evil—he fled France after the Nazis began rounding up Jews. He founded Neve Shalom in 1950, as a place where members of the three Abrahamic religions could live together, as a testimony of what was possible. The message resonated deeply with Raymonda and Ruth.

At the ceremony, the two friends took their shovels and were ready to start digging a hole for trees when Raymonda spotted an Israeli flag flapping white and blue in the wind. If she were to be shown in an Israeli newspaper, with the Star of David in the background, it could spell trouble.

She dashed over to the back seat of the Citroën and pulled out a long green and red Palestinian flag she and her daughters had made out of scraps of cloth. She draped the illegal flag, an act punishable by a year in prison, over her shoulders like Superman's cape.

"Raymonda, take that thing off!" Ruth banged her shovel into the dust.

"Why?"

"Because trees aren't politics, for heaven's sake." Ruth merely wanted to plant the saplings, smile for the cameras, and call it a day.

Raymonda gripped the flag tighter around her shoulders. *Yeah*, she was thinking. *That's convenient for you to be above politics. No one's going to shoot you down for being a collaborator.* To keep from shouting, Raymonda hummed to herself a Janis Joplin song she heard on Abi's Peace Radio: "Somethin' came along, grabbed a hold of me, honey, and it felt just like a ball and chain."

"Everything is politics here, Ruth," she finally told her, refusing to back down. "Trees, rainclouds, pantyhose, everything." Their eyes locked, and Raymonda wondered if their friendship would end—over a symbol. She saw a smile forming on Ruth's face. "OK, Raymonda, hang your pantyhose on a flagpole."

"I have a better idea, Ruth. You plant a tree under your flag, and I'll plant one under mine." It was a sort of impromptu two-state solution, even though Raymonda's real dream was for everyone to live in the same state, as equals.

Ruth was willing to go along, but the other Israelis now chimed in with indignation and catcalls. Even a few pinecones were tossed in Raymonda's direction. The level of the hostility rose to such a pitch that the organizers, people of good will hoping for peace and not a lynch mob, called off the event.

40

The Quest

Dayan left the Ministry of Defense in 1975, never to return. Over cheeseburgers, at California Café, Raymonda joined Abie, Amos, and Uri in uncorking champagne for the occasion. Amos, his wavy hair starting halfway back on his head, shared stories of war crimes, his and Moshe's. One of the last things he said before he nodded off in his chair, drunk, was that he and the general deserved a firing squad. "But Dayan has to go first."

The new top man in the Ministry of Defense was Shimon Peres, at the time deemed a civilian security hawk little better than Dayan, and in some ways worse because he lacked Dayan's virtue of candor. Of the two, poetry-loving Dayan was by far the more natural fighter—Peres never said, as Moshe did, "I know nothing more exciting or dramatic than war." Dayan's military ethos wasn't a product of arrogance; unlike Peres, a francophone who never bothered to learn Arabic, Dayan liked the culture, language, and mentality of the people regrettably living atop ancient Israelite pottery shards. He felt in his bones the tragic nature of the Arab-Jewish competition over the same territory, in ways that Peres didn't, or at least not yet.

Peres picked up the pace of settlement expansion in the West Bank and beefed up censorship laws. The relative press freedom in the West Bank, Dayan's legacy, covered novels and glossy celebrity magazines, but anything smacking of support for Arafat or evidence of the ha-Nakba ran afoul of laws 87 and 97 that barred anything deemed to endanger "public

159

order." What really got the system baring its teeth were public calls for civil disobedience, such as strikes; and when the newspaper Joe Nasser had worked for dared call for one, Peres's response, citing undisclosed "PLO terrorist threats," was a total closure of the West Bank, a hermetic clampdown with half the IDF patrolling the streets to make sure it was enforced. The Palestinians of Nablus hadn't experienced such heavy-handed repression since King Hussein sent in his Bedouin tribesmen.

For Raymonda, it brought back memories of reading *Nausea* during the Jordanian curfew. A welcome loophole to this closure was that Israelis could still move around freely. Uri and most of his friends had beards, so they just had to slap on yarmulkes for soldiers to wave them past checkpoints. Avnery showed up at Raymonda's with some friends who had hacked electronics in the army. From them, she learned how to transmit voice recordings by connecting up her "Kalashnikov" to the telephone line. The beautiful thing about the hack, or so they assumed, was that it was impossible to trace. Shin Bet phone taps were useless. The trick enabled Raymonda to transmit taped interviews on Peres's siege to the San Francisco radio station she had visited the previous year. The station broadcast the interview, a report duly and vigorously denied by the Israeli government. Once other news agencies picked up the story, Peres found himself under diplomatic pressure to end the clampdown.

Raymonda redoubled her efforts at engaging with the Israeli left, and the stream of activists, Palestinian and Israeli, converging at her house became a torrent. The upswing in the number of cars with yellow plates, parked in front of the house, attracted the attention of the "rejectionists" who had picked up the pace of murder. A fellow Palestinian brave enough to sit down with Israelis, Aziz Shehadeh, who as a young lawyer in Jaffa had worked with Raymonda's father Habib, attracted unwelcome attention. Meeting with Israelis was a sort of acknowledgment that Israel was an established fact. Palestinians should seek to establish their separate state. In a radio broadcast from Damascus, militants lambasted him as a "traitor, a despicable collaborator. . . . You shall pay for your treason. We shall silence you forever." Abu Nidal even tried to assassinate Arafat and his main political advisor, Abu Mazen, for being too "conciliatory" with their talk of an "olive branch" replacing the gun.

Daoud responded to a series of threatening anonymous phone calls by wanting to shut the front door to Israelis—he didn't want to become a widower. The five children sided with their father. Like their mother, they had been raised by nuns, but they didn't have the example of Jewish friends, survivors of the Holocaust, to balance out the rage of seeing friends arrested, or in Diana's case, being dragged on the ground by her hair. Suha watched on as soldiers looped belts around the necks of demonstrating students at her Rosary Sisters School and herded them into military trucks, like wayward cattle on the way to the slaughterhouse. Her political heroes were Jesus, Che, and Arafat.[53]

"Mama," Suha said sharply when an Israeli leftist showed up one day, wearing an army uniform, "I don't think we should welcome soldiers into our house." Her voice rose several octaves into a shout.

Raymonda did her best to reason with her, telling her that she shouldn't assume all Israelis thought alike, and reminded Suha that Uri and Abie had also been soldiers. What choice did Israelis have, anyway? They had to serve.

"Yes, mama, but when they're in uniform they can't disobey orders, can they? They have to kill." They were in the kitchen at the time, and the eldest son Gabi (Jubran) chimed in and reminded Raymonda that during the war in Europe, the French branded as a traitor anyone who received Nazis.

"Gabi, Israelis might be our enemies but never say they are Nazis. They aren't."

Raymonda decided to take her chances again with the Shin Bet, by returning to Beirut to get an explicit endorsement for engaging the Israeli left. Badly scarred Bassam Abu Sharif set up a meeting with Abu Mazen. The armed drivers picked Raymonda up at her hotel and drove her back to the Fakhani district, heavily fortified because of the civil war raging at the time.

The loud chatter in the basement room, the nerve center of Arafat's movement, stopped the minute she entered, dressed in a knee-length silk dress and her customary high heels. Her hair flowed freely down past her shoulders in the Bridget Bardot fashion. She recognized few of the faces now riveted on her; Arafat wasn't in the room.

Gentlemanly, Abu Mazen stood up to welcome her. In introducing her to his men in the basement, he mentioned her engagement with the Israeli left. At once, there were objections. "Which Israelis?"

Raymonda remained standing, and without a hint of trepidation, she mentioned Uri Avnery, Abie Nathan, and Ruth.

"But they are Zionists," a large man in military dress interjected.

"What are you talking about," Raymonda faced the man and said. "I AM A ZIONIST!" She herself was shocked at what she had just said, but she continued. "Do you even know what Zionism is? The word comes from Zion—it is about a longing to return to the Holy Land. There isn't a day that passes that I don't think about Acre and Haifa. Just because Jews feel an attachment to what they call Zion doesn't mean that a man such as Uri Avnery wants to steal our land, or oppress us. Why can't two peoples love the same land?" Her quest, she told them, was to find a way to do so.

Of all the men in the room, Abu Mazen understood her the best. He was a refugee from the Galilee. A short rather colorless man, he was nodding along, cautiously but affirmatively, as she made her case. It made no sense, Raymonda continued, to shun all contact with the other side, as if all Israeli Jews were like Dayan or Sharon. Just look at universities in Europe and the United States. They're rebelling against their elites; young Israelis are turning against theirs, and we should support this. "We all know that eventually Jews and Arabs will have to find a way of living together."

Abu Mazen followed up her speech by calling her a "very courageous woman" because she was "willing to risk her life to meet with Israelis." It was a ringing endorsement from the man who would go on to become chief architect of the two-state solution with Israel.

41
House Arrest

On August 12, 1976, an Israeli officer showed up at Raymonda's front door with the diktat from the military governor, barring her from leaving her house—the Tawil family had by this point moved to Ramallah. A policeman, furtively taking in the sight of her shapely figure, stood outside the door, and the military ordered her phone disconnected, cutting her off from the outside world. Her "Kalashnikov" was silenced.

As they isolated her, the Israeli government propaganda services leaked stories about her undefined "illegal activities," how she was stirring up tension between Christians and Muslims, and how, in a further twist of the knife, she was carrying on a series of romantic liaisons. The Iraqi-born Binyamin Fuad Ben-Eliezer, military governor of the West Bank at the time, taking a surprisingly sophisticated tack that would become part of the Israeli repertoire, played off Arab male prejudices and feelings of "honor." He told village elders that a woman cavorting with Israeli men was a threat to sacred Arab tradition, a despiser of the Almighty Himself.

Daoud had little choice but to put on a brave face. What the authorities didn't factor into their plans was Raymonda's network of Israeli friends. Together with Uri, Ruth came by often, and the churlish soldier outside the door, jaw dropping, didn't dare block her. Like chastened schoolboys, they looked down at their boots when she said they were being "absolutely silly."

Amos turned up, always ready to share a bottle of spirits. Abie was tireless in his efforts to get the word out on Raymonda's house arrest, by broadcasting reports over his pirate radio station; Abie Nathan was the one Israeli the Tawil children couldn't wait to see. Each visit, they slipped him scraps of paper with titles of pop songs they wanted to hear: Suha's favorite was "Hotel California."

The *New York Times* ran a story on the case, accompanied by a flattering caricature of her as a lioness in a cage. Barred from going through the front door, an Italian television crew crawled over a wall and interviewed her through the bathroom window in the back of the house.

House arrest had lasted for two months before the authorities summoned her to the military governor's office. It was October, and the entire country was a dusty brown after half a year of no rain. The air was dry and smelled of smoke. The military policeman led her into the building, up a flight of stairs and to a spacious, bright room, lingering a moment before swiveling around and shutting the door behind him. Yigal Carmon sat in a chair with his legs crossed and his hands laced behind his head.

Carmon, the Ministry of Defense expert on Arab affairs, was an intellectual and a historian, and part of his job was to monitor what was written about Israel in the Arab press. He might have been her persecutor, but he was also a sharp-minded professional, eager to understand her.

His office chair squealed as he swiveled it around to face her. Raymonda noticed on his furrowed temple a thick blue vein beating. "It seems," Carmon said without further ado, gesturing to her to take a seat, "that house arrest is not enough for you, Mrs. Tawil." He cleared his throat. "You are still opening your mouth too much!" He delivered the line smoothly. His unblinking face was made almost anemic by the sunlight pouring through the windows of his office. He sat with his hands clasped on one knee. At first, she thought he was nodding off: trained interrogators can look both asleep and watchful, cunning like a rattler.

With a racing heart, she knew she had to stand up to him: showing weakness would only make matters worse. If she wanted Israeli men to respect her, she needed to strike back. In the toughest voice she could muster, she said: "You'd better listen to me and people like me! If not, you'll have another Yom Kippur fiasco on your hands. Your son could be killed in it! And then, when you're staring down into a hole in the ground, you'll remember me and my warnings."

Carmon, sucking on the end of a ballpoint pen, tried to say something, but stopped. Pointing in the direction of the door, he said with an almost pleading whisper, "Please get out." It must have been one of the shortest interrogations in the history of the occupation. The impression he made was of a man forced to repress someone he admired.

More draconian orders arrived a few days later, barring her from welcoming visitors, sealing her off from the outside world. There were now two soldiers stationed out front, preventing anyone from entering while another kept watch over the backyard. General Ben-Eliezer, who was slandering Raymonda as a "loose woman," passed by to check in with the soldiers and warn them not to be "seduced" by her "smiles and hospitality"—Raymonda kept them stocked with coffee and cake.

The next time the military permitted her to leave the house was for a trip back to the military governor's building, to hear the official charges against her, which included the usual crimes against the state: organizing strikes, transmitting information illegally, taking part in demonstrations, and wearing a PLO badge on her lapel. It took the judge half an hour to run through the entire list.

42
The Comedians

Isolation made Raymonda want to shriek at her children and Daoud; it slowly began to entomb her, day by day, like a chrysalis. Journalist friends kept writing about her case in the press. The only good thing to come out of forced isolation was the time she had to jot down notes for what her co-writer turned into *My Home, My Prison*.

At one point in late December 1976, someone must have decided that the price of keeping her under hermetic isolation was doing more harm than good, and she was released with a variety of warnings of future arrests and expulsion if she returned to her troublemaking.

Ruth, sitting in the Tawil living room the next day, asked Daoud whether he would marry Raymonda if he had to do it all over again. He chuckled, shook his head, and in a soft voice replied, "No. Way too much drama for a conservative banker," he said, a lie belied by his eyes shimmering with affection and by the way he held Raymonda's hand.

One of Raymonda's first trips back to Jerusalem was to see Assi's darkly comic *Feast for the Eyes*, a film about a failed poet who kills himself. Critics read into the film a metaphor for the collective suicide the youngest of the Dayan children believed his country was mindlessly committing.

In Ramallah, activists from all over the world and the West Bank, along with Ruth, Uri, Amos, and Abie, and a gaggle of other left-wingers resumed their regular pilgrimages to the Tawil's house. The Israelis were brimming with excitement at the new political organization they were creating. They believed their group would break the power monopoly of the labor and right-wing parties. It was the first Zionist group to call openly for two states, one Jewish and one Palestinian, and Ruth's support was considered a coup for the group. Then as now, Ruth wasn't sure it made much sense to carve out a separate Palestinian state when it seemed easier, and better, for everyone to live together as equals. But she was happy to support the leftists. At least they were doing something.

The two-staters gathering at one-state Raymonda's house, with their noble but wishful thinking over stuffed grape leaves and wine, badly misread the political map in Israel. Their group was never more than a boutique party with a voter base more or less equal to the bohemian theater and cafe population of Tel Aviv. In 1977 Ezer Weizman forged the Likud Party by cobbling together various right-wing groups; and, with the hardboiled Greater-Israel nationalist, Menachem Begin, at its helm, the Likud came to power. To Ruth's dismay her ex-husband joined the government as foreign minister. Yitzhak Shamir, an erstwhile Irgun fighter with strangely reptilian eyes, also joined the cabinet. Sharon picked up the Ministry of Agriculture. Ruth's dear Ezer, as chief architect of the most right-wing government in the history of the country, was the new minister of defense. Ruth wanted to march over to the Ministry of Defense and shake some sense into Ezer. Seeing him and Moshe smugly next to Begin felt like a betrayal far worse than cavorting with other women. "Cheating on me, that's one thing, but cheating on the country!"

Israelis on the left called Begin every libelous name in the book: fascist, demagogue, dictator, and so on; many quoted Ben-Gurion when he compared Begin to Hitler.[54]

The California Café crowd, with their boundless vilification of the Begin-Dayan-Weizman-Sharon-Shamir government, became even more marginalized when Egyptian President Anwar Sadat announced his imminent arrival in Jerusalem. He was to appear before the Israeli Knesset. Word of the unimaginable act reached Raymonda in the middle of a conference, organized by the *New Outlook* magazine at the Tel Aviv Hilton. She and the manager of the hotel, a former governor-general in the West Bank, were at one another's throats because she wrote "Palestine" on her plastic nametag. He barked into her face that there was no such entity.

"If you . . . you . . . you keep the name . . . name Palestine on that badge," stuttered the general-turned-hotel-manager, reaching over and yanking it off her neck, "I . . . I will b-b-b-blow up this hotel."

"OK, go ahead and blow it up," she shot back. "Then the dead of Jaffa will rise to fight you." The five-star hotel was built on top of the Muslim cemetery of Jaffa, expropriated after 1948.[55]

She and the stuttering manager were going back and forth, just as the announcement was read over the hotel loudspeaker that Anwar Sadat was going to visit Jerusalem. The manager lost his stutter. "You win, Raymonda." He handed the badge back to her. "Write Yasser Arafat, if you want."

Sadat made his visit, and Moshe spearheaded the subsequent peace talks with the Egyptians. Over the coming months of intense negotiations, he had the final adventure of his life that included one secret meeting with Sadat's men that required him to travel undercover with a mustache, wig, and sunglasses, and to move between cars and far-flung Middle-Eastern airports.

With her ex-husband now racing around the world in his unlikely career shift as peacemaker, Ruth wanted to go on a long journey, much the way she went to the Congo in 1960. The Ogowe River was out of the question because Albert Schweitzer was dead, so she took up an offer from the Inter-American Development Bank to create handicraft projects in Latin America, extending her know-how accumulated at Maskit to a dozen poverty-mired countries. She resigned as head of Maskit, and was off.

Ruth's eight years at the bank were the longest stretch of time away from home since she was in London as a child. She got the job when she was already over sixty, closing in on what most people look forward to as their golden retirement years. In and out of luxury hotels and palaces so often over the years, she felt most at home in squalid, outlying villages with cackling chickens where she communicated with her hands and feet, and where no one had ever heard the Dayan name, though her ex's legacy managed to shadow her in the most unexpected places. Manuel Noriega, dictator of Panama, gave her a big kiss because her husband was one of his greatest heroes.

Letters she keeps in a shoebox and composed in neat Hebrew hand-writing follow Ruth's movements throughout her years at the bank. There are a hundred pages from the Andes, Tierra del Fuego, or Port-au-Prince, letters that read like something out of Bruce Chatwin.

At one point she was drinking a cocktail in an Argentine hotel bar, with a picture of Jesus on the wall, when over the radio came the news that a Turk tried to assassinate the pope. There was such a commotion—she didn't understand a thing until a man in a business suit said to her, "Pray for the pope, señora, pray for the pope," as if her Jewish prayers would fly through the Pearly Gates quicker than their Catholic ones.

One letter has her riding on a mule for a week, in the barren mountains of Bolivia in pursuit of a small indigenous tribe, and encountering, on a perilous rocky trail, a group of handsome Spanish priests devoting their lives to the *damnés de la terre*. Their mysterious self-sacrificing charisma, their "reverence for life," brought to mind Schweitzer. The main difference between Ruth and the priests was motivation. The secular Ruth wasn't on the prowl for isolated tribes to save souls, not hers and not theirs. "I'm a solitary ship lost at sea, floating from port to port," goes one letter. "I have no close friends and I am dependent on the whims of revolutions and dictators."

Ruth blossomed in the anonymity. She didn't need to have an identity, not as wife-of, not as an Israeli. Her most emotional missives are from Haiti, a country ruled in those days by Jean-Claude Duvalier a.k.a. "Baby Doc" and his cronies known as the "dinosaurs." Ruth felt at home in the country the instant she stepped out of the twin-engine plane into the fly-filled, sweltering airport in Port-au-Prince crowded with half-starving beggars, their hands groping after her.

From the airport, she rented a Citroën and headed off to a hotel operated by Abie Nathan's ex-wife Rosie, a lesbian and disciple of the celebrated African-American dancer and mambo priestess in the voodoo religion, Katherine Dunham. Rosie had gone native, except for the tattoos and butch look of closely cropped hair.

Every morning, Ruth set out from the hotel into the slums navigating steaming streams of sewage, holding her Maskit shawl over her nose and taking in the dazzling colors of the homes and the people. "I'm on my way to a madhouse," one of her letters begins. "Every day, my mind is captivated by the colors and the way of life—the natural goodness here. It is as if the heavens have opened and produced life, coconuts falling from the sky." Haiti mesmerized her with its colors, singing, dancing, voodoo and art.

In the evenings, Ruth headed over to the legendary gingerbread-style Hotel Oloffson, the watering hole for the Haitian elite. Graham Greene set much of his novel *The Comedians* in the bar, to get support for her work in the slums. Greene writes of "nights with the discord of violence instead of jazz." Ruth's visits coincided with a spate of political murders.

At the Oloffson Hotel, Ruth hobnobbed with the elite mulattos and intrepid expatriates who continued to live in the country. She followed all the gossip on the island because one of her friends, a Palestinian from Nazareth, was Baby Doc's sister-in-law.

43
Crossing Boundaries

R uth often returned to Israel, and when she did, Raymonda gave her plenty of hugs along with a long list of requests for favors. With the Likud in power, settlement construction shot up; there were harsher crackdowns, and more and more Palestinian nationalists ended up placed under house arrest or in prison, or were simply tossed across the frontiers, to Jordan or Lebanon.

With Weizman as her brother-in-law, Ruth could pull strings, and she normally did whatever Raymonda asked. Sometimes without knowing it, Ruth facilitated the work of the PLO.

In January 1978, the World Council of Churches invited Raymonda to the United States for three months. Daoud didn't even try stopping her this time. On her way, she attended a symposium in Rome on human rights in the occupied territories. Following the symposium, she added a new role model to her list that included Fadwa Touqan and *Ms. Magazine* founders, Gloria Steinem and Letty Cottin Pogrebin. She met Oriana Fallaci, the former Second World War partisan. Fallaci was one of the most brazen, outspoken journalists in the business.

From Rome, she flew to Paris. Avnery had a surprise for her. Her cab driver pulled up in front of a home, in the suburbs, belonging to the Palestinian heart surgeon, Dr. Issam Sartawi. Uri was waiting for her inside, and with him was Matti Peled, the IDF general who had once described the "bullets and missiles" coming out from Raymonda's "rosy lips."

Sartawi's and Raymonda's lives overlapped at a number of points: born within months of one another in Acre, he had fled the city with his family, in 1948. He ended up in Baghdad and, later, in Cleveland in medical school. Radicalized by the Six Day War, with the PFLP leader George Habash and Bassam Abu Sharif, he was involved in the operation that nearly killed Assi at the Munich airport. Eventually, recognizing that terrorism was no way to further the Palestinian cause, he began reaching out to Israelis and Jews. One of his biggest backers was the Austrian-Jewish Chancellor Bruno Kreisky.

Raymonda, Avnery, Sartawi, and General Peled ended up at a restaurant where they conferred on how best to achieve a political solution to the Israeli-Palestinian conflict while doing justice to the Palestinian refugees of 1948. They also discussed the growing plague of Jewish settlements in the West Bank. At one point in the conversation, Sartawi excused himself and headed to the restroom, leaving his attaché case under the table. It was full of PLO secrets, which he later told Avnery, with a broad smile, "If I revealed to any of my friends that I left a briefcase full of PLO secrets in the care of a Zionist, they wouldn't believe me."

"If I told any of my friends that a PLO terrorist put an attaché case under my table and went away, and I remained there without grabbing it, they'd think that I was crazy," retorted Avnery.[56]

In New York, Raymonda stayed at a luxury hotel, on the Upper East Side, across the street from the Guggenheim. The clandestine talks she had had in Paris must have whetted her appetite for high-stakes diplomacy. She arranged an illegal tête-à-tête between Arafat's top representative at the UN, Zuhdi Labib Al-Tarazi, and Ruth. Raymonda thought Ruth, flying up from South America, might be the perfect courier to deliver a message from the PLO to prominent Israelis in the government.

Working amid the squalor of third-world slums, and being far from Israel, made Ruth more empathetic to the Palestinian cause, and more indifferent to opinions of grandstanding politicians, as well as Israeli law. She had no qualms about sitting down with Arafat's UN man.

Al-Tarazi, a Greek Orthodox Christian, was a well-known figure in diplomatic circles. The Patriarch of Jerusalem made him a Knight of the Holy Sepulchre. But when Jimmy Carter's ambassador to the UN, Andrew Young, ran into him at a luncheon and had the temerity to talk to him, the *New York Daily Post* ran the headline, "Jews Demand Firing Young." Carter dumped him.

Like so many of Arafat's men, threats came from all sides, not just from the Mossad and Abu Nidal. Though no militant, the Jewish Defense League threatened Al-Tarazi's life often enough for American authorities to station a guard with a submachine gun in front of his apartment building in New York City, and the windows of the apartment were bullet-proof because people had already tried to assassinate him.

Sitting on the leather sofa in the living room, with Frank Lloyd Wright's Guggenheim masterpiece visible through the window, al-Tarazi handed Ruth a personal message from his boss Arafat, which expressed his willingness to cut a peace deal with the Israeli government, on the condition that Israel recognize the PLO and agree to the establishment of the Palestinian state on the frontiers of the armistice of 1949, including East Jerusalem. This was the first time such a formal offer was ever mentioned by a Fatah leader, and Ruth knew it.

Raymonda felt faint because Arafat's new line meant the end of the dream of a single democratic state. Ruth swallowed hard as well, but more out of excitement. Was this the beginning of genuine peace? She bolted up from the sofa and stood as erect as a soldier at attention. "Mr. Tarazi, I will deliver this message to my brother-in-law, Ezer Weizman."

There was an awkward pause. Raymonda fixed her gaze on Ruth. "Ruth, there is something you need to know. Weizman's men are trampling on our rights." Ruth sat back down before stiffening her back and coming to his defense. "I don't believe a word you are saying. Ezer is a NICE MAN!"

"Yeah," rejoined Raymonda, "and Moshe is just a farmer! Weizman's acting like a MONSTER." Tarazi and Raymonda presented evidence: Not as deft as Dayan in his personnel choices, Weizman hired a certain General David Hagoel to be his commander. Like Conrad's Captain

Kurtz, Hagoel ran the territories as a personal fiefdom, doing as he pleased. The trigger for bringing up Weizman's misdeeds that afternoon in Manhattan was the order Hagoel gave to soldiers to fire tear gas into the classrooms of schools, forcing children to jump out a window. But the evidence failed to sway Ruth, especially the accusation about the tear gas; in fact she was shocked that Raymonda would believe such gruel propaganda. "Our boys don't do such things."[57]

"If you want proof, just go and see for yourself what's going on. Go to Ramallah. Here, take the address of the mayor." Ruth promised Raymonda and Tarazi to check out the story.

She made a special trip back to Israel. As soon as she returned, she got in her Saab and drove to Ramallah to meet Karim Khalaf, the green-eyed mayor.

The mayor told her story after story of demolitions and other abuses. Children testified about the tear gas incident.

Appalled, she headed straight for the hospital—Weizman was recovering from an operation—and gave him a piece of her mind. "They call you a monster. Do you know what? You deserve it! Shame on you!" She had to refrain from swinging her handbag at him. "After what happened to Saul . . . how could you!"

Weizman loved Ruth. The fact that she stood in front of him shivering with emotion, and mentioned the sniper attack on his son, was all it took to get him groaning out of bed. Snapping out orders for a change of clothes and a helicopter, he flew at once to Ramallah. He spoke to Mayor Khalaf, with Raymonda present, and heard the same appalling tales.

Weizman stared at his men with a blank expression that quickly boiled into rage: his bad temper was legendary. With a sweep of his hand, and turning to his officers and chief of staff, he asked if the stories were true. He spoke with crisp military cadence and cracked his knuckles loudly. The officers said nothing, which Weizman assumed was an admission of guilt. He barked out commands to his underlings to loosen their stranglehold on the Palestinians.

An article the following day in the *Jerusalem Post* quoted Khalaf praising Weizman as a wise man. During Ruth's next visit to Ramallah,

Mayor Khalaf thanked her for standing on the side of the oppressed. Two years later the green-eyed mayor lost his right leg when West Bank settlers booby-trapped his Cadillac.

Raymonda began touting Ruth's "good witch's" power in bringing out Weizman's humanity. His chief of staff, by contrast, was shocked at his boss's "transformation of opinion," and his alarming talk of "concessions and compromises" on Eretz Yisrael. Weizman shifted from being an ardent proponent of settlements to a principled opponent. He began looking for ways to establish a secret conduit, through Ruth and Raymonda, to Arafat.

44

The Good Witch

Ruth returned to the jungles, mountains, favelas, and hotel bars of Latin America, with frequent trips to Washington, DC, where the bank had its headquarters and where Moshe, absorbed in the peace negotiations with Egypt, was in and out of the White House.

Sitting down with Tarazi encouraged Ruth to strike out on her own. During her next trip to Washington, she read an op-ed in the *Washington Post* by the Georgetown professor Hisham Sharabi. The silver-haired member of an aristocratic family was an academic superstar — Bill Clinton was his student. Unhappy with what he wrote, she rang him up.

She told him her name — stone silence on the other end — and invited him for lunch. "It's on me." Ruth made sure he knew she was divorced from Moshe. He sounded uncomfortable because she put him on the spot; he had to agree.

Ten minutes later his assistant called and, with a deep baritone voice, wanted to know why the ex-wife of Foreign Minister Dayan would want to speak with Professor Sharabi. What about?

"Just because," she began. "Because I want to discuss the nonsense he wrote in the *Washington Post*."

"Nonsense? Yes, I see."

The man with the deep voice joined Professor Sharabi, and the three met in a hotel lobby. At first, Sharabi barely looked at Ruth. He picked at his salad with a fork and, when he finished, he stared down at his fingernails. She guessed what was swirling around in his brain: What the hell am I doing here with Mrs. Dayan? In those days, Palestinians got killed as "collaborators" for less. She decided to break the ice a little:

"Listen, in your article you ticked off our crimes, one by one. Be my guest and rake us over the coals, though if you ask me I could do a much better job of it. You got your facts wrong, that's all." He was still staring down at his hands. "Do you know Raymonda Tawil?"

The professor looked up and began slowly nodding his head.

"Well, so do I, and you know what else? She's one of my best friends. You can say we're soul mates. We put her under house arrest, you know. I visited her in Ramallah. You may know her husband Daoud."

Sharabi kept nodding. "A fine man."

"I said to Daoud, 'Daoud, now Raymonda must feel like she won the lottery. She finally has what she's always wanted. It took her years of trying, and finally she's a martyr, a media star. Mazel tov.'"

The professor's nodding transformed into a grin, and he was soon laughing into his fist. Ruth, too, started laughing so hard her stomach hurt. She asked him if he thought Israelis and Palestinians could make peace. "Our two peoples, I mean. Isn't it time?"

"Yes, yes, yes, Mrs. Dayan, you are entirely right. Maybe you and Raymonda are proof of what's possible."

A few weeks later she got another phone call from one of the Israeli organizers of the upcoming *New Outlook* conference in Washington.[58] On Raymonda's behalf, he asked if Ruth could persuade Ezer Weizman into permitting the mayors of Nablus, Ramallah, and Hebron to attend the conference. The government had stubbornly refused, until then.

"Of course," she said. She got ahold of Ezer and began to raise hell. It didn't do any good. "Ruthie, I can't," he kept apologizing every other sentence. His hands were tied. The mayors couldn't leave Israel. People in the Shin Bet told him it would be a "security danger."

The conference took place at the International Inn. Sharabi stood in for the mayors, and Raymonda gave a rousing speech on peace. Ruth was there with Abie, Uri, Amos, some Peace Now activists, Edward Said, I. F. Stone, and other prominent American Jews. Jimmy Carter invited Said and Raymonda to the White House for dinner.

Seeing Sharabi and Raymonda on the stage made Ruth more resolute than ever to use her and Raymonda's powers to "bang some sense" into politicians' heads. There was still one top politician Ruth avoided. One afternoon while still in Washington, she was sitting with Abie when he spotted Moshe surrounded by a clutch of security men. Abie nudged her, suggesting she give the fellow a hug because he was finally promoting life instead of destroying it. She had never stopped loving him. She also knew that speaking with him would tear open the wounds that had been healing in the jungles and mountains, far from Israel. She stayed riveted to her seat, and Moshe and his entourage disappeared through double doors.

Mistrustful, reluctant Begin, submitting to heavy American arm-twisting, and with Dayan and Weizman pressuring from inside, eventually agreed to hand back the Sinai. The peace deal, for which Begin and Sadat shared the Nobel Prize, was supposed to lead to a general Israeli-Arab peace treaty. This never happened. Polish-born Begin deemed "Judaea and Samaria" to be the eternal property of the Jewish people. Lands where long ago our kings knelt to GOD." He wasn't about to deliver this sacred patrimony over to "beasts walking on two legs," the Palestinians, and their "bloodthirsty" leader Arafat.

Moshe, his schizophrenic respect for Arabs and atavistic attachment to their lands in full force, flatly refused to consider wily Arafat to be anything other than a terrorist. The most he was willing to offer Palestinians in the Occupied Territories was a sham autonomy, with no control over the Jordan Valley and the hill country. The IDF would continue guarding the borders, ruling the airspace, controlling water, and settling the empty space. Moshe's vision of wagonloads of settlers, like in the American West, rumbling across the Green Line can be seen in his protégé Arik Sharon's detailed scheme. In 1979, he wanted 1.5 million Jews settled in the West Bank.

Dayan's response to the victory of moderates inside the PLO, men such as Raymonda's son-in-law Ibrahim Souss, Sartawi, and Sharabi, in winning Arafat over to the two-state solution, was ratcheting up settlement activity.

The killing continued. In Paris, Mossad agents eliminated two of Ibrahim Souss's PLO colleagues, both moderates, and like Dr. Souss, supporters of a two-state solution.

45

Militants for Peace

The combination of Abu Nidal, the Israeli security services, and the rogue Jewish terrorists who blew up Major Khalaf in his Cadillac, should have made Raymonda more cautious, but she still behaved as if she were somehow immune from physical attack. The Virgin Mary protected her, she told Ruth. She surely needed divine help when there were as many as thirty activists and journalists, Arabs and Jews, crammed into her house.

No longer trying to constrain Raymonda within the bounds of propriety and common sense, Daoud offered to rent an office space for her. With his refined indignation and tenderness, he complained that since her house arrest their salon had turned into a political club or a campsite. "I love you, my dear, and I'll love you even more if you open your own office and let us live in peace and quiet."

She didn't need much convincing, and Raymonda quickly found the perfect spot a hundred meters from Damascus Gate, on Salah al-Din Street, named after the great Muslim warrior who liberated the city from the Crusaders.

The timing was right, too. With Begin brandishing his Nobel Prize, and Dayan feted as warrior-turned-peacemaker, she needed to expose the way the Israeli government was redoubling its colonizing ventures in the West Bank. But to launch such an ambitious project she had to return to Beirut and consult with Arafat.

She left for Amman, and from there flew to Beirut. From the airport, a company of Force 17 men zigzagged her through the maze of gritty streets in West Beirut until they pulled up in front of the nerve center of the Palestinian resistance. Minutes later she had her second encounter with the legend.

She spoke, and he nodded along. The gist of her proposal was this: Over the years, the Israelis had built up an integrated information strategy with a highly professional press office, regular reports sent to foreign governments, and an army of tour guides and "experts" leading journalists and VIPs around the conquered territories. All the Palestinians had to offer in response were scattered reports, for the most part poorly written, laced with hyperbole, or so slapdash and cavalier with facts, sprinkled with outright fabrication, that foreign journalists, overworked and less interested in fact-checking than drinking cold Maccabee beer at the American Colony Hotel bar, preferred to rely on the Israeli government press offices.

A Palestinian press office, if done right, Raymonda said, not only could reach Israelis and people in the West; it could influence the politicians. We could counteract one of the Israeli government's most valuable assets.

Arafat squeezed a tennis ball as she spoke. She repeated to him what she had been saying for years. The Palestinians' secret weapon was that the Israelis are a free people. "Do you know what that means? They'd rather get a suntan on the beach than fight us. Some Israelis can be our allies." She gave this man who knew next to nothing about real-life Israelis a crash course. Yes, Israel has its fanatics. Yes, it has Begin and Sharon. But it also has communists and disciples of Bakunin, its Uris and Amoses, it has its Abies who agonized endlessly over the morality of their state, its crazy painters and poets and prophets. She mentioned Ruth and Assi.

"Ruth Dayan?" Behind Arafat's shades, his glowing eyeballs were expanding.

"Yes, Ruth Dayan."

Sipping his black tea, he stared into space for a moment. "You are right. We need militants for peace, like Mrs. Dayan."

Raymonda's press office was in full operation. For the first time, people in Israel and abroad got credible reporting from the West Bank. A nation arose from virtual non-existence by having a presence within pages of *Le Monde*, the *New York Times*, *Frankfurter Allgemeine*, and the *Times of London*.

46
Ms.

Across from Raymonda's desk, a large square window looked out onto the honking traffic of Salah al-Din Street. To clear her mind and plot her moves, nearly every day she ambled three blocks up to the American Colony Hotel, a well-known meeting place for spies from various intelligence services. Conversations were less likely to be bugged in the crypt-like bar downstairs than in her office.

She ordered drinks and handed out copies of the latest bulletin or translations in English, French, and Hebrew from the press office's newspaper *Al Awda* (The Return). Raymonda was willing to talk to Israelis, meet with them, protest together, and even risk her life, for the sake of peace. But her dream of a return to Acre was still alive.

With Arafat's blessing, the press office brought fresh vigor to a Palestinian East Jerusalem, showing strains from the comprehensive Israeli system of pass laws, permits, zoning, and multiple and sundry acts of bureaucratic malfeasance and chicanery. Gone were the salons and nightclubs and the genteel old families of the pre-1967 city. The city was full of garbage, pot-holed streets, bands of feral cats, and sagging electrical wires. Because the idea was to compete with the Israeli government press office on the other side of town by attracting foreign journalists, Raymonda made sure the office had the best coffee and aperitifs in town. Daoud dipped deeper into his savings to buy Italian furniture, French wallpaper, and plush clover-green carpet.

The office functioned as a sort of human rights switchboard, with more than a dash of full-throated feminism. For hours every day, Raymonda and her coworkers worked the phone with villages and towns and cities, talking to mayors, activists, anyone with information to share. This allowed the office to come up with a complete documentary of events: lists of the arrested and beaten, the homes ransacked and property confiscated. With the "Kalashnikov" hooked up to a phone line, Palestinian voices were heard over the airwaves.

As for feminism, her mantra was "When our women have the chance to get out from under masculine domination, you'll see what they'll do for Palestine."

Her fame grew. Vanessa Redgrave wanted her opinion about Arafat, to which Raymonda replied that behind his Smith & Wesson .38, Arafat was a man of peace. In a documentary she financed, *The Palestinian*, Redgrave is seen dancing with a Kalashnikov. *Saturday Night Live* did a skit with Jane Curtin as Redgrave and John Belushi, in tails, a bowtie, and dark shades, in the role of Arafat.

Part of Raymonda's careless sense of invulnerability, curiously, related to her feminism, which simultaneously aroused the ire of many Arab men.

When Letty Pogrebin of *Ms. Magazine*, a committed Zionist, came to Israel with a group of fifty other American feminists in March 1978, she wanted to meet Raymonda because of her reputation as a rebel against "Arab patriarchy," and a believer in Jewish-Arab coexistence, making Raymonda a "feminist heroine." Pogrebin, repressing the "hatred" she frequently harbored against Arabs for "hating Israel"—her grandfather was killed in the 1939 Arab uprising in Tiberius—invited Raymonda to address her group at the King David Hotel in Jerusalem.

A devoted reader of *Ms. Magazine*, Raymonda jumped at the chance. Of all people, American women needed to hear the Palestinian side of the story. Raymonda had on her most glamorous spring outfit, her *Cosmopolitan* Magazine look, as Pogrebin introduced her to the women sitting in the gilded reception hall. Israeli feminists in the audience nodded their heads in solidarity as Raymonda spoke about the evils of the occupation and the need for a peaceful state of Palestine existing side by side with Israel.

Then the fireworks began. It was a repeat of her America trip, with the same lurid accusations, the same frothing mouths.

"Israel is a democracy. How can you expect us to hand our land over to terrorists?" one woman wanted to know. An Israeli feminist tried to defend Raymonda but couldn't because a black Baptist woman launched into a tirade. "I hate you Arabs." She had her chest thrust forward. "You SHITS were the ones that sold us as slaves. No Jew has ever kept a black under the lash." Raymonda, dumbfounded to find herself suddenly cast in the role of the slave trader, paused to gather her thoughts.

Are you out of your mind, she wanted to say. By the time she regained her composure, others were piping up with their own recriminations and heckles. The best Raymonda could come out with was that Palestinian "freedom fighters" would never give up the struggle for independence.

"Baby killers," screeched multiple voices at once. "What do YOU know about FREEDOM?"

She had expected a roomful of Vanessa Redgraves and instead got hard-line Likudniks. Their lack of empathy pushed her to the edge of tears. She wanted to run out of the room, and would have if she hadn't had a vision of her mother behind a sewing machine telling her to live without hatred, and to be strong. Never buckle.

"What if," began Raymonda, in what according to Pogrebin's account was delivered with the "vocabulary of feminism" and "cadences" of a revivalist—"what if there remains somewhere in the Jewish state, some-how, some remnant of the great Jewish tradition of humanism? Some bits of the power your noble culture has in the diaspora where you are a minority, and you have no army. You call us Palestinian savages! The Israeli prime minister, you should know, bombed this hotel in 1946. Yesterday's terrorist is today's prime minister."

More boos.

"And . . . and . . . and today's freedom fighter will be tomorrow's presi-dent of Palestine. His name is Yasser . . ."

BOOOOO!

Raymonda raised her voice. "His name is Yasser Arafat. And you talk about terror! The Israeli government has dehumanized us. We had a culture in Palestine for centuries. We knew English, French, music, and art. We were a light in the desert. Now we have lost everything, a people without a country. We are the Jews of the Arab world. Israelis are the Prussians . . ." Other Palestinians had said as much, just never in front of a mainly Jewish audience at the King David Hotel.

The line about the Prussians nearly caused a pogrom, and Pogrebin held back a mad stampede of angry women, hotel cutlery in hand. STOP! She bellowed this so loudly that the women quieted at last. She asked Raymonda why the Israelis put her under house arrest.

"I'll tell you why. It was because the military authorities look at me as a malevolent propagandist for peace. Because I am telling everyone that the only way to prevent rivers of blood is for Jews and Arabs to sit down and talk, as equals. My mission is one of love, and Dayan and Begin want to muzzle me for it."

"Does that mean you condemn terrorism?"

"Do you say the same thing about Soweto?" She quoted Sartre's line about terrorism: a "terrible weapon but the oppressed poor have no others." Which was the last thing Raymonda said before storming out of the hotel. [59]

Three days later, Pogrebin and the fifty feminists boarded a bus and headed for Tel Aviv. On the highway, along the coast, they encountered the smoking remains of an Egged bus. Fedayeen, sent by Arafat's sidekick Abu Jihad from Lebanon, had landed by sea and hijacked the bus using Kalashnikovs and rocket propelled grenades. One of the terrorists was a nineteen-year-old woman from the Sabra refugee camp in Beirut. The aim of the "operation" was to capture hostages to be swapped for Fatah militants in Israeli prison. The operation turned into a bloodbath with over two dozen Israelis killed.

Pogrebin had to dispel suspicions among many of the women on the bus that they were the real targets of the attack, and that Raymonda had somehow communicated their itinerary to the Fedayeen. [60] The smoke and blood and death Pogrebin saw that day, in fact, convinced her that Raymonda was right in what she said at the King David.

47
The Tomb of God

"If the prisoner is beaten, it is an arrogant expression of fear."
—Ghassan Kanafani

Two weeks after the Coastal Road Massacre, Raymonda heard the screeching sound of military jeeps, a dozen of them, in front of her home. Soldiers, guns drawn, forced Daoud and the five children to one side as they handcuffed and blindfolded her. They drove her to the Moskobiya police headquarters where Joe Nasser had, according to Father Michel, been held. Palestinians call the place the "Tomb of God" or the "Torture Factory." Where monks once tried to reach the divine, interrogators now worked at breaking minds and bodies.

She was fingerprinted, and a female guard, a Moroccan Jew named Rose, led her through a heavy steel door and shut it behind her with a loud metallic clang. There, behind a simple wooden desk sat a small man who introduced himself as Yossi. He had dark eyes, and his lips were grimly pressed together. A long scar extending down the length of his right cheek gave him a sinister look in striking contrast to his necktie and the neat row of pens and pencils in the pocket of his button-down Oxford shirt. His voice was calm and refined, each syllable intoned carefully like a pharmacist reading from a prescription. "Mrs. Tawil, we're going to have the opportunity to get to know one another well over the coming days. . . . If you don't cooperate with us, you can stay here for years."

Yossi wanted to know about her activities in Rome and Washington, and about her discussions with Arafat in Beirut. "We know you met him." This last word came out with distaste. Raymonda wasn't dressed for interrogation, the Italian silk scarf didn't fit the setting, nor did the Chanel maroon blazer or the matching coat with a fur collar, or the velvety black high heel Italian boots. "Who are your contacts in Italy? You have to tell me what you discussed with Arafat. Who else did you meet in Beirut? We need names."

In the same calm, steady, emotionless voice, he accused her of raising money to buy weapons for the PLO. "We've been watching you for years. We know EVERYTHING about you. You think we're stupid? We know all about your little trick with the phone line." There were a few more similar comments, followed by a cigarette or shot glass of steaming Arabic coffee, and he began again with the same line of queries and accusations.

She denied everything except the phone line transmissions to the San Francisco radio station: she wasn't a member of the PLO, had no secrets to reveal about Arafat, and had never raised a nickel to buy so much as a bullet.

The only thing she said about Arafat was what she liked most about him: "It's how he speaks. To me, at least. Some people find his monologs tiresome; I can listen for hours." She also mentioned something that got through to her interrogator's unflappable exterior: that Arafat was willing to cut a deal with Israel. With a sharpened No. 5 yellow pencil pulled from his shirt pocket, Yossi scribbled into a notepad.

The five-hour interrogation session was just starting.

"I know you like to smoke," he said with a cool smile while opening a fresh pack and, smoothing out the cellophane, placed it next to a tin of biscuits. "And I'd love to give you some coffee. Against regulations, so sorry." He asked about the news agency, and with what struck her as feigned impatience he tapped his pencil on the desk and, upping the ante, accused her of aiding a "terrorist organization." For the next five hours, she denied every version of the absurd accusation. "You are alone, madam," he said like a bad actor reading his lines. "No one cares about you. No one will rescue you from this place. You will rot here. Smell the air. You can smell the rot already."

Rose escorted her to a concrete cell, Number 12, with a sink green with mildew, an iron bed, a square wooden table, a rickety metal folding chair, and a single florescent light bulb that never went out. Because of the damp cold, she slept in her coat and boots. The stench from chain-smoking inmates and the acrid scent of vomit seeped into the mattress, into the very peeling paint on the walls.

Each day Yossi, polite and impeccably dressed, circled like a raptor until he came up with a hole in her story. After each interrogation, Rose led her back to her isolation cell, and she sat on the bed and listened to the intruding insects buzzing in and out of the bars, and the sound of water drops dripping from the sink. Sometimes she heard groaning sounds outside her door of prisoners being dragged down the hall.

Raymonda started losing weight, her hair fell out in clumps, she took on the smell of the mattress and sink. Yossi warned her that her comparison of Begin to Hitler was enough to keep her buried alive for a year.

"For Christ's sake, I was just quoting Ben-Gurion! Why don't you dig up Ben-Gurion and grill him?"[61] The only time she knocked Yossi from his unflappable equilibrium was when she said about Begin, "Deir Yassin was a kind of prelude for him."[62] The interrogator leaped up from his chair, grabbed her by the dress, pushed her against the wall, and barked into her face that she was a "danger to the State of Israel." He then let go of her, ran his fingers through his hair, told her he was sorry, and sat back down and apologized again. "My God," he moaned.

After finishing one of the sessions, a guard marched her upstairs and handed her over to a different officer who seemed to be a Russian, or who reminded her of a burly figure brought to life by Arthur Koestler in *Darkness at Noon*, a Soviet-style jail-keeper.

The man was of gargantuan stature, a feature further brought out by his emotionless agate eyes and his shoulders, as thick as a steer's, and long arms that looked strong enough to bend the iron bars of her cell. Like Yossi, he had a long scar on his left cheek visible beneath his light blond stubble. The size of the gap-toothed hulk, or rather, the vision of what he could do to her, almost made her faint: he was opening and shutting his hand in a strangler's grip. But he spoke with an extraordinarily soft voice. When she reached him he said, half-turning, "boker tov" — good morning — and took her gently by the arm and led her to a room, as if they were heading to a dance floor.

For forty-five days, Raymonda was in solitary confinement. She awoke one morning early to the sound of jangling keys and the squeaking of the opening cell door. Rose led in a Palestinian woman charged with stabbing her father to death because he had been serially raping her and her sisters for most of their lives. For long hours between interrogation sessions, Raymonda learned about her life in an isolated village, wholly under the control of her beastly father and a mother who knew but couldn't prevent what her husband was doing. How the only way to stop him was with a long butcher knife. It felt like liberation, she said, to drive it into the detestable body she was so familiar with, over and over.

The international campaign for Raymonda's release was in full swing. She learned about the efforts of Jean-Paul Sartre and Simone de Beauvoir through an article smuggled to her, wrapped in a stale piece of pita.

The Shin Bet refused to allow Ruth to visit. Even Minister of Defense Weizman, encouraged by Ruth, got the same response: his visit would endanger "state security."

Yossi was soon joined by other interrogators — at one point seven men faced her. Their final attempt to get her to talk was to use shame. Thinking that the worst indignity for a Palestinian woman was to have any association with a "whore," they threatened to put her in a cell with a prostitute. "How dare you," she snapped. "A woman is a woman. Why do you humiliate us?" Judging by her initial response, they must have thought the shame trick worked, but instead of baring her teeth at them for "daring" to lock a "respectable" mother of five up with a prostitute, she blasted her seven interrogators with a flurry of citations from Simone de Beauvoir. She threw in a few words from Paulo Freire's *Pedagogy of the Oppressed*. "What sort of woman are you?" her interrogators asked with an amazed respect.

In the middle of the night, guards brought in three Jewish prostitutes, from Algeria, Yemen, and Morocco, into the cell next to hers. Raymonda listened to the way they cursed the guards–in Arabic. And then all three began singing a song of Umm Kulthum, "Enta Omri," "You are my life."

"Who are you?" they asked Raymonda. "Are you the terrorist?"

"No, I am a Palestinian, and I love my country just like you do."

"You're not here because you planted bombs?"

"No bombs," Raymonda laughed. "Why are you here?"

"Because the government of Israel promised us milk and honey and we got shit instead. We are on the streets because our families need food. You think we love this country? All of us curse the day we came to this place."

For the final interrogation, Yossi handed Raymonda over to a tall, strikingly handsome man with hay-colored hair. He was the director of the prison, a man named Shimoni.

Shimoni had a very different style from the Shin Bet men. He ran through the same stock questions—meeting Arafat, her secret rendezvous in Rome, her telephone hack. At one point, after she repeated her usual replies, he began to say something; then, with a cunning smile, he seemed to change his mind and made a sharp cutting gesture with the side of his hand. At first he struck only air. He drew close to her, pointing his finger right in her face. "So, Mrs. Tawil," he said almost snorting, "I don't think you realize the trouble you are in."

"The State of Israel is in trouble if you keep . . ." Before she could finish he slapped her on the face with such violence that she fell out of her chair. She scrambled clam-like on all fours, but he grabbed her again and, with one knee on the ground, he balled his fist and hit her in the face, slashing open her cheek. She could barely breathe out of her nose and mouth because of the blood.[63]

In the split second before losing consciousness, Raymonda returned to the Acre of her childhood: fluttering through her mind were images of the Crusader walls jutting out into the sea; the white spray from crashing waves and sparkle in the surf; the playful acrobatics of swallows; the buckled old woman selling flowers from large yellow baskets; the midday

Angeles ringing from the church tower. She also saw a man in a huddle of clothing sprawled out on the sidewalk in front of her family's villa in Haifa in 1948. He was face down against the quarried granite, his legs crossed at an unnatural angle, one arm, the one with the gun, nearly touching the door, as if he was trying to knock when the soldiers shot him. The man was stiff with rigor mortis.

And then the world went black.

She woke up in the infirmary. Once news reached the Red Cross of her condition—doctors feared she could die of a brain hemorrhage—international pressure mounted for her release. Journalists came to the hospital, and the newspaper pictures of bandaged-up Raymonda were a PR disaster.

Encouraged by his sister-in-law, in the middle of May Weizman gave a news conference announcing her immediate release. Ezer had a second announcement: he was firing General Hagoel from his post in the West Bank.

Rose gave Raymonda the official news of her release. "You will be freed tomorrow." Here her voice trailed off, and there was a pause, during which Raymonda could hear her breath; it was almost like she was holding back tears. "You are such a great woman, a woman with the same kindness of women of my country." She meant Morocco. Rose had big, walnut brown eyes, black hair down to her side, and a perfect set of white teeth. "I will miss you. You have to remember, Raymonda, that we are your sisters. In Arab lands, we lived together for centuries. It wasn't like now."

Raymonda could have dismissed this as a case of Alice's Walrus and Carpenter, who wept salt tears over the oysters they gobbled up, but she sensed Rose's sincerity. Her tenderness. They were sisters, women from the same Middle Eastern family.

48

A Furious Aura

"The eyes are not here
There are no eyes here
In this valley of dying stars
In this hollow valley
This broken jaw of our lost kingdoms"
— T. S. Eliot, "Mistah Kurtz — he dead: A penny for the Old Guy"
from "The Hollow Men"

The first time Raymonda read the book *Moshe Dayan: Story of My Life*, she was still in the hospital. In the epilogue, Moshe is wandering around a canyon in the Negev known in Hebrew as Nahal Beersheeba. Seeing what looks like a cave, he attaches a rope to the bumper of his jeep and clambers down, and begins sniffing around like a dog looking for a buried bone. What he finds is an Iron Age scene: potsherds, bones, flint blades, and an ax head. "This was their land," he writes about the ancient troglodytes, "their birthplace, and they must have loved it."

> When they were attacked, they fought for their birthplace.
> And now here was I, at the end of a rope, having crawled
> through an opening in a cliff-side across their threshold
> and inside their home. It was an extraordinary sensation.
> I crouched by the ancient hearth. It was as though the fire

had only just died down, and I did not need to close my
eyes to conjure up the woman of the house bending over to
spark its embers into flame as she prepared the meal for her
family. My family.

Raymonda was barely able to hold up the book, and even though it
made her wince in pain, she laughed at Dayan's imaginary "family." A
light bulb went off. "My God," she said to herself. "The great general with
so much power over us is stark raving mad." She almost pitied him.

Dayan was diagnosed with colon cancer shortly after quitting Begin's
government in 1980.

During the final family gathering on Joab Street, a brood of grandchildren clamored over the pirate's chest of Roman sarcophagi, Byzantine
gravestones, and bronze church bells. The parting gift the warrior-troglo-
dyte gave his children that day was a macabre swansong: "At the end of
the day/ Let each of you cultivate our ancestors' land/ and have the sword
within reach above your bed. /And at the end of your days/ bring it down
and give it to your children." Yael brushed off his ode as "clannish and
almost primitive in its brutal lack of any shred of light, only fighting, till the
end your days, and of our children's days. This was his gift, his inheritance."

Assi's showdown with Moshe was one of the greatest theatrical scenes
of his career, a soliloquy, or rather a rant at his father's bedside. The verbal assault could easily be slipped into an Israeli version of *King Lear*, or
Tennessee Williams's *Cat on a Hot Tin Roof*, with Moshe in the role of
"Big Daddy."

Though the two had had nothing to do with one another for years,
the prodigal son was running low on cash—cocaine was an expensive
habit—and knowing his millionaire father could afford it, thought he
could wheedle some money out of him and decided to swing by Zahala.
Assi noticed his shrunken figure. "So it's true, you are dying."

Moshe was clearly in no position to slap his children around any more,
so Assi spilled out decades of resentment:

"Listen, I want to tell you a few things." His voice climbed into a high,
reedy, inquisitional register. "I want to tell you that you were OK, you

were quite a father till the age of sixteen. Since then just one thing I remember, that you are a SOB, you are the worst person, full of yourself, full of shit. You are the one who invented screwing as a national item; who sends his bodyguard to give my kids chocolate on their birthdays. They don't know much about you. But I'll tell them. You are the generation that lost sight . . . of what we were . . . Because at a certain point you thought you were King David."

Assi, as emotionally crippled by his father as his father was by the Senegalese sniper, kept firing:

"Anyhow I want you to know that I simply hate your guts . . . You were interviewed in the paper, and you said that if you could live again you'd never have a family. I hope you understand what that means to me. That I was your mistake. Things have changed. Now you are my mistake."

Ruth knew Moshe was ill, but made no arrangements to return to Israel. Yael assured her there was no hurry. Even when he fell into a coma, Yael said nothing. Ruth therefore wasn't in the country in October 1981 when the farmer she still loved, the "firstborn son of redemption," died a millionaire, despised by his sons Assi and Udi; only Yael clung to her stubborn, ambivalent love. Her memoir *My Father, His Daughter* opens with the image of his corpse in an intensive-care unit with the EKG machine displaying a straight green line, emitting a high, piercing whine. His heart is no longer beating; the trigger finger stiff and bluish; tubes and electrodes feed into the emaciated body of the Homeric hero, whose "maimed face," scarred by a sniper's bullet, "is turning yellow." His left eye, scrolled open, is a cloudy gray marble. "I have seen many dead faces, tranquil or accepting, amazed or tortured, childish or wrinkled. Father's conveyed angry frustration, as if he didn't mean it to happen quite then, and for the first time was caught unaware, deprived of the last word. Those things unsaid and unaccomplished hovered there, almost palpable. This furious aura has haunted me ever since."

Ruth caught the first plane back in time to attend the funeral on the hill just above Nahalal.

The general's death began to ease the rivalry that pitted daughter against mother. Yael could still not discard her caricature of Ruth as weak and plagued by a "martyr's complex," an absurdity given her mother's globe-spanning efforts at improving the lives of women, from the women threatened with "honor killing" in the West Bank to weavers in Haiti. But Yael grudgingly admitted that her mother, "poor and too generous," was the only parent with the indefinable quality called love. "Mother flooded us with gifts from the nothing she had, and father had charged us for everything. I was amazed at this remarkable woman."[64]

49

Borderline Case

> "Even victors are by victories undone."
>
> —John Dryden

The day after the funeral, Raymonda told the AP and UPI newswires: "Nobody rejoices at a man's death, even if he is an enemy. But Dayan was a conqueror and an enemy, and nobody will forget his severe hand, the collective punishments."

Meanwhile, Begin and Sharon were still in power. Raymonda would later need a box of Kleenex to sit through Steven Spielberg's *Munich* because many of the Palestinians killed by the Mossad were friends. If the Munich massacre was the catalyst for the killings, why did the Israelis wait ten years after Munich to blow up or gun down so many moderate Palestinian intellectuals, writers, poets, translators, and journalists, many who had nothing to do with terrorism?

Her first death threat on European soil—she had accumulated a raft of them in the Holy Land—came in 1981. Along with imprisoned Nelson Mandela and Simha Flapan, the Israeli behind the *New Outlook,* she won a peace prize named after Austrian Chancellor Bruno Kreisky.[65] Pro-Israel groups all over Europe went to work slandering her as an anti-Semite. In Vienna, anonymous bomb threats forced her to switch hotels three times.

As a sign of just how ecumenical the threats against her were, Abu Nidal, after having just dispatched an Austrian socialist politician and head of the Israel-Austria Friendship League, sent a pair of hit-men, a Libyan and a Tunisian, to kill her for "collaborating with the Zionists."

She was in a Viennese restaurant with her daughter Suha when she noticed two dark men nursing a tea, their eyes fixed on her. She had seen enough spy movies to know the meaning behind the hard stares. Their badly fitting polyester suits were incongruent in the upscale restaurant.

The idea that Suha could get caught in the line of fire made her heart race. As soon as she was able to think clearly, she asked Suha to go to the ladies' room. "You need to get to a phone. Call this number"—it was the number of the PLO representative in Vienna. "Tell him we have a big problem. They have to come."

The Abu Nidal men missed their chance when a carload of armed men showed up in the nick of time.

Raymonda was still in Europe when the Mossad targeted Majed Abu Sharar, her mentor in politics who was among the first Palestinians to extend his hand to the Israeli left. She knew him well, having stayed with him in Beirut; she introduced him to his wife. The iconoclastic Marxist, a man immune to nationalist jargon and sloganeering, believed in engaging the Israeli left. He used to say, "In these days, death is present in every action we take, in movement, and in halting, but I would rather die moving." In October, he went to Rome to attend a writers' conference with progressive writers and politicians from all over the world, including Uri and Amos. The bomb that killed him was hidden under his bed in a hotel on the Via Veneto.[66]

In July the following year in Paris the Mossad struck again, this time targeting Ibrahim Souss's assistant Fadl Danni. It was early in the morning. Kissing his young French wife and five-month-old son as he did every morning, he got in his Peugeot and edged away from the curb. A bomb planted in the chassis of the car detonated.[67]

Back in Ramallah, late-night visitations by IDF soldiers, pounding on the door with the butt of their rifles, turned into such a regular occurrence that Raymonda stopped locking the front door. "Just come on in."

The most memorable interrogation session she had was with military governor Fuad Ben-Eliezer. He tried to blackmail her with "photos" he assured her would "scandalize" her family. "Oh, I hope they are lovely." Raymonda was taunting him in a combination of Arabic and Hebrew. "They must be nudes. Are they nice? They turn you on, right? You can't fool me, General Fuad. The trouble with you," she said briskly, "is that you're an Arab. And you Arab men have rather embroidered sexual fantasies, if you know what I mean. Go ahead and make them public," she added with a wink. "Be my guest. Oh, I can even help. Take Uri Avnery's telephone number. I'm sure he'd be more than happy to put them on the back cover of his magazine. Or centerfold, even better." For this little bit of cheek, Prime Minister Begin slapped yet another travel ban against her.

On Raymonda's birthday in June 1982, with Dayan's grave still fresh amid the poppies on bucolic Shimron Hill, Prime Minister Menachem Begin, on a flimsy excuse, ordered the invasion of Lebanon.[68] Sharon, despite a truce that had held for a year, was determined to shoot his way through West Beirut and "put Arafat in a cage." Begin likened the assault on Arafat's headquarters to the siege on Hitler's bunker. In fact, Begin and Sharon wanted Arafat dead, and the man on the ground in Beirut charged with the task of tracking him down was Uzi Dayan, the son of Moshe's brother, Zorik, and now a commander of a commando force specializing in intelligence, espionage, and reconnaissance behind enemy lines.

The Lebanon War coincided with the original Hebrew version of Raymonda's *My Home, My Prison*, and it was a bestseller in the Israeli army despite the propaganda smearing her as the Palestinian Tokyo Rose. Conscripts at checkpoints asked for her autograph.[69]

The following year, 1983, the Israeli playwright Ruth Hazan, inspired by *My Home, My Prison*, wrote *Mikreh Gvul* or "Borderline Case," as an imaginary debate between Golda Meir and Raymonda. In the play Golda, with her stringy hair the texture of a Brillo pad piled into a bun, looked like the owner of a cheap diner.

At one point the former prime minister (dead for five years by now) stamps her feet and exclaims, "You don't exist," playing off her famous refrain that there is no Palestinian people. The Raymonda character unbuttons her blouse to show a bit of cleavage. "I don't exist?" you say, pointing at her ample breasts. "My dear Golda, let me assure you I do, as did my parents, my grandparents, and their parents' parents' parents' parents all existed in Palestine, long before you showed up from Milwaukee." She next grabs her by the throat and snarls: "Maybe I should just strangle you!"

Golda squirms, but in the end Raymonda decides to release the gasping prime minister from her clutches. With Golda on the ground rubbing her sore neck, the Raymonda character announces a more effective weapon than either terror or the slavish acquiescence to power. "I take a third way, the way of dialogue."

"Borderline Case" was a smash hit, and the theater troupe performed all over Israel, mostly at left-wing kibbutzim. In Tel Aviv, eight hundred IDF officers turned up for a performance, many of the officers having just returned from the fighting in Lebanon. Adding to the drama of the evening, earlier that day a terrorist detonated a bomb in the open-air Jerusalem vegetable market, and the carnage provoked calls of "Mavet le-Aravim," Death to the Arabs.

Backstage a young soldier was in the restroom with Raymonda because security was so tight they wouldn't leave her alone. "Aren't you afraid?" she asked.

"Afraid of what? Why should I be afraid?" With a flick of her wrist Raymonda pulled a shot of cognac.

The soldier seemed incredulous. "Because . . . because . . . Do you know who is there? The chief of staff, the leaders of the IDF." From her tone of voice, you'd think she was talking about Jehovah and his heavenly hosts.

"So what! I'm not afraid of them!"

Minutes later Raymonda was on the stage for the performance of a lifetime. At that moment she was the most recognizable, most celebrated

Palestinian woman in Israel. She was both admired and feared—and her name was high up on someone's list to be eliminated.

She introduced the play by reading out some prepared thoughts, but mid-sentence the notes fluttered to the floor. She still had the sweet taste of cognac on her tongue, and out came fire as from a blast furnace. She faced the officers. "One of your soldiers just asked me if I am afraid of you." She was pacing the stage. "O, I know what you can do," she pointed out into the audience. "You are all so manly, so handsome, so strong, aren't you? O, you officers of a mighty army! Under your control, you have tanks and guns and missiles. You have the power to impose your laws; our destiny is in your hands. I look at your uniforms, your medals, badges, the stars on your shoulders—but when I close my eyes, I strip you down and see you as men; and now I address you in the name of humanity. Before you look at me through a riflescope, stare into my eyes. Do you feel, do your hands tremble, do you sense the palpitation? If you do, don't pull the trigger."

There was a storm of applause.

So far, so good, Raymonda was thinking. Now I should tell them what I really think. When will I ever have eight hundred officers in one room, eating out of my hands? Let the fireworks begin! L'pozez akol!

"You may haul me off to jail for what I am about to tell you. Yes, I know that your law makes it a crime to associate with the PLO. You know something? Before your invasion, I went to Beirut to meet with Arafat. I wanted to see the brave Palestinians who are fighting officers like you. I wanted to find out who they were. You know what else? I just came from Tunis, and I sat with Arafat and the Fatah leadership, with the people you just expelled from Beirut."

She could still hardly believe her eyes. The officers were sitting upright in the cushioned seats of the theater waiting for her to speak.

At that moment five generals, the top brass in the hall, shot up from their seats and marched out. A handful of others followed.

"What did I say?" she called after them. "You brag about your democracy but you don't want to hear the truth. You don't want to know that peace is only possible by sitting down with Yasser Arafat." She raised her voice. "OK, you don't want to LISTEN to me."

The generals slammed the door of the auditorium with a resounding boom.

She turned her attention back on the rest of the officers. "Do you want the war to continue? If you do, then let war be the answer. I'll stop now." She was about to say something else when an officer with the distorted beet-red expression of a man stubbing his toe sprung from his seat and informed her matter-of-factly that Arafat was a terrorist, and "so are you." The man surely wanted to continue along this vein when his seven-hundred-and-ninety-something fellow officers told him to shut up, and the chastened little man with the red face sat back down.

From all parts of the audience Raymonda heard, "Go on! We want to hear you out, Raymonda!" This was when she told them not to be like the "Nazis who just take orders."

Raymonda's words were so forceful and yet so emotional and so visceral that there was no doubt in the mind of the officers that she was telling the truth.

Following the last word about taking orders, there was a protracted silence, as though the officers were either stunned, speechless or were about to rush onto the stage and drag her off to prison. Then the applause broke and rolled over her in a wave, long and sustained, giving her for a brief instant a feeling of total control over the occupiers.

50

Beyond the Walls

With Moshe safely interred on Shimron Hill, Ruth returned home to Tel Aviv. She was there for the premier of Assi's latest film, *Beyond the Walls* (1984), which was nominated for an Academy Award for best foreign picture, and can be seen as an allegory of a land forcibly divided into Jewish and Arab halves, by leaders playing on people's fears and prejudices. The setting is Israel's Central Prison. Mohammed Bakri, Israel's leading Arab actor, plays the lead role of Issan, a PLO leader serving a life sentence for terrorism; Assaf, Assi's character, is a leftist in jail for meeting the PLO in Europe. Behind bars, Assaf witnesses suicide and corruption, and finally, an unlikely coalition between radical Arab nationalists and Jewish criminals. A murder engineered by the prison director leads the Arabs and Jews to join ranks to oppose the real criminals sitting upstairs in the prison administration building.

Raymonda saw the movie right after it opened and phoned up Ruth choking with emotion at the film, "a masterpiece," an assessment Ruth shared.

Meanwhile, other members of the Dayan clan were rising to prominence. Assi's cousin, Yonathan Geffin, a poet, songwriter, and playwright, came out with a book on the Yom Kippur War titled simply, *The Failure*. On his Peace Ship Abie Nathan played Geffin's song "Ihyeh Tov," "It'll Get Better," over and over until it became the Israeli anthem of peace and one of the most famous songs in the country:

We will yet learn to live together
between the groves of olive trees
children will live without fear
without borders, without bomb-shelters
on graves grass will grow.

Jonathan raised his son Aviv, a future international rock star and a member of what he terms the "screwed up generation," in an atmosphere of orgies and cocaine. In 1984, Aviv made his public debut on Israeli television when he sang a song written by his sister.

51
The Bomb

The warning signs were unmistakable. Back in 1983, Raymonda's friend Dr. Issam Sartawi attended the same congress of the Socialist International in Portugal as Shimon Peres. Men dispatched by Abu Nidal followed him to the lobby of the Montechoro Hotel and murdered him. Two years later, unidentified assailants knifed to death Sartawi's fellow believer in dialogue, Aziz Shehadeh, in his home in Ramallah.

Raymonda was more of a provocation than both men because she didn't just attend conferences with Israelis but was also frequently seen tooling around with Ruth Dayan. Just as bad in the eyes of conservative men was her feminism and how she considered securing women's rights part and parcel of Palestinian national liberation. What good would it do to get an independent state if women remained in the harem?

Raymonda's reputation as feminist troublemaker attracted the attention of Dial Torgerson, the *Los Angeles Times* Middle East correspondent, who was doing a story about a European women's rights organization and the "underground railroad" run by the nuns of the La Crèche convent, a dangerous operation smuggling women threatened by their families out of the West Bank to Europe. Raymonda, with a long history of following stories of women murdered by their families, helped Torgerson in his research.

In her Salah al-Din press office, she was seething with rage about what she called the "scourge" of Arab society. As an example of this "epidemic

of killing," she told Torgerson about a man arrested in Nablus with his
sister's head in a bag.

Torgerson's article attracted media attention, and soon foreign and
Israeli journalists crowded into Raymonda's office. Honor killing became
a red-hot issue, and Raymonda was one of the few Arab women willing to
speak openly about it. A Hollywood producer even showed up and asked
her to write a movie script.

There were many Palestinian nationalists rankled by her message that
a woman's right to life towers over a man's need for honor. Reproaches
against her became even more vitriolic once Zionist organizations began
using honor killing as proof of Palestinian backwardness, cruelty, and
inability to manage their own affairs. Echoing what colonial regimes have
always said about the "natives," some Israelis began touting the occupation as morally necessary. Fatah leaders demanded that she stop with her
feminism until after they sloughed off the occupation.

She refused, and the pressure built. The men working in the press
office threatened to go on strike—against her. "You are not allowed to talk
about these things," they said. "You are encouraging prostitution!" An old
friend, with close ties inside Fatah, warned her that she should consider
"leaving the country" for her own safety. There was "talk" on the "street"
that something unfortunate could happen to her. A stray bullet from a
moving car, maybe, some "accident." A week before the car bomb, an
anonymous caller warned that she was putting her life in danger.[70]

The Israeli government, too, was running out of patience. Two days
before the explosion, she agreed to debate the Israeli diplomat Abba Eban
at the American Colony Hotel in Jerusalem. The topic of the debate
was 1948: French Television would air it live in France. The idea of
being on the stage with Eban was frankly terrifying for her. Not only
was he the chairman of the Foreign Affairs Committee in the Knesset,
not only had he been the longtime Israeli ambassador to the UN and
high-ranking member of the Knesset for the Labor Party, not only was
he famously loquacious with a ready witticism for each occasion—he
coined the bon mot "Palestinians never missed an opportunity to miss an

opportunity"—but he was also a lawyer with a razor-sharp mind and an astounding gift for language.[71]

It was like stepping into the ring with a prizefighter. The day of the debate, she boned up on some facts about the conflict and downed half a bottle of cognac.

The TV cameras were set up in the Pasha Room upstairs. Eban was a large, impeccably dressed, walrus-looking man with round glasses and soft eyes; Raymonda put on bright red lipstick and a polka dot dress.

It must have been the cognac. Soon into the debate, triggered by Eban's canard of Arabs attacking the Jews in 1948, therefore having got what they deserved, she asked him point blank: "And what about the four hundred villages the State of Israel bulldozed off the map to make room for your kibbutzim and supermarkets and universities?"

He denied it.

"Oh really, shall we drive over to Deir Yassin and take a look around? I'll bring my friend Amos Kenan."

At that point, Eban unclipped the microphone from his lapel, stood up, and left the Pasha Room, with the television crew and the audience gaping in astonishment. It may have been too much for him, not her words, not what she said, but the sudden confrontation with what his country had done, acts hidden away in archives and people's memories, not allowed to be brought up, and certainly not in front of French television cameras.[72]

The following morning at five came the familiar banging sound on the front door of the Tawil family home, a message from the military governor relaying an order from the new Prime Minister Yitzhak Rabin barring her from leaving the country.

The car bombing took place forty-eight hours later. She had just returned home with Daoud. They went inside the house, turned off the lights, and crawled into bed when they heard a blast powerful enough to cut the power supply on the entire street. Outside the upstairs bedroom window, she saw a wall of red flames and dense billows of black, acrid smoke. Throwing on a nightgown, she flew downstairs and out the door to see a heap of twisted metal; the powerful bomb had blown the car to shreds. Neighbors in pajamas watched as their cars caught fire.

Daoud stood rooted in the garden aghast. "Christ!" his eyes opened wide and he shook Raymonda, her nightgown black with soot, by both shoulders. "I told you years ago to stop this suicidal activism of yours. You must want to get us ALL killed."

Raymonda couldn't respond because the blast sent a clear message. She had tried someone's patience too far. If she kept it up, she'd end up as human confetti.

The next morning, the military governor swung by the house and, viewing the crater left by the bomb, with great self-assurance informed Raymonda that "your people did this." She accused the Shin Bet. Only the Israeli security service could have built such a bomb.

It was then that Father Michel De Maria came to mind. Once her nerves calmed down enough to steer a borrowed car, she returned to the village church.

Sensations from childhood surged back again as she stepped into the small stone chapel, breathed in the frankincense, and stared at the candles illuminating the altar and making the icons glow. The old man took one look at her and knew why she was there. As if in a trance, he described a "terrifying" scene in which her whole family could have been killed in the car.

"The Israelis wanted me dead, didn't they."

"Raymonda, how can you be so naïve?" he replied without naming the bomb-makers. He said "outsiders" were responsible. "They wanted the inferno to be a lesson to others. Don't you normally park the car close to a large gas balloon in the garden, in front of your house? If it had been parked there, the gas balloon would have destroyed your house and those of your neighbors. Many people would have died, you and your family and some of your neighbors."

With his hands the old priest, his curls now mostly white, made patterns in the air, as if writing a letter. "For the love of God, Raymonda, you don't need me to understand their message." He spoke as if he had a mental picture of the bomb-makers. "This time God has spared you. Many times, they've almost taken your life. You are protected, yes, but time is running out." The next words came out as a reprimand: "Why are you still in this country?"

"You once said I have a mission, father. To fight against hatred . . ."

"Yes, that remains your mission, just do it from the outside. You must leave with your family. Otherwise, you will die; there is no doubt. Do you want your children to lose their mother just as you lost yours?" He was silent for a moment, waiting for the effect this might have on her.

"Leave! I can't let them win—they already took away Acre and Haifa from me. I want justice."

She noted a sepulchral sadness in his face when he told her about a future of bloodshed, "because people shut their hearts to God and embrace hatred rather than love. This Holy Land . . . it is filled with darkness."

"Father, how can this be? Won't there be peace?"

Taking her by the hand, he replied: "Just go away."

"And my mission?"

"Raymonda, what life has taught you—talking to your enemies because you have compassion for them—that is what you must take with you to the outside."

Raymonda closed her eyes and breathed deeply. "Okay," she said. "Where am I supposed to go?"

He turned and left the room. She tried to call him back, but he closed the door behind him.

Ruth was with Raymonda during the frantic days that followed. Her life was clearly in danger. Prime Minister Rabin's travel ban prevented her from leaving. She was trapped.

Ruth approached Rabin, asking him to reverse his decision. The French-Arab Friendships Association had made Raymonda their "Woman of the Year" and invited her to Paris to receive the award. Laconic Rabin grunted "No." President Francois Mitterrand turned to Shimon Peres, Rabin's foreign minister, to get the ban lifted. Peres brushed him off. Bruno Kreisky and German Chancellor Willy Brandt tried, also in vain.

Fearing for her friend's life, Ruth headed back to Rabin, and this time she refused to leave his office until he granted Raymonda an exit permit.[73]

52

A Debt of Love

"The only reason to fight death, to avoid danger, and to
prolong life is not in order to achieve something but rather
because of a kind of responsibility. A debt of love to those
who may benefit from the fact that I am alive."

—Yael Dayan, *My Father, His Daughter*

On the eve of her departure, Ruth invited Raymonda to meet Yael at
the Philadelphia restaurant, off Salah al-Din Street. In their long
friendship, it was usually Raymonda who asked Ruth for a favor. Now it
was Ruth's turn.

An Israeli soldier, in a tank, had been killed in Lebanon, and Ruth
wanted her help in getting the remains returned. Raymonda suddenly
had political pull because her chosen place of exile was to be Paris, and
her daughter Diana had married Ibrahim Souss. Dr. Souss had an open
line to Arafat.

Another reason for the lunch was to introduce Yael to Raymonda. Yael
had inherited a number of Moshe's qualities, some good and some bad;
what she didn't pick up from him was greed for land and indifference to
nuptial vows. Unlike Udi and Assi, she was a devoted partner and mother.
And few people in Israel despised the gun-toting settlers fanning out
across the West Bank as much as Yael, who was beginning to emerge from
her father's shadows, becoming his much-improved successor, his missing

eye, by assiduously ignoring his swansong about the "sword within reach above your bed."

What she lacked was real human contact with Palestinians—which Ruth set out to provide.

Raymonda, with the ethos of turn-the-other-cheek drilled into her by the convent sisters, wanted nothing more than to embrace Yael. Yael was far more reluctant, and Ruth had to drag her to the restaurant.

The three sat at a round table with a green tiled surface and clawed iron toes gripping the marble floor. Yael emptied a packet of sugar into her tea. Raymonda studied the clockwise movement of Yael's writing hand, so strong, her skin perfectly smooth. At first she could hardly speak. There, the woman she had so admired since her early years in Jordanian captivity was dressed simply but elegantly, trim, sparkling with life, and smelling of Allure Sensuelle. Her eyebrows looked plucked in the style of a French fashion magazine, high and noble, and her almond-shaped eyes were bright and smart. It was the clenched jaw that communicated Yael's ambivalence. Ruth sensed the lack of chemistry between them.

"So," Yael began. "What should we talk about?"

Raymonda searched for words. "Whatever. You, perhaps."

"Me?" She tossed back her head, her face looked suddenly as hard as granite. "I'd prefer to talk about you."

What Yael came out with over a lunch of hummus and grilled lamb, with Ruth biting her nails, was the standard lines about how Arafat was a pathological liar. She was delivering these lines smoothly, without rancor, like a judge reading an indictment. She didn't mention any specific atrocity, only that Arafat, as a kind of dark wizard, was at fault for driving their peoples into war after war.

Ruth remained silent, not wanting to intervene and unwilling to side with Raymonda against Yael even if that was what her conscience was telling her to do.

Yael's hand was shaking enough for her sparkling water to spill over the side of the glass. Ruth handed her a cigarette. It wasn't what Yael said that startled Raymonda most; she had heard it all before a thousand times. It was the unbridgeable chasm that seemed to separate them. It was as if their primordial loyalties and the inability to understand the other's experiences closed the two off from one another.

At first, unsure how to respond, Raymonda stared into her face and pictured her as an infant with her father rocking her in his arms.

Trying her best to keep her voice calm, Raymonda finally said: "My family was expelled from our lands when I was a child. My father tried to return, and your soldiers nearly killed him because he wanted to go home. And today? We don't have some ideology telling us we own Tel Aviv. Keep Tel Aviv. Take it." Raymonda put down the fork and scribbled "Tel Aviv" on a napkin and handed it to her. "We just want the same freedoms you have. We want to be free."

Yael listened, puffing nervously on her cigarette. "I'm sure I'd feel this way if I were you," she finally said under her breath, without moving her lips.

Yael was relaxed, sipping arak with the voice of the Umm Kulthum singing in the background. She looked around the restaurant and made a comment about the open, mixed atmosphere of the place, with Arabs and Jews and foreigners sitting in the same place without one group lording over the other. Raymonda, turning to Ruth, asked if she remembered when Umm Kulthum performed at the Alhambra Cinema. The art deco building, the crown jewel of a sophisticated, cosmopolitan Jaffa, seated over a thousand people, and no one cared who was Jewish, Christian, or Muslim. "Remember that? Before these idiotic wars turned our beautiful country into a hell."

Raymonda reached over and held Yael's hand. Raymonda met her now warm gaze and thought: It's so easy. Peace takes no more than a human touch.

53

"Better a Living Woman Than a Dead Hero"

Just as Raymonda's fierce tongue landed her in exile, Ruth took her quiet humanitarianism to apartheid South Africa as her greatest project of all. It began with a phone call from the South African ambassador who delivered a message from the hidebound Afrikaner Foreign Minister Pik Botha. He wanted Ruth to create a Maskit for Bophuthatswana, one of the "homelands" engineered by the South Africans.

Ruth was in a bind. Clara, one of her closest friends, had for years been a major ANC supporter. The boycott movement against apartheid was building up steam—Bruce Springsteen's E Street Band was spearheading it. She told the ambassador that she detested apartheid and didn't want to work for the "whites."

"Don't worry," he assured her. "You won't see any white faces in the homelands."

When Ruth arrived in Johannesburg, the high veld was baking. The embargoes against the South African regime were having an effect, and the once proud white city was turning seedy and dangerous. Wearing her favorite twenty-year-old Maskit dress, she rented a car and drove to the sprawling township of Soweto, a vast ramshackle city, and hotbed of ANC support. "Necklacing," that is to say, putting a tire around someone's head and lighting it on fire, was the preferred way of dealing with collaborators. From Soweto, she headed to Bophuthatswana.

For the text two years she traveled back and forth between Tel Aviv and the homeland creating an African Maskit, bigger and better than the original.

The letters Ruth wrote from Africa or Tel Aviv to Raymonda were addressed to a Paris apartment on rue Raffaelli in the sixteenth arrondissement. What for thirty years had defined Raymonda as a woman in a man's world—the salon, the press office, a theater filled with admiring officers—had been stripped from her. Father Michel's words on her "mission"—counteracting the hatred between Palestinians and Jews—became fixed in her mind as she rebuilt her life. This was probably just as dangerous for her in Paris, the assassination capital, as it had been in the West Bank.

Through her son-in-law Ibrahim Souss, Raymonda was in regular contact with Arafat and his right-hand man, Abu Jihad, the man behind the coastal road killings, but now a convert to the moderate wing of Fatah. Raymonda was, for him, an important asset because she knew the Israelis so well.

Perhaps the most dovish man of all Arafat's men was Dr. Souss. To bring the entire organization over to the side of the moderates, Souss sought formal French recognition of the PLO. To this end, Raymonda found herself shuttling back and forth between Paris and Arafat's office in Tunis. One of her trips could have easily ended in a fireball.

In October 1985, she was reclining in the lobby of the Abou Nawas Hotel, on the seashore in Tunis, with her brother George and the poet Mahmoud Darwish. Father Michel had been spot-on when he told Christmas that George would live in far-away places: from his base in London, he ran businesses in Kuwait. He was in Tunis with Raymonda because he wanted to meet Arafat.

Raymonda was more relaxed than she had been for years because she was far, she thought, from harm's way. The previous evening she, George, and Darwish had shared martinis and bowls of jumbo shrimp with some of the Fatah people Raymonda came across in Beirut, characters straight out of Fellini's *La Dolce Vita*. These men, "veteran fighters from the mountains and deserts of Jordan and Palestine, men who had survived Israeli missiles and daggers flung by rival Palestinian factions," were cultivated, their minds sharp and curious; and they had a stockpile of jokes. Their joie de vivre was not what you'd expect from guerrillas.[74]

So where did their lust for life come from? That was the question they debated that morning in the hotel lobby waiting for the Force 17 men to escort them to PLO headquarters. They never showed up. Raymonda phoned Arafat's office, but the line was dead.

Raymonda conjectured that the life-loving fighters around Arafat had come under the salutary influence of Beirut's beaches, nightclubs, and cafés. They had learned to combine fighting for freedom with a liberated lifestyle, so unlike the monkish Arafat whose only luxuries were pots of fresh Langnese honey and *Tom and Jerry* reruns.

They were still chatting in the lobby when word came of an Israeli air strike on Arafat's Tunis headquarters and apartment. What? How could the Israelis bombard the capital of a peaceful, neutral, tourist paradise? How could the Americans permit it? Never. In fact, President Reagan gave his tacit nod of approval for the Israeli retaliation raid for a Fatah attack that killed three Israeli tourists on a yacht. Lyrically dubbed "Operation Wooden Leg" after Captain Ahab, it was carried out under the leadership of now Prime Minister Shimon Peres—his Likud rival, Shamir, was minister of foreign affairs. Using intelligence received from the spy Jonathan Pollard, Operation Wooden Leg killed 270 people, including many of the men Raymonda had shared a convivial evening with the night before. Shimon Peres called the carnage an "act of self-defense. Period."

The attack seemed to signal the Israeli desire to kill Arafat. Ezer Weizman knew better. "Yasser Arafat is alive today," he confided to an American professor, "because we want him alive. Don't believe the news reports. We knew where he was. We always know where he is. If we wanted to put a missile through his bathroom window while he was sitting on the toilet, we could do so . . . and we know when he's on the toilet."

The raid didn't kill Arafat, and it left alive his chief military strategist Abu Jihad. Raymonda was convinced that Abu Jihad was the chief reason she was still alive. He had a checkered history, from guerrilla training with Che in Algeria to the bus massacre that Letty Cottin Pogrebin and her delegation from *Ms.* magazine had witnessed. But like Sartawi, he realized terror wasn't going to end the Israeli occupation of Palestine. Israelis needed to be engaged, and he pushed the more militant factions inside the PLO to adopt a political, two-state solution.

Abu Jihad gave the green light to Raymonda to fly back to Tel Aviv in 1986 to sit down with Weizman at the Tel Aviv Hilton, a conversation Ruth managed to arrange from Bophuthatswana.[75]

Ezer wanted to hear if Arafat and Abu Jihad would be willing to enter into dialogue with Israel, an unexpected thing to hear from a minister in the Peres-Shamir-Rabin government that had just pulverized PLO headquarters.

Ezer knew that the Israeli talk of autonomy in the West Bank was a sham, and inside the cabinet he began pushing for unilateral separation from the conquered territories before addled messianic settlers hijacked government policy. Israel had to vacate the Biblical homeland of Judea and Samaria in order to stop the "zealots" and "fanatical dreamers" from undermining the State of Israel and its democratic achievements. Israel needed a two-state solution with the Palestinians.

At the Hilton, Raymonda repeated to Weizman what Tarazi had already told Ruth: that Arafat was willing to consider a ceasefire with Israel as a prelude to direct negotiations, leading to two separate states. It was a political direction she grudgingly accepted even though it meant no return to Acre and Haifa.

Raymonda wasn't back a week in Ramallah when someone, late at night, threatened her in Arabic over the phone that "if you do not leave the country within three days, you will end up like Aziz Shehadeh," in other words, dead.[76] This time she didn't bother going to Father Michel. She knew what he would tell her. Morris Draper, the American consul general at the time, echoed more or less what she'd already heard from Father Michel: "Get the hell out of this place, Raymonda, and never, never come back. Better a living woman than a dead hero."

54
Uprising

Yitzhak Rabin must have regretted letting Raymonda out of Israel. Soon after she arrived in Paris, the Minister of Culture, Jacques Lang, invited her and Amos Kenan to address the Assemblée Nationale. The house was packed with the intellectual elite of France and the world. Mitterrand sat next to Ruth's latest hero, South African Bishop Desmond Tutu. Raymonda and Kenan were supposed to address the assembly separately, each making a statement on peace and the two-state solution. "What are you going to say?" Amos leaned over and asked her just before he spoke. She retorted that she wanted to talk about the return of refugees to their homes. "Never, never, never," he blustered. There was booze on his breath. "Have your state, but just don't swamp ours with all these people . . ." He lost his train of thought.[77]

With Tutu in the audience, she was determined to stick to her guns. "Amos, maybe we should have two states, I don't know. What I can tell you for sure is that people have the right to return to their homes in Acre and Haifa and the Galilee." There should not only be peace; there should be true friendship between Israelis and Palestinians. But she added something she had heard from Dvora's mother so many years earlier: once peace comes, the expelled must be permitted to return. This was the essence of Raymonda's speech before the French nation.

Raymonda could see Kenan wincing at her words. It was his turn to speak. He pulled out a small flask, took a swig, and zigzagged his way to the front, embracing her on the way. "I'm an Israeli," Amos said with clear,

217

steady, strong words, avoiding the issue of refugees. "I'm asking for the Palestinians to have their state and for the PLO to be their representative."

That day, the Assemblée voted to accept PLO as the representative of the Palestinian people, and to call for a separate, independent Palestinian state.

An interviewer on French television asked Raymonda following the event, What's next for you? Without thinking, she announced she was going to create a PLO press bureau, in France. Though this was the first time the idea crossed her mind, since everyone agreed it was a good idea, she flew to Tunis to discuss the matter with Arafat and Abu Jihad, and the two men promised to provide the funding for an office she then opened on the Avenue de la Grande Armée, close to the Arc de Triomphe.

She had barely opened up for business when the first Intifada broke out in the West Bank and Gaza in December 1987. Ruth had wrapped up her South Africa Maskit and was mostly living back in Tel Aviv. Hardly a week passed without the two women talking over the phone about the bloodletting of what people called the "children's revolution" because they were the ones throwing rocks at soldiers. From her years of working with craftspeople in the West Bank, Ruth knew hundreds of people in villages and cities, and dreaded the harm meted out to them. When she got the chance, Ruth let her old friend Yitzhak Rabin know that brute force alone wouldn't stop kids from throwing rocks.

Ruth passed on to Raymonda the message from Weizman that he urgently needed to talk again. Raymonda got the go-ahead from Abu Jihad, now her main backer inside Fatah. But in April 1988, ten days before Raymonda left Paris for Tel Aviv, the Israeli inner cabinet, dominated by Shamir, Rabin, and Peres, decided to put an end to Abu Jihad's career.

A family man, Abu Jihad was reclining on the sofa with his wife Um Jihad, in their middle-class apartment in the Sidi Bou-Said neighborhood of Tunis. The children were in bed, and the two were laughing about the latest gossip, that Anthony Quinn was considering playing Arafat in a Hollywood movie. Hearing a noise, Abu Jihad, pistol in hand, went to the door. The head of the Mossad team was standing there, wearing a surgeon's mask and gloves. Abu Jihad tried firing off a shot, but the man coolly, without words, emptied the clip of bullets into him. Not a word was said. A second commando, disguised as a woman, videotaped the scene.

A cold fear gripped Raymonda when she heard the news. By killing the strategist of civil disobedience, the Israeli hawks proved they would stop at nothing to preserve the occupation. She felt as if the Israelis had also signed her death warrant. Who was going to protect her against Abu Nidal or a host of other enemies wanting to teach the feminist, with the acid tongue, a lesson? Why risk her life and the life of her family? She called up Ruth and canceled the follow-up meeting with Weizman.[78]

Ruth ran up a sizable telephone bill trying to get her to change her mind. Ezer finally got on the line and snapped out an order. When that didn't work, he pleaded long enough for Raymonda to acquiesce.

At the Hilton bar, the first thing she asked, before even shaking his hand, was about the killing. "Abu Jihad encouraged me to contact you!" The suspicion of him being a "monster" was creeping back. "How many more Israelis have to lose their sons?" She was referring to his son Saul.

His face was pale as parchment. He took his elbows in his hands, glanced around the lobby, and then refocused back on her. "Listen," he said. "It's complicated."

"Complicated? Seems simple to me. You killed a man who . . ."

He cut her off. "Raymonda, I fought that decision." He raised both arms as though he was being held up at gunpoint. "But what was I to do? Do you think I could have sent Abu Jihad a telegram warning him? I want peace, Raymonda, but I'm no traitor to my country. Don't ask me to be." He leaned forward to grab the finger of Scotch left in his glass.[79]

"Well, shame on you, on you all!"

Weizman dropped his head and stared down at his empty glass. The tough old soldier was biting his lower lip.

"OK, Ezer, why are we here now? What do you want from me?" Weizman, ordering another drink, revealed an approach that would eventually succeed with Oslo, but in 1986 was still unthinkable in Israeli government circles: Israel and the PLO should recognize each other's legitimacy and the two sides should enter into secret negotiations for a two-state solution. "What do you say?"

Her long years of contact with decent generals, including a few psychotic ones, gave her the ability to assess the seriousness of the offer. *My God*, she thought. *This could be it!*

From her Paris office, Raymonda sent a message to Arafat, asking him if he agreed to have indirect contact with Weizman. Using an encrypted code, Arafat conveyed his willingness. She then asked Arafat into agreeing that his new Number Two, Abu Mazen, conduct secret talks with Weizman in Moscow. The meeting never took place because the Soviets didn't give Weizman an official state invitation, a necessary cover for the illegal meeting that, if exposed, could have opened him up to charges of treason.

Arafat and Weizman were in fact so eager to get started that they spoke directly over a tapped line: Weizman didn't know that someone in the security apparatus deemed him enough of a threat to snoop in on his phone conversations. In January 1990, word leaked of his telephone call with the arch-terrorist. The Shamir, Peres, and Rabin triumvirate, lashing out at his "betrayal," sacked him from the government. Weizman, in his inestimable RAF manner, cursed the three of them as "sons of bitches."

That Weizman lost his job at least proved his sincerity to Arafat. Just as Raymonda had been telling him for years, some Israelis sincerely wanted to come to terms with the Palestinians. Arafat contacted Raymonda and told her he was now open to dialogue; he even asked her to set up a meeting with Ruth.

"Anytime, any place," was Ruth's natural response, but since even muttering the name of Arafat in Israel was like waving a copy of *Mein Kampf*, she asked Defense Minister Rabin for his okay, to which his answer was a predictable no.

55

Living with History

Arafat, in constant fear of assassination, spent most of his time in his Dassault Falcon 20 jammed with weapons in every available spot, including the lavatory. With the military option no longer realistic, and with an uprising in the territories in full swing, he was sold on the idea of gaining broad diplomatic respectability. The man spearheading the campaign, in Paris, was Dr. Souss, Arafat's soon-to-be brother-in-law. A musician Arafat nicknamed "the pianist," Souss won over French President François Mitterrand through his performances of Franz Liszt and Frederic Chopin, his poetry, and his book on Jewish-Arab reconciliation, *Letter to a Jewish Friend*.

Dr. Souss's friendship with President Mitterrand turned Paris into the central diplomatic hub in the Palestinian effort to shed the old image of wild men menacing international airliners. The first official meeting between Mitterrand and Arafat took place in 1989, at the time when crowds in East Berlin were using sledgehammers to bring down the Wall.

"I have come in the spirit of your revolutionary tradition," Arafat said to the French parliament during his visit, reading a speech largely written by Souss. "I have come searching for the peace and liberty of my people. Peace for us, and peace for the Jewish people. Peace and co-existence between our two peoples."

At Raymonda's request, Souss hired Suha as an emissary carrying sensitive documents back and forth to Arafat's headquarters in Tunis. She was an excellent French-Arabic translator, having been raised with both languages at home. While studying French literature at the Sorbonne, she had begun working as a journalist; she even made a name for herself in France by interviewing the Egyptian feminist rebel Dr. Nawal El Saadawi, whose book *Women and Sex* was banned in Egypt when it came out in 1971. She had sat in a dungeon for months for writing her book.

At the time, Suha had plans to marry a French lawyer, a suitable match for the stylishly coiffed blonde with her haute couture outfits and her well-turned ankle.

During her trips back and forth between Paris and Tunis, monkish old Arafat, who preferred crumpled military surplus outfits to a suit and tie, set his bulbous eye on her. Suha succumbed, less to Cupid's arrows than to the aura of a legend. To what she called "living with history."

The entire courting game was short and necessarily clandestine for the simple reason that Arafat's men were dead set against her. The Arafat brand, that of a selfless hero wedded to the revolution and sitting in the trenches with his troops, had no room for a Valkyrie-type intellectual in Giorgio Armani stilettos.

When Suha broached the topic, Raymonda let her know it was a bad idea. Raymonda had, after all, struggled most of her life to win her independence from men, and now her dear daughter contemplated tying the knot with a man who was charismatic, but also well over twice her age and a constant target for a hail of bullets. There was also the small matter of character: given his line of work, Arafat was necessarily secretive and equivocating. Raymonda's hero, the Italian journalist Oriana Fallaci, noted the way he "contradicts himself every five minutes. He always plays the double-cross, lies even if you ask him what time it is." Hardly a formula for nuptial bliss.

Undeterred, Suha pressed on with her plans. Following Arafat's request, she told no one, not even her mother.

It was a secret wedding that took place in the Tunis bunker: no white lacy dress, no layered wedding cake, no champagne, no flying grains of rice. In a sop to hardline Muslims, she went through a perfunctory conversion to Islam. Nor was the crusty bridegroom one to carry her over the threshold of his closet-sized digs in Tunis. There were bodyguards everywhere: even on the roof of the building, men peered through binoculars, looking for Israeli helicopters.

Raymonda was kept in the dark; all she knew was that Suha was mysteriously living full-time in Tunis. In July 1990, she was on a plane flying to Vienna to attend Bruno Kreisky's funeral when one of the top PLO functionaries, a man close to Arafat, sat down in the empty seat next to her and whispered that she should "control" her daughter. "We are a very conservative society. Fatah is a liberation movement, but we don't allow girls to behave this way."

"Which way?" Raymonda had no idea what he was talking about. The words "girls" and "behave" made her want to eject the man from the jet.

"Your daughter, Raymonda, is the mistress of Yasser Arafat." The way he said "mistress" sounded like misogynist gossip. Joining fury at the way the man spoke was a dread of her daughter being branded with the same scarlet letters as she had been. The Fatah man chipped in that Suha's "life may be in danger."

On the ground, Raymonda checked herself into a Viennese hospital because of heart palpitations she feared could lead to a heart attack like the one that had killed Christmas. No, she wasn't going to allow men to destroy Suha's life. From the hospital she called Suha, at Arafat's office in Tunis, and insisted she return to Paris. "This has to stop. Do you know what people are saying about you?"

Arafat got on the phone and without saying a word about the marriage or the rumors assured Raymonda that he was "a serious and honest man."

"Then why don't you tell me, me and the world, if you've married my daughter?" There was dead silence on the other end. Click.

From Vienna, Raymonda flew directly to Tunis to confront a man she had supported for decades and continued to believe in—as a revolutionary leader, at least.

She arrived at his office during a meeting between Arafat and his main advisors. Raymonda demanded to see him, raising her voice loud enough to penetrate the bunker's walls. Arafat, rubbing his eyes in disbelief, left the meeting to see what she wanted. He didn't exercise anything close to the level of dictatorial control as Saddam, Assad, Mubarak, Gaddafi, and other Arab leaders; over the years he had learned the art of light banter with foreign journalists and leftist supporters. Still, he didn't tolerate dissent within his own ranks and his own people, and he certainly didn't put up with women telling him what to do—which was exactly what Raymonda had in mind.

In an adjoining room, Raymonda repeated to him what she had heard on the plane and demanded to know if he'd married Suha.

"You are not my mother, so don't mix into my business," he screamed at her. The poet Mahmud Darwish, in the meeting in the next room, registered each and every word of an unprecedented row. Raymonda shouted back, "This is my daughter . . . people are saying she is your mistress. YOU MUST TELL PEOPLE THE TRUTH."

He tried to deny they were married, but Raymonda exercised her legendary tenacity until she forced him to pull from his pocket the marriage certificate, signed by a sheik. "There, are you happy?"

"NO, I AM NOT. You are not just the father of our nation; you are the husband of my daughter. You have a duty to defend your wife. One of your men told me her life is in danger. You cannot let your wife be denigrated as a mistress!" No one had ever given Arafat so much cheek. "You have to tell our people about the marriage."

He looked chastised for an instant. But afraid of stirring up opposition within Fatah ranks, not to mention enemies such as Abu Nidal, by compromising his guerrilla image, he called in his Force 17 people and ordered them to escort Raymonda out of the building and to lock the door behind her.

Seized again with painful heart palpitations, Raymanda checked herself back into a hospital. A controlled leak to the young Israeli journalist Gideon Levy, through Ibrahim Souss's office, informed the astonished world about the marriage.

56
Ring of Fire

The revolutions in Eastern Europe in 1989 brought hope but also fresh dangers. Ruth had met Suha a hundred times and thought such a beautiful and intelligent woman, a sophisticated and freethinking feminist, would have a salutary effect on the old revolutionary. By 1989, Arafat had renounced terrorism and embraced diplomacy as the only way to win Palestinian independence. She was seeing flickers of hope after two years of intifada.

Ruth's worries were more on the Israeli side, as the Likud government continued to tighten the screws on the Palestinians. The government strategy was to hunker behind the slogan of "security" and a "war against terror," as a cover for rapid settlement expansion and thus to prevent a two-state solution. Prime Minister Shamir and his Likud colleagues denied there was any such thing as a moderate Fatah leader—all were terrorists. Shamir's government strictly enforced Israeli laws barring contact between Israelis and the underground movement.

Raymonda saw Suha less and less because she was married to the world's most wanted man. He spent most of his time traveling, and when he was in Tunis, the two moved from one cramped place to another in order to keep potential killers guessing. Suha's makeup was in one safe house, high heels in another and the collection of avant-garde French poetry in the third. She couldn't even speak freely on the telephone because everyone knew the lines were tapped. To leave the guarded compound she needed clearance from security. "Can I go out? Is the road open?" Little wonder Suha began suffering from headaches and hypertension.

"When I go to see her," Raymonda told a reporter, "frankly speaking, I feel like I am in a jail. It's like being in jail."

Raymonda soon reached out to Father Michel one last time. In the spring of 1989, one of Arafat's top men phoned Raymonda to say that Arafat's Russian-built plane had crashed overnight somewhere in the Libyan desert during a sand storm. Was it shot down? Was he dead? No one could say.

Cascading thoughts tumbled through Raymonda's mind. What would happen if he was dead? Arafat was willing to sit down with the Israelis and negotiate a political solution to a conflict that had raged since before she was born. With all his flaws, this monkish warrior, this man who reached out to Weizman, embraced Abie Nathan, and still wanted to meet Ruth — he was the only Palestinian leader able to fulfill Raymonda's "mission" to get Palestinians and Israelis to talk.

Raymonda immediately called Ruth to see if she could find out anything from Weizman. He knew nothing. The Israelis knew nothing.

She next picked up the phone and called up a cousin in Kfar Yassif in Israel and asked him, in the middle of the night, to wake up Father Michel in Rama and ask him about Arafat's fate. The cousin did as she requested, and the old priest, who rarely slept anyway, was up waiting for him.

"Tell Raymonda there is no need to worry. Yasser Arafat is alive. I see him in the desert; there is a circle of fire around him" protecting him.

Arafat was found wandering around the wreckage of the plane two days later. The circle of fire Father Michel referred to was a shallow ditch the survivors of the crash dug, filled with airplane fuel, and lit on fire as a signal for rescuers and to ward off hungry jackals.

57
Oslo

In 1990, Abie Nathan, the Jewish "Don Quixote" who, as *The Guardian* commented, preferred to "light a candle than curse the darkness," sat in an Israeli prison because he had met with Arafat. From Paris, Raymonda had been the matchmaker.

Nathan got out and at once returned to Tunis to create "hope and understanding." This time, the Israeli authorities sentenced him to eighteen months in prison. Nathan went on a long hunger strike that nearly killed him. After three weeks Arafat sent him a note from Tunis, requesting that he end the fast. The struggle was important. More important was that he stayed alive. Nathan kept it up for forty days. Ruth was, again, one of his faithful guests.

He got out, and like a boomerang, he went back to Tunis. Nathan was awaiting trial in Tel Aviv when the 1992 parliamentary elections brought the Labor party back to power, headed by Yitzhak Rabin. Ruth spent election night celebrating Yael's election as a Labor MP. The Dayan legacy lived on, this time with a sharp turn to the left. In one of Yael's first acts as a politician, and in defiance of the law that put Nathan behind bars, she flew to Holland to meet one of Arafat's advisors.

Raymonda remembered the conversation with Yael at the Philadelphia restaurant, her lovely face contorted by suspicion; and now Yael was taking calculating, pragmatic, jack-knifing steps in the right direction. Not like Ruth with her emotions but rationally with her mind she agreed with Uncle Ezer: Israel had to give up her father's territorial war booty.

Raymonda felt like dancing: it was as if she and Ruth, indirectly through Yael, were helping overcome the abyss of hatred and mistrust separating Palestinians from Israelis. "You did it!" she shouted into the telephone to Ruth. "Bravo!"

Rabin not only didn't send Yael to prison for meeting the PLO, he scrapped the law that forbade such contact, ironically the same day the Knesset legalized prostitution. Rabin, who six years earlier had supported the killing of Abu Jihad, and had said that the dream of all Israelis was to wake up one bright morning and all the Palestinians would be gone, knew he had no choice but to deal with Arafat.

At once Raymonda, directly and through Suha, began working on Arafat to invite Yael to meet him face to face. It didn't take much convincing, and Yael's visit to Tunis, in late January 1993, stirred a din of objections and recriminations back in Israel. Images of the daughter of Moshe Dayan standing shoulder to shoulder with a man they had always equated with Amalek, the Biblical enemy of the Jewish people, shocked Israeli television viewers and newspaper readers the next day.

Raymonda did another jig in honor of Ruth's defiant, insolent, liberated daughter. Right-wing Israelis dismissed the trip to Tunis as a self-promoting stunt, seeing in it a spiritual connection to the Knesset's recent legalization of prostitution. "Yael Dayan has hastened to Tunis to embrace the greatest enemy of the Jewish people since Hitler, PLO chief Yasser Arafat! The legalized degradation of women was thus followed by the legalized degradation of a nation. Or to put it another way: by placing whores on the same level as decent women, the law also placed Arab thugs on the same level as Jews."

In the foreign press, the story of the daughter of the war hero meeting with his former mortal enemy made for perfect copy. He was "nicer" than she had expected, she told The Independent. "He has a public appearance that is not very appealing. But that quickly disappears. He is a good listener. Very quick. Humorous and gentle." She began telling people that if her father were alive, he too would be sitting down with Arafat. You make peace with enemies, not friends.

Her Uncle Ezer soon had a new platform to push for peace. With Rabin's backing, in March 1993, the Labor and leftist parties in the Knesset voted him president of Israel, an ostensibly ceremonial role, but one he used to promote his peace agenda. President Ezer and First Lady Reumah had traveled far since they met on his botched Irgun mission, in 1946.

With her sister installed in the presidential mansion on Jabotinsky Road around the corner from Villa Leila, Ruth wandered the old neighborhoods. Cafe Atara on King George Street, where she and the wife of the Mossad chief used to sit in the mornings, was still around. Ruth walked to her parents' old house where she was raised, and to the tall stone building from whose rooftop she watched the 1929 riots. Another fifteen minutes by foot, through Damascus Gate to the other side of the walled city, was the kindergarten her mother ran in the 1930s for Arab and Jewish children. It was now a parking lot. On these long peregrinations, Ruth reflected on Moshe, the flawed hero. She agreed with Yael: were he still alive, he would join his friend and sometimes rival Rabin in making peace with Arafat. Of this, she had no doubt.

From the presidential mansion, Ruth made long calls to Raymonda; she even put Ezer on the line. Ruth predicted that her friend's exile would soon be over.

Raymonda, mindful of her "mission," wanted nothing more. With Weizman, Yael, and Ruth, who continued to go on her tireless trips into West Bank villages, she was certain she could fulfill her "mission" of bringing Palestinians and Israelis together. There would be peace once the two sides got to know one another.

Daoud refused to entertain the idea of returning to anything like her salon days when activists camped out in the family living room and death threats got slipped under the door at night. Besides, none of the children lived in the West Bank any longer.

Neither Ruth through Weizman nor Raymonda through Arafat had any inkling of the secret negotiations going on in Oslo. When news of an agreement between the two sides came late 1993, Ruth rang up Raymonda with the animated tone in her voice of *We finally did it!*

"Raymonda, when are you coming home?" There was such euphoria in the air. Ruth felt it; Arafat felt it—he was describing Rabin as the "Israeli de Gaulle." Switching from rocks and Molotov Cocktails, schoolchildren in Ramallah were handing out olive branches to IDF soldiers.

Raymonda prevaricated on the phone and even sounded somber as if they were discussing a funeral and not final peace. Oslo meant no more settlements, no more hijacked planes and raids on schools, and, for Raymonda, no more exile. She should come home and resume their work, Ruth said. It wasn't about a tree-planting ceremony like earlier years. Now they could really be partners. True soul mates. "Raymonda, we've done it!"

Why "we," Raymonda wanted to reply but stopped herself. The two of them had had nothing to do with Oslo. The agreement had been done in secret by a closed group, of men, mostly by academics no one had ever heard of. How could such a secretive pact work? For two generations, both sides had spent their best energies demonizing the other, killing one another, assuming the absolute worst and, as Father Michel said, spreading the poison of hatred. And now an agreement, which just a handful of people had read, was supposed to wipe this away? Raymonda didn't criticize the agreement because her son-in-law had signed off on it. But she wasn't going to toss confetti, either.

And what about the spoilers, Hamas, on the Palestinian side, and the vitriolic right among the Israelis? Ariel Sharon, with the young politician Benjamin Netanyahu, vowed that once their party regained power, they would refuse to abide by the agreement with Arafat, a man they continued to portray as the terror chieftain. Arafat "deserves a bullet in the head," intoned a member of the Knesset from one of the religious parties. A former chief rabbi, agreeing with him, said it was every Jew's religious duty to assassinate Arafat. The Council of Jewish Settlers offered 30,000 dollars for anyone who captured him "dead or alive."

"Are you coming home?" Ruth wanted to know.

"Return? Not so fast, Ruth." Daoud, she explained, preferred Paris.

Daoud, the six-foot aristocratic gentleman who had been in his wife's shadow for years, all the while bankrolling her free-spirited ways that had pushed the family into exile, wasn't nearly as passive as he seemed. Through all the years, he sat on the leather sofa, legs crossed, his polished shoes tapping in impatience but also absorbing what the activists were saying. Now, before almost anyone else, he put the pieces together and assessed Oslo as a ruse. "The Israelis were building a big mouse trap for us," he told Raymonda. "This Oslo thing sold off Jaffa, Acre, Haifa, Nazareth to the Israelis, and for what? Scraps of territory in Gaza and the West Bank? You tell Arafat," he pointed his finger at Raymonda, "that the Israelis are going to put him and us into a cage. Arafat agreed to reestablish apartheid here, under our noses."

Daoud had no intention of going back under those conditions. "I'd rather die in Paris."

For the official ceremony, slated for October, President Bill Clinton chose the south lawn of the White House. Rabin and Foreign Minister Shimon Peres represented Israel. Arafat could invite his closest allies, and he asked Daoud and Raymonda to attend. Daoud put his foot down, solidly and implacably: No, he wasn't going to a ceremony celebrating a bad deal. For the first time in their marriage, he won the battle of wills; Raymonda too declined the invitation.

She got a taste of the new reality of Oslo after she and Daoud flew to Washington, DC to watch the festivities on television. Back in Paris, someone broke into the Tawil apartment, and, stealing nothing, emptied out Raymonda's desk, closets, and cabinets, rifling through utility bills, lingerie, and linens looking for something they obviously didn't find. French police combed the apartment suspecting the intruders had also planted a bomb.

58
Life According to Agfa

Abie Nathan was so wrapped up in the Oslo euphoria that he sank his peace ship. McDonalds opened its first fast-food outlet in the country, and Starbucks soon followed. There was the new Israel, the new Middle East.

Assi commemorated the Rose Garden ceremony with a line of coke and a screenplay about two lovers, an Arab and a Jew, in the Galilee. The dystopian story ends with the Jewish state "going down the tubes."

His aunt Reumah and President Ezer couldn't make it to the premier of Assi's *Life According to Agfa* (1993), considered by critics his best film. Ruth sat in the front row watching a film that ends in a bloodbath committed by a broken-legged IDF commander named Nimrod and his gang of soldiers in a seedy Tel Aviv bar named "Barbie," Hebrew slang for a mental asylum.

The film has the dark, nihilistic violence of *Taxi Driver* coupled with the existentialist mood of *Deer Hunter*. In making it, drugged out Assi was a prophet on a mission, a mission described by his producer as a sort of futuristic nostalgia: "When the Zionist experience comes to an end, and we're all living in Europe and all sorts of other places, I think that this film will express beautifully the existence we had here." "It was this point in time in Israeli reality," added an actress who played the barmaid in the film, "where it seemed like the end of the world was near, and we had come to warn people. We were sure we were headed for the end of

232

the state, that a terrible disaster was looming; we felt we were doing something that went beyond a film."

Shortly after the release of Assi's follow-up film, *An Electric Blanket named Moshe*, he was arrested and hospitalized for psychiatric observation. Police accused him of splashing acid in their faces.

If Assi was the ideological gravedigger of Israel, Yael remained the pugnacious believer; and she knew that helping build a Palestinian state was the only way to prevent the Zionist dream of statehood, because of the settlements, from degenerating into an apartheid regime.

Along with a thousand Peace Now activists, she joined the PLO's Jerusalem man Faisal Husseini, the son of the guerrilla leader Abdel Kader al-Husseini, on a march across the Green Line to the West Bank. The group held symbolic "peace talks" in a town just across the old Green Line. In response to a phalanx of army jeeps blocking their advance, Yael grabbed a mike and said in a strong, unhesitating voice, "Faisal Husseini's father and my father fought each other to the death. Today I am proud to stand next to him in a peace meeting. I am sure that his children and mine will live, each in his own country, in peace. . . . I'm grateful they set up a roadblock. They've demarcated the border. This is not Greater Israel. . . . The State of Israel ends here."

Yael's activism made her a target for hate mail and even death threats. She once got a letter in the mail with six bullets inside.

59
Separation

In Israel for every Ruth or Yael there were a hundred bearded believers excoriating Rabin for embracing "Amalek." Many people, brainwashed for years to hate Arafat, accused an out-of-touch elite of forcing Arafat down their throats. Some rabbis went well beyond calling for Arafat's death; the ancient cabbalistic curse they directed against Rabin wished on him a painful death.

On February 24, 1994, the American-Israeli doctor Baruch Goldstein, graduate of Albert Einstein School of Medicine, walked into the Cave of the Patriarchs in Hebron and emptied a clip of bullets on the Muslim worshippers, killing 29 and wounding 125. To prevent reprisals, Rabin responded by introducing new roadblocks and a hermetic closure of Palestinian towns and villages. The Islamic movement Hamas lashed out at Arafat for his peace deal: he was less a liberator than a traitor, a collaborator with the Zionist enemy. His chic blond wife was further proof of how removed he was from Islamic purity.

Five months later Arafat and Suha flew from Tunis to the Sinai in Egypt, got into a black Mercedes, and were escorted by Egyptian security to the border with Gaza. Israeli soldiers waved Arafat through. From the border to Gaza City, fifty thousand jubilant Palestinians lined the streets tossing rose petals and showers of white rice. Raymonda stayed behind in Paris to tend to Daoud, who was gravely ill. The genteel ex-banker, who considered Oslo to be a national catastrophe, wasn't about to swap Paris for gun-infested Gaza. "No, I will never go back," he repeated by phone once more to his son-in-law. "Jaffa is my home, not Gaza and not Ramallah. Give me Jaffa, and I'll change my mind."

According to the terms of the Oslo agreement, Arafat wasn't a triumphant Salah al-Din bringing liberation to the country, but at least he didn't have to crawl on his belly under barbed wire as in the old days. The most recognizable Arab leader on the planet, the subject of a dozen biographies, hundreds of studies, tens of thousands of news reports, and a myriad of cabbalistic incantations, was the liberator of a few postage-stamp-sized enclaves in the Gaza Strip and Jericho, for which he was feted by the masses with their flags and smiles and sadly misplaced hopes.

Oslo changed the logic of the conflict. The Israeli military still controlled 90 percent of the West Bank, and thousands of Palestinians still languished in prison. In this respect, there was no liberation—far from it. But nor could Fatah carry on an armed struggle against a country it had agreed to settle its disputes with through negotiations. Arafat and his men needed to strike a balance between cooperation and resistance, international respectability, and the support of the street. Finding a workable formula became equally urgent and elusive.

With fanatics on both sides vowing to kill one another, Rabin and Arafat ordered their security services to separate the populations, the theory being, the less contact between Israelis and Palestinians, the less chance for violence. From Raymonda's perspective, and from Ruth's, the precise opposite was needed. The less contact Israelis and Palestinians had, the more suspicion remained the primary prism through which they viewed each other.

As usual, Ruth preferred actions to words. A week never passed without her jumping in her ancient Saab and sputtering off to Palestinian towns and villages, working with groups of women making rugs or embroidered bags.

Arafat and Suha lived in cramped quarters in Gaza, one of the poorest territories on earth. Revolutionaries in Algeria moved into mansions after they turned out the French; Lenin got the Kremlin. Arafat insisted on taking over a concrete building with the charm of a furniture warehouse. He and Suha had vastly different esthetic standards. She said to *Vogue* that he took one look at her shoe collection and likened her to Imelda Marcos, the wife of the Philippine dictator. As for their living quarters, "luxury," he told her, "was in your father the banker's home, not mine." The compromise they worked out was for the monkish ex-guerrilla leader to live upstairs in a room with a cot, leaving her to decorate the entire second floor more to her francophone sensibilities.

When Suha became pregnant, she returned to be with Raymonda and her gravely sick father in Paris. Daoud died in June 1995. Raymonda buried him in Montparnasse Cemetery close to the graves of Samuel Beckett, Jean-Paul Sartre, and Simone de Beauvoir. Standing next to her children, Raymonda stared down at the casket, tears streaming down her face. Her mind turning to his literary graveyard neighbors, she reflected on the complexities of the heart. In a more ideal world, she never would have married the older man. They had come to love one another, not the passionate, romantic love Raymonda had always wanted, but a love based on affection, admiration, and loyalty. If he bristled against her foolhardy activism, he also admired her defiance and courage, her boundless exuberance.

A month later, Suha gave birth to a daughter named after Arafat's mother Zahwa, in a private American hospital in Paris.[80] It seemed like half the Paris police force was on hand after an anonymous caller had threatened to blow up the maternity ward. Burly French police, slipping a bulletproof vest over the baby, took mother and daughter to a different floor. "My God," Arafat exclaimed when he arrived by armored car from the military airport. "This is the first day of her life, and it's already starting." How many babies are born wearing a flak jacket?

Arafat was beaming the first time he took Zahwa in his calloused, liver-spotted hands. Over the years, a plethora of distortions, half-truths, and fabrications had slipped into the press about him, that he enriched himself, that he was the owner of seven airliners, that he was a psycho with bottomless hatred in his heart. Behind his masks, and he had hundreds of them, was a sentimental and warm man. With Castro and Mandela, here was one of the last survivors of the anti-colonial struggles, rocking his infant daughter in his arms.

But the new father had little time for his young family, because Hamas launched a campaign of suicide bombings against Israeli civilians to revenge the 1994 Goldstein killings in the Hebron mosque. Rabin's response, naturally enough, was to beef up roadblocks and checkpoints.

The perverse logic was deepening: peace through separation and ever-tighter control over people's movements: peace through strangulation.

60
"I Cry for You"

In November 1995 Ruth's hip was aching too much for her to stand for hours at Israel's biggest peace gathering ever, so she sat in her easy chair at home and watched a crowd of 300,000 gather in the Kings of Israel Square in Tel Aviv on a gentle, warm evening. Against the background of the ugly modernist city hall building, young Israelis held up banners with a message of Peace Now! Over the previous weeks, angry right-wing protesters in Jerusalem had held up posters of Rabin wearing an SS uniform. In Tel Aviv, the mood was festive and triumphant. Few doubted that humanity would triumph over atavism and hatred.

On the stage Assi's cousin, Aviv Geffen, sang his exquisite ballad "I Cry for You." The crowd roared.

Aviv, Israel's biggest pop star, wrote and sang about the same themes as Assi's best films: love, peace, death, suicide, politics, and the perversions of religion. "I prefer Pink Floyd's 'The Wall' to 'The Wailing Wall,'" goes one of his one-liners. As for macho Israeli culture, he diagnoses its obsession with guns and missiles as a "U-turn in evolution." He dodged the draft.

On that balmy Tel Aviv evening, Rabin, the most unlikely peace-warrior of all, stood on the stage and gave the draft dodger a hug. Joining the old man and the rock star with mascara in the square, with the sweet smell of honeysuckle—and marijuana—wafting through the air, were Ezer, Yael, and hundreds of thousands of Israelis.

Ruth mopped up tears with tissues. She had known Rabin since the 1930s, and she had helped raise Aviv. History was making a full circle. At seventy-eight, she felt that what she had fought for for much of her life, peace and justice, was finally coming about. "I Cry for You," she sang along. She knew the song by heart. "What should I do, should I cry for you? Should I cry? Should I die? Should I try to forget?"

Rabin's fine-boned assassin, son of a Yemenite kosher butcher, waiting backstage, slipped through security by claiming to be Aviv's personal driver. Aviv responded to Rabin's hug with a kiss on each cheek, and five minutes later the prime minister was on his back, bleeding to death from bullets fired from a Beretta pistol. "The killer didn't just kill a person," Aviv responded when word came from the hospital that Rabin was dead; "he killed a dream."

Two days later President Weizman, too distraught to respond, stood next to the two Schwarz sisters and the special guest, President Bill Clinton, at Rabin's funeral. His eulogy was laconic: "Together we ate a few good things, and drank a few good things."

Raymonda never saw Arafat, an imperturbable veteran of many battles, won and lost, more shaken than when the Shin Bet contacted him in his cramped presidential compound in Gaza to confirm the news reports. He must have understood intuitively that the bullets eliminated the best chance for the two peoples to come to terms. Nor was the chairman afraid to put his emotions on public display for a man who had become his partner. "I am very sad and very shocked for this awful and terrible crime," he told the press, his lower lip trembling, his eyes watery and red, his face ashen. Arafat sensed dark days ahead.

Ruth celebrated her eightieth birthday in 1997 in a traumatized, and transformed, Israel. In July 1997, two Hamas militants, one wearing a Yankees baseball cap, entered into Mahane Yehuda vegetable market in Jerusalem and detonated the plastic explosives duct-taped to their abdomens, killing sixteen Israelis and wounding nearly 178 others. There was grimly familiar carnage of body parts spread across market stalls onto the clothes and hair and skin of terrified pedestrians.

The Likud was back in power after this. A series of other suicide bombings followed. Per agreement, the Israeli army had already withdrawn from
the large Palestinian cities and handed its central prison in Ramallah,
the Muqata, over to Arafat. The new government, headed by Benjamin
"Bibi" Netanyahu with Ariel Sharon as the strongman in the cabinet, further restricted Palestinian movement while opening up fresh territory for
the expansion of what were now 140 Jewish colonies. Thousands of villas
with red-tiled roofs proliferated across the West Bank and East Jerusalem.
Each new suicide bombing sprouted fresh checkpoints and settlements
encircling cantons—Bantustans as Daoud would have said. Uzi Dayan
was the IDF's deputy chief of staff in charge of the tightening matrix of
checkpoints. If Sharon was the hangman, Uzi was the weaver of the rope.

Begun with such fanfare, the signatories to the Oslo peace process
entered into a prolonged period of feinting, jabbing, counter-jabbing,
and occasional blows. Negotiations between the two sides dragged out
interminably, and the idea that the peace agreement would lead to a full
Israeli withdrawal seemed less and less likely.

Yael continued pushing for peace to smaller and smaller audiences,
without fail Ruth always at her side. For Ruth's eightieth birthday, in an
Israeli newspaper, Yael published a letter called "After my own heart."
An extraordinary piece of writing, the letter touches on Ruth's uncanny
energy and indefatigable hope when most people would stew in bitterness at a world gone badly astray. Despite a lifetime of "tears, insults, and
fears," her life is "a wonderful poem where every chapter is interwoven
with youth and age, contentment and curiosity, childish innocence." The
modern-day Candide is out there every day handing out "fragments of a
better future to all those who had lost hope."

Raymonda had, by this point, returned to Palestine and was living in
Ramallah. Shortly after arriving back in spring 1997, she spotted Father
Michel in the lobby of the Grand Hotel in Ramallah. He was living in a
home for retired priests and was accompanied by younger men on either
side of him, holding him by the elbows. "Father Michel!" Raymonda
called from the other side of the lobby, quickening her pace in his direction. He looked at her, smiling without speaking.

"Father Michel, oh my God! For ten years, I've wanted to thank you." The priest, with a shock of white hair, his tall frame slightly bent over, looked at her with effervescent eyes. "Thank you for saving my life!" Had she not heeded his warning in 1985, she certainly wouldn't have survived.

Nodding, Father Michel reached out and took her hand; there was tenderness in his touch. It had been nearly fifty years since he first told her about her "mission."

She asked him about "hatred in the Holy Land," and if anything would change. He shook his shaggy gray head of hair, turned his back, and shuffled off without saying a word. The encounter would be their last; he died a short time later.

In the West Bank, what had been the stage for Raymonda's feminist-nationalist rebellion was now strangely vacant, as the spy novel atmosphere of the 1970s and early '80s gave way to a bureaucratic deal between the IDF and the Palestinian Authority's security apparatus. There were more people than ever in Ramallah because of the stream of people returning from exile; martini bars and Mercedes dealerships were on their way. But the spirit had changed. A dull, sullen depression had descended on erstwhile activists.

She felt isolated—Suha was in Gaza and the other children were scattered around Europe. For Raymonda, there was no going back to the glory days of the "Kalashnikov" and hacking phone lines. Abie was ill, and western journalists didn't need her for a scoop—they went directly to Arafat or his men.

In matters of civil society, Raymonda was light years ahead of Arafat and his cronies in assessing the needs of the moment. An inveterate media aficionado, she never missed a trend. The media landscape was changing fast, and the Palestinians had to be on the cutting edge of the change. Boiling over with ideas, she drove to Arafat in Gaza with a new concept.

She might as well have been speaking Chinese. Arafat sat behind a card table he used as a desk and bounced a tennis ball on the ground as she expounded on *Al Jazeera*, the Internet, email, bloggers, and chat rooms. "Have you ever heard about the *Drudge Report*?" She proposed to start modestly, with a news and current events magazine simply called

Falasteen, harkening back on the country's first pan-Arab newspaper in Jaffa. A new *Falasteen* could counter the Israeli PR machinery by letting the world know what was happening on the ground.

He kept bouncing his ball. "You, Raymonda," he said in a cheerful and yet serious tone, "you are too independent, you refuse to obey orders and rules, you're a free thinker—and you know me, I admire your freedom. You just can't speak on behalf of Fatah. That I can't allow." Arafat was wary of the phenomenon General Matti Peled once described as "bullets and missiles firing from rosy lips." No way was he going to permit his mother-in-law to direct her liberated mind at his regime. Soon she'd be dredging up honor killing, abandoned babies, abusive husbands, the perversions of Sharia Law. Recruits would sign up for Hamas's war against the "infidels."

She did manage to wheedle out of him enough money to hire a small staff for the paper, nothing more.

Suspicions among Fatah leaders that her feminist tongue was "damaging the cause" surfaced in the most sensitive of places: Israeli television. Israelis were eager for gossip and insider scoops on the life of the man whose fate, for better or for worse, was tied to their own. Journalists from an Israeli TV station approached Raymonda, cameras rolling, wanting to know about her relationship with Arafat, to which she retorted, chest thrust out defiantly, that "no one created me, no one made me, not even Arafat. I am my own woman." She also said something about not having been thrilled at her daughter's marriage to the man whose title was now President Arafat.

She thought she was complying with Arafat's order to keep her "free spirit" out of PLO business. His advisors didn't have such a generous interpretation and understood the interview as an act of breaking ranks. They began blocking her access to her son-in-law.

Even Suha barely saw her husband because he was a notorious workaholic. ("He gets up early," she told a reporter. "He leaves early, never gets back until way past midnight.") Whenever she tried to focus his attention to normal marital matters, such as their daughter, Yasser would switch on *Looney Tunes*. The only freedom she had in straight-laced, Islamic, dilapidated Gaza was driving around in her latest model BMW convertible, which was more food for critics despite the fact that she was usually on her way to a clinic she ran for handicapped children in a refugee camp.

The stranglehold of checkpoints, the collapsing Palestinian economy where the best jobs were on construction sites for settlements, and the pervasive feeling that Oslo was a boondoggle, made it easy for Hamas to caricature President Arafat as an Israeli stooge. The last thing on his mind was bouncing sweet little Zahwa on his knee.

The grim reality of Oslo exceeded Daoud's pessimism. Arafat was being squeezed from Hamas militants, wanting only to murder Israeli civilians in the name of their virulent Wahabi strain of Islam, which in turn enabled the Netanyahu-Sharon-Uzi triumvirate to cage him in, more and more. Ezer Weizman, with his powerless, ceremonial presidential post, could do little to help.

The more settlements expanded, the greater the support for Hamas and the message of violence; and the more Arafat scrambled to win back support on the street, the more he and his nine security forces turned "liberated" Palestinian areas into armed fiefdoms. The man Ruth met in the Washington hotel lobby, Georgetown Professor Sharabi, described Oslo as a "catastrophe for the Palestinians."[81]

Islamic holy warriors blowing up pizzerias and the Bibi-Uzi-Sharon chokehold brought out the street fighter in Arafat. During a gathering in Bethlehem, with the Church of the Nativity behind him, he stirred up the crowd with calls for "Jihad, Jihad, Jihad." The Israeli right, expert in the art of PR, got this out to the world.

Hamas bombings, and with Arafat bellowing out "Jihad," marginalized people who still believed in peace. Ruth, Yael, and Avnery appeared to most Israelis, even the young who had gathered by the tens of thousands to light candles on the site of Rabin's assassination, to be little more than crusty old has-beens. Whatever public declarations they made sounded like whistling in the wind.

Part IV
1995–the present: Walls

61
Three Kisses

It was only natural that Ruth, over eighty, would think back on her childhood in Jerusalem. She was a lonely little girl and unhappy at the school where her parents sent her. At the age of eleven, she had had enough. She sold her schoolbooks for money to buy bread and cheese for sandwiches, and she headed out to the Turkish-built train station on the edge of town. A bearded man, wearing a tarbush, sat in the ticket booth, looked at the few coins Ruth had left and asked her, with a sympathetic look, where she wanted to go. Tel Aviv, she replied.

"I'm sorry, my dear girl, you don't have enough fare."

"One way."

"Not even for that."

Ruth, her plan thwarted, set out by foot, walking along the tracks. Barefoot. An Arab signal worker found her a mile out of town and took her back to her parents.

She had always bristled against gates and gatekeepers, and the man whose job it was to control her movements in the West Bank was Uzi, a man she once cradled in her arms after Druze fighters shot his father Zorik in a field.

Ruth didn't hide her feelings about the iron necklace of control Uzi operated. Instead of swinging her purse at him or his boss Sharon in righteous motherly anger, when Ruth ventured into the West Bank she typically put on the peach-pit necklace, maneuvering around checkpoints in her car, with soldiers following her through the scope of their rifles.

Ignoring security warnings of terrorist attacks, she continued working with Palestinian women embroidering pillows to buy food for their families. As always, she preferred acting to grandstanding.

If she wanted to see Raymonda, she headed to the West Bank because Raymonda hated using her Israeli-issued VIP card, for it smacked of an elitist arrangement between the Israeli military and what was now called the Palestinian Authority, a bankrupt oligarchy.

Ruth often complained to Ezer about the stranglehold on Gaza and the West Bank. She wasn't just channeling Raymonda when she warned him of an explosion if it continued. Oslo was supposed to bring peace, not a new intifada. "You need to invite Arafat to your home," the presidential mansion decorated with rugs from the Maskit factory in Umm al-Fahm.

President Weizman's basic humanity, his down-to-earth jocularity, and his loose tongue made him the most popular politician in the country. Yael winced at his occasional machismo: he said during a visit to a shelter for battered women, "forty-five years I am married to Reumah and not once have I dreamed of slapping her around." Adding to the folksy love he earned among average Israelis, Jews and Arabs alike, was personal tragedy. His badly maimed son Saul died in a car accident with his wife.

Weizman used this popularity to put Netanyahu, a man he disdainfully dismissed as "dumbfounded and wrong," in his place. "There will be a Palestinian state," he declared breezily, irrespective of the blinkered opinions of Likud Party fantasists. Just as the prime minister sidelined Arafat as a "terrorist," Weizman followed his sister-in-law's sage advice by inviting the former archenemy to the presidential mansion. "Look," Ezer said to Arafat over a pot of tea, "You fought me, and I fought you, but I think it is time to sit down and talk."

Accompanied by Yael, Ruth finally got her chance to meet Arafat face to face during a visit to Suha in Gaza in 1999. An Israeli television crew was there to capture on film the widow of Dayan chatting with the Palestinian First Lady. Ruth's plan was to have lunch and then visit the widow of Abu Jihad. Ruth and Yael arrived with the Norwegian diplomat Terry Larson, one of the architects of Oslo.[82]

Ruth, Yael, Raymonda, Larson, and Suha sat chatting on the second floor of the shabby concrete presidential mansion. On the wall in Suha's section of the building hung framed images of Jesus, Pope John Paul II, and the young man Arafat with his swarthy unshaven face and beguiling smile.

The four women and the diplomat were still chatting when through a set of double doors Arafat appeared, his eyes blinking excitedly. "Why didn't Suha tell me you were coming?" he oozed in a familiar voice as if they were old friends. He aimed straight for Ruth, who bolted up from the sofa in time for him to grab her and give her a warm hug. The cameraman took a close-up of the two.

He was so excited that he began kissing Ruth on one cheek, then the other. He repeated his kisses three times and told her how proud he was to have had her deceased husband as a foe. He was the "best enemy a man could hope for," a real "Bedouin warrior." The living quarry was singing the praises of the dead hunter.

Ruth was wiping away the tears as Arafat lauded Moshe, words that confirmed her complex love: though abusive and deceitful, Moshe was also a great man, magnanimous and heroic; and if he were alive, he and Arafat would together make a peace of the brave.

62
Suha

Ruth's visit to the presidential palace in Gaza brought out the best in Arafat—his boyish, spontaneous, exuberant side. But the Tawil women received less and less of his warmth, as more and more Palestinians sided with Hamas against Oslo.

Some of his top advisors wanted to force Suha into the role of a meek, docile, and most of all silent "Arab wife." They didn't trust a woman raised by a notorious feminist who for twenty years had bedeviled the "liberation movement" with her refusal to toe the line, with her brazen defiance of male privilege.

The advisors were far from pleased when Suha began exerting herself in a manner unheard of from the first ladies of Egypt, Syria, Iraq, or Libya. She channeled Raymonda by quoting her manifesto from the Palestine press agency days, "When our women have a chance to get out from under masculine domination, you'll see what they'll do for Palestine."

With Raymonda, Suha paid a visit to La Crèche to meet the women and their children. The two listened in horror to stories of women too afraid to give their names out of fear their families would find out where they were, kidnap them from the convent, and butcher them. In Gaza, Suha became a magnet for women threatened by their families, because the old Jordanian laws still on the books made honor killing a minor offense with, if at all, a few months behind bars. She took women into her home to save their lives, and asked Arafat to intervene on their behalf. To his credit, Arafat sat down with the women's fathers and brothers and stressed the virtue of mercy.

To handle the long line of desperate women outside the front door, Suha opened up a center for abused women in a refugee camp where she heard tales of lives getting worse, not better, under the regime of "liberation." She grew more and more pessimistic about the PLO's grip on Gaza; she saw a "black" future—or one colored the green of radical Islam. She could barely contain her rage at the gambling casino launched in Jericho by Fatah men whose business partners included Israeli politicians. "I hate it . . . right across from a refugee camp, no less."

As if anyone asked you, retorted her husband's men.

In February 1999, she ruffled more feathers by giving an interview to The *New York Times*. The article, "Suha Arafat Is a Very Different Sort of Palestinian Freedom Fighter," describes how the "Arab Militant in High Heels" maneuvered her blue BMW on her way to the children's clinic, "blond hair flying," with veiled women and donkeymongers looking on. Suha's deadpan line, "every beautiful flower ends up surrounded by weeds" hardly endeared her to PLO men. Boiling under the surface, what she said about her husband's allies was even worse: "It is a man's world, and very closed—like a family with a lot of intermarriages, and, well, you know the result of that."

A far more severe rupture between the First Lady and the president took place later that year in November, in the presence of Hillary Clinton. Suha gave the American First Lady a warm kiss and then claimed that Israel was causing a leap in cancer rates among Palestinian women and children through poisonous gas and toxic waste, which to most Americans sounded like gruel propaganda. Hillary, given the press reaction back home, had no choice but to blast her as an "anti-Semite," which couldn't have been further from the truth: Suha had inherited from her mother immunity to that particular mental disorder. As a personal favor to President Clinton, Arafat demanded that Suha retract the statement. She said no.

No one would dare attack Suha directly. Those who wanted to silence her chose to go to what they assumed was the source of her dangerous humanism.

They got their chance two weeks after the *New York Times* article appeared when an Israeli journalist, a buxom natural blond named Daphne Barak, turned up at Raymonda's front door wearing her signature tight-fitting dress with spaghetti straps. She had made a career of interviewing A-list celebrities—Mother Teresa, Benazir Bhutto, Michael Jackson, Jane Fonda. Raymonda didn't invite her in and explained that she had to be discreet because of the hell she got from the interview she gave to the Israelis in 1995.

"What do you mean?"

"I said things some people didn't like."

"Like what?" Barak had a pad of paper out and began scribbling notes.

"Well, for starters that I was against Arafat marrying my daughter."

With that, Raymonda, full of apologies, shut the door and Barak fabricated an entire "interview" which wound up in a mass circulation Arabic newspaper in London, and included a few lines in Raymonda's mouth about Arafat's regime being riddled with corruption and cronyism.

Whatever Barak's motives for her inventions—Uri Avnery suspected that Barak was a Mossad agent[83]—the damage was immense. The day after the interview appeared panicked neighbors reported seeing a long-bearded man skulking around Raymonda's house in Ramallah. Raymonda then got a phone call, and the man on the other line warned her that she should return to France "for your own safety." Raymonda recognized the voice: the caller was one of Arafat's top advisors. He told her that her life was in danger.

The heart palpitations flared up again.

Raymonda hung up the phone. Swallowing anti-stress medication to prevent a heart attack, she grabbed her VIP pass and maneuvered past checkpoints on her way back to Israel. She headed north to a region she considered her lost home. She drove to the village of Rama to visit the grave of Father Michel De Maria. His words came back to her about hatred in the Holy Land. She spent the night in her mother's native village of Kfar Yassif and, from a cousin's home, rang up Arafat's office.

The advisors didn't want to pass him the phone. "Do you know where I am? I'm in the Galilee. If you don't pass me to President Arafat, I'll give a press conference here in Israel." She employed her *L'pozez akol* voice.

Arafat asked her what she wanted. "I didn't say those terrible lies to the press. Someone is trying to destroy me . . . us . . . you . . . us all. One of your men threatened me and said I had to leave our country. Where should I go? Do you want me to go back into exile?"

He denied his men said any such thing.

"Shall I give you his name? I'm sure he's standing right next to you."

She heard muffled sounds on the other end. "Raymonda," Arafat said, this time with intimacy and warmth. "I believe you. Palestine is your home. You must stay."

63
The Angel

Suha's clinic for handicapped children, her visits to the nuns in Bethlehem, and her interventions on behalf of women threatened by honor killing, were sporadic, scatter-shot efforts at change, noble efforts but nowhere close to the ambitions of a woman reared on a steady diet of feminist rebellion. Deeper and more revolutionary changes were needed. Without success, Suha prodded her husband to toss out laws that more or less sanctioned the murder of women.

The response she got was the predictable equivocation of a ruler keeping two sets of books. In theory there wasn't a single feminist precept Arafat didn't agree with—yes, women should be equals, yes, they should control their own bodies, yes, their lives are more valuable than male codes of honor. All the while, he kept his eyes on the street. He didn't want the Islamists to suspect him of acting against Islam at the behest of his Christian wife. It was the same refrain Raymonda had heard a thousand times: Don't interfere; women's rights will have to wait.

In January 2000, Zahwa came down with a serious enough fever for Suha to take her to Paris for urgent treatment. Mother and daughter decamped to the Neuilly quarter. It was a safe place far from the coming cataclysm.

Months rolled by. Ruth was one of the few Israelis Raymonda still saw. Unlike most Israelis, she ignored warnings by her government that the West Bank was a lawless and dangerous enemy territory. A jungle. The specter of the widow of the great general showing up on a Hamas website with duct tape wrapped around her face kept Shin Bet people awake at night.

With Suha gone, people who needed something from Arafat turned to Raymonda. Arafat spent most of his time in the Muqata in Ramallah, the former Israeli prison and now presidential headquarters. By this point, Raymonda knew how to deal with Arafat's advisors—she ignored them by walking straight past the burly security men, sweeping into his office unannounced, usually at least once a day.

Whenever people had medical problems and needed money, they came to her because Arafat never said no to her; she just had to explain the reasons people needed help. Millions flowed from the presidential coffers to poor people with cancer or mental disease, or whatever. Quietly, without drawing too much attention, the president saved lives of scores of women threatened by their families for "dishonoring" them.

Arafat's generosity was in the context of a failing regime. President Weizman blamed the Likud government for the stalemate in the peace process. "I have reached my red line," the exasperated Weizman said in a 1999 television interview. "I'm not willing to help Netanyahu any longer. It is impossible that everyone is angry at us—the U.S., Europe, President Mubarak, King Hussein—and only we are right."[84] Some said that Weizman was working behind the scenes with opposition parties to force the grandstanding prime minister, a former furniture salesman, into calling for new elections. The Labor Party, led by Ehud Barak, won.

Someone probably wasn't too happy with Weizman's dovish ways. Leaked reports of minor financial shenanigans led to his resignation that summer.[85] Barak, while donning Rabin's peace mantle, also had to watch his back. Just as he launched land-for-peace talks with the Syrians at Shepherdstown outside Washington, DC, Uzi Dayan, on behalf of the new leader of the Likud, Arik Sharon, led top American politicians around the occupied territories to prove that Israel could never return the land to the Arabs. The occupied territory was too important for Israeli security.

The last time Ruth saw Raymonda before the Second Intifada broke out was as Barak left for Camp David for an ill-fated encounter with Arafat. Driving her thirty-year-old jalopy across the archipelago of checkpoints, she turned up at Raymonda's house in Ramallah, wearing a summer dress the color of cotton candy. Though for decades she had rubbed shoulders with many of the world's most famous designers, she still preferred the old Maskit wardrobes she lovingly called her "rags."

If she could have gotten away with it, she probably would have shown up barefoot. Ruth's gray hair showed her age, but her iridescent green eyes, her fast and determined walk, her sinewy personality had remained constant since her first encounter with Raymonda in St. Luke's Hospital.

Before Ruth even had a chance to say hello, Raymonda told her three mourners inside her house needed "your angel's help." The father of a large Christian family had just died, and his children wanted permission for their siblings and close relatives in Jordan to attend the funeral, which was in three hours' time. The relatives were already at the King Hussein Bridge, but the Israeli soldiers wouldn't let them through.

Raymonda was speaking rapidly and, before reaching the front door of the house, she forgot to share an important detail about the supplicants— that they belonged to a prominent family whose most famous member was Georges Habash, the founder of the militant organization Popular Front for the Liberation of Palestine (PFLP), and Arafat's most outspoken foe on the left. Like Daoud, Habash, likening Oslo to a poker game, rejected the Accords. Habash called Oslo a legal ruse used by the Israelis to get Arafat to give up his best available cards. While Arafat was off the Mossad hit list, Habash, otherwise known as "al-Hakim" or "the doctor," was still a marked man for the hijacking of the Air France plane in Entebbe. He was the one who, in 1970, had dispatched the gunmen who had nearly killed Assi in Munich.

Raymonda introduced Ruth to the three mourners; only then did she come out with the name "Habash." Ruth's raised eyebrows signified that she knew she was standing in front of relatives of Public Enemy Number One. The guests, after politely greeting Ruth, turned back to Raymonda and asked if she could call Arafat and get him to act.

Next to Ruth was one of the mourners, a well-heeled gentleman in a finely tailored black suit. She asked him in English what was happening. The two of them huddled together, trading whispers. Ruth was shaking her head, and then she was nodding. Her face showed a range of emotions: first sadness and then an understanding smile, and then back to sadness. Her empathetic genius was again at work.

"Let me help!" she suddenly announced in a loud enough voice that everyone stopped, their heads cocked in her direction. "Just give me the names of your family members in Jordan. I'll see what I can do."

If you go through Ruth's address book you'll find the telephone numbers of most of the leadership elite of Israel, and in Raymonda's house she made use of her best contacts in the military to help out the family of a man whose group tried to kill her son. There she was, dabbing away tears while she speedily, carefully jotted down the names, one by one; then picking up the home phone, she called Uzi because he was the master gatekeeper. At the time he was on the front lines in Lebanon.

Uzi Dayan! The mourners could hardly believe their ears.

Ruth contacted an office within the Ministry of Defense, and within a few minutes she was connected directly to him. Ruth hung up and said, with her good-witch magic, that Moshe's nephew promised to contact the commander of the King Hussein Bridge across the Jordan and get permission for the family to pass. It seemed to make no difference to Uzi that the Habash family was involved.

After the family gave their effusive thanks to the "angel" and left, Ruth told Raymonda the story of Uzi. Ruth knew some of the scars Raymonda had been carrying since she was a little girl, the expulsion, the killing, and the destruction of her family. Now Ruth told her about Uzi's scars. Just as Raymonda was a terrified little girl in a convent, not knowing if her parents were dead or alive, Uzi's father Zorik lay rotting in a field.

Epilogue
Great Wall of Zion

On the way back from Camp David, Arafat passed through Paris and instructed Suha to stay put in France. The Israelis were pushing him to betray his principles, he told her. "I do not want Zahwa's friends in the future to say that her father abandoned the Palestinian cause." He was going to show the Israelis he couldn't be cowed by their power. "I might be martyred, but I shall bequeath our historical heritage to Zahwa and to the children of Palestine."

Arafat naturally had his contingency plans for a faceoff with the IDF, even if he knew there was no winning a military confrontation with Israel. He probably wanted a limited shootout. Ehud Barak had his contingency plans to nip armed resistance in the bud.

The so-called Al Aqsa Intifada began with Sharon's march up to the Haram al-Sharif and his words, quoted from an IDF commander after the war in 1967, "The Temple Mount is in our hands." There were protests, and the following day trigger-happy soldiers shot dead seven unarmed protesters on the plaza surrounding the Dome of the Rock, and wounded more than one hundred. Violence quickly metastasized: over the following days forty-seven Palestinians died, and 1,885 were wounded; five Israelis died at the hands of the Palestinians.

The Islamists were quick to organize a spate of suicide bombing and guerrilla attacks. To keep the support of the street, Arafat gave orders to his security forces to open fire at Israeli forces. His chant "Jihad, Jihad, Jihad" went well beyond theatrics.

This militarized Intifada was all the right wing in Israel needed to recast Arafat in his old role as a moving target. The *Jerusalem Post* wanted him put in Adolf Eichmann's glass cage in a grand trial for his "crimes against humanity," as a prelude to the gallows. The spread of Palestinian terrorism into Israeli cities swept away the Labor government and brought into power Ariel Sharon. Now his national security advisor, Uzi labeled Arafat "the problem" and "the obstacle to a solution."

Other members of the Dayan clan did what they could to keep a bit of humanism alive. Ruth indefatigably continued her humanitarian forays into the West Bank. Assi's latest film was about a West Bank settler-rabbi wanting to take over the Temple Mount. Yael clung to her view of Arafat as a peace partner. Aviv Geffen the rock star teamed with an Arab singer-songwriter to record the song "Innocent Criminals." "You say the Arabs are primitive / say the Arabs are aggressive . . . The Arabs demonstrate, the police take their lives."

Raymonda was still in Ramallah, walking over to the Muqata every day to visit her son-in-law. In 2003, the steady stream of suicide bombers, some dispatched by Fatah leaders, triggered an Israeli campaign of targeted assassinations. Eventually, the IDF reoccupied West Bank cities and laid siege to the Muqata in Ramallah. For fun, during the invasion, soldiers in Markova tanks flattened Raymonda's BMW parked on the street.

She could no longer see Arafat because of the tanks in the street. Soldiers shot a neighbor in the head while she was hanging out the laundry on her balcony.

"*Tiftach*—open up!" Raymonda heard one morning. Dressed in a night robe, she unlocked the door and soldiers—it seemed like an entire company of them—filed into the house.

"What do you want?"

"We're here to get him."

"Get who?"

"Get out of our way." They pushed her to one side. A nervous eighteen-year-old stood guard while the others searched the house.

"Who are you looking for?"

"Arafat," said the soldier guarding her. "The one who wants him is the Fat Man," army lingo for Prime Minister Sharon. "We have intelligence that you smuggled him out of the Muqata, and he must be here," under a bed or crouched in the bathtub or hiding in a closet.

"Are you insane?" she scoffed. "Not even the birds can fly out of the Muqada without getting shot. How am I supposed to get him out?"

Soldiers tore apart the house, looking everywhere for him. They even opened the stove and refrigerator, as if he were hiding in a yogurt container. One of the soldiers with a Russian accent called out from her bedroom, "Here's the man. It's him." It was a picture of Arafat holding Zahwa in the hospital in Paris.

Two days later, Raymonda heard over the military loudspeakers outside, "In one hour we are going to blow up the Muqata." Sharon decided to take out a nemesis he had hunted down for nearly half a century. Upstairs in the Muqata, Yasser was rubbing his prayer beads and repeating like a mantra that he was willing to die a martyr's death. The only thing of value he owned, much more than his life or even his family, was his honor, and he wasn't about to allow the Fat Man to take it from him.

Within minutes, a different set of loudspeakers belonging to mosques all over Ramallah instructed people to go to the streets to save their leader by defying the curfew and forming a human shield around the Muqata. Shots rang out from outside as the first people to answer the call were shot down.

Raymonda's cell phone was still working, and she called Ruth. "You must do something!" she said, looking out through shattered glass at the soldiers in their jeeps. "Ruth, do you hear me? Are you there? Call this bloody Sharon of yours. He's going to kill Arafat. Call Uzi! For Christ's sake, do something."

"Raymonda," Ruth replies, "what on earth do you imagine I can do? You think I can just call up Arik and order him to stop?"

"YOU CAN'T JUST SIT THERE, YOU MUST DO SOMETHING!" Her words turned into shouts. "He's going to kill him in less than an hour." Eliminating Arafat would turn the Holy Land into even more of a caldron of hatred than it already was, she reminded Ruth. An inferno. "Ruth, we are running out of time."

"Well, I have a surprise for you. I am NOT Arik Sharon!"

It was President George Bush, not Ruth, who yanked the leash on Sharon and kept Arafat alive.

After Arafat fell mysteriously ill in October 2004, Raymonda navigated the rubble of the Muqata to spend with him what would be his final days in the "liberated" homeland. She saw him for the last time when he left to a Parisian hospital, where he died in November.

Raymonda, too, soon left Palestine, never to return. She wasn't around to witness the way Uzi Dayan headed up the so-called Public Council for a Security Fence whose mantra was that a wall be built between Israel and the West Bank according to "demographic principles," with as much empty land on the Israeli side and as few Arabs as possible. Working under Sharon, he transformed his concept into watchtowers and a twenty-foot-high, reinforced concrete barrier that fit together like Lego pieces and separated families and friends, a Berlin Wall snaking its way through the middle of the Holy Land. The Great Wall of Zion.

At a backyard party thrown by the rock star Avi Geffen, Uzi and I discussed the Security Wall. He was so sure of himself, so emphatic with a sort of serene yet determined smile on his face. I wondered what went on in the mind of this man, so honest and mild-mannered and intelligent, when he inspected his walls with his engineer's eye.

Since I first met Ruth and Raymonda in 2009, we've spoken dozens of times about the injustice of putting masonry between peoples whose worlds are so interwoven that separation, far from being a natural product of mutual antipathy, has to be forcibly imposed from above. The largest impediments to peace they both believe, more than terrorism, are laws and barriers preventing Jews and Palestinians from meeting. Right-wing Israelis and the holy warriors of Hamas share the same fear: empathy.

Raymonda's pet theory on the Wall goes like this: Separation, be it the old law forbidding Israelis to cavort with Arafat and his ilk or the more draconian laws of more recent provenance making it illegal for Israelis to venture into Palestinian areas, have less to do with security than with preventing human contact, because contact leads to understanding. Moshe Dayan and his generation, though they fought war after war with them, nevertheless knew, respected, and understood Arabs. Today's technocrats ignore the human factor altogether.

"If we want to be secure in this country," Ruth said to me in May 2013, "we'll have to tear them all down, all the damn walls. Moshe realized this, believe me he did, but when I tell this to Uzi, he thinks I'm loony. You may not like Moshe—that's your problem. But there isn't one Palestinian—not one!—who wouldn't prefer his Open Bridges over what they have now." Ruth made this declaration sitting as usual in her easy chair. From my position on the couch the colorful painting from Haiti hanging behind her looked like a nimbus. She struck me in fact as exceptionally saintly that morning.

During my last trip to visit Raymonda in Malta, in summer 2013, we got Ruth on Skype and Raymonda read to us a passage from her and Ruth's old friend, the Israeli historian Meron Benvenisti: "Man is a tree in the field—that is not us. Our love of the land is a love that we imposed on the land and foisted on the land. With the Arabs, it is the opposite. Their love for the land truly sprang from the soil. Love of the fig, of the tree, of the house."

"Yes," Ruth smacked her lips. "Meron is right." That was all she said. All she had to.

"That's why we need this book you're writing," Raymonda chimed in.

In the years since beginning the project I had visited Ruth a hundred times in Tel Aviv, and had flown off to see Raymonda twice in Dubai, twice in Malta, and once in Baltimore. But we rarely discussed what they wanted out of the book. This book. They certainly couldn't expect a happy ending with Raymonda living in exile and Ruth shouting at the television each time the nightly news comes on.

"So Ruth, what do you want readers to take away from the book?"

"Ask Raymonda. She's the one who put us up to it." Ruth was pointing at the computer screen as she spoke. I thought back to the first time I met Ruth and how she told me about a "very special lady" with a "mission." What also came to mind were the many spats between them I had been witness to, and for the simple reason that Ruth is a proud founding member of an admirably successful state, a secular miracle most people in the world continue to see through the prism of the film *Exodus*, a story of overcoming all odds and rebuilding an ancient nation from the embers of the Holocaust. Raymonda, living in exile, belongs to a people still occupied and whose pre-1948 lands and cities remain well beyond reach or recovery.

"First of all," Raymonda cleared her throat and began, "let me tell you that I understand people like Uzi." Thus spoke again a woman raised by nuns. "They are so fearful . . . Much of what they do is also driven by guilt. They know they have wronged us but can't see any way to stop. It's like a sleepwalker attacking a man on the street, and when he wakes up he realizes he's strangling a perfect stranger. He just can't stop because if he does the stranger will turn on him. So he keeps squeezing."

"Is that the reason right-wingers feared you?"

"Oh, those people. Sharon till the bitter end—in a coma he probably still has nightmares about people like me and Ruth; and it's getting worse because the two sides no longer meet. At least in the 1970s and '80s we could join forces with the Israeli left. And that was what terrified the right." Raymonda was too much like the best Jewish intellectuals in the diaspora, humanists fighting for rights and equality and basic dignity. "We drove Sharon and his friends crazy. Why do you think they sidled up to the Islamists? Islamic holy war, because it sounded so far-fetched at the time, was music to their ears. Anything but the secular, educated Palestinians, and in particular people like me calling for non-violent resistance. They'd rather have suicide bombers."

If Israel really wanted peace, the country would name streets after Raymonda and Ruth. The two would have their own TV talk show. Women, proponents and products of a dialogue, would be celebrated instead of ignored and exiled.

"Raymonda, you didn't answer my question. What do you want out of this book? In a sentence or two."

Raymonda thought for a moment. Outside the window, down on the beach, there was a procession for some Catholic saint. Fireworks lit up the sky.

"Let me tell you why I admire Ruth so much. It's because, like me, she's a product of the history of our country. She's full of contradictions—who isn't in that place?" Raymonda was pointing out toward the sea. "She still loves Moshe, and she sees in him the farmer and not the general. But she's honest. She doesn't go around apologizing for what and who she is, or pulling out bones from archeological digs to make a point. Most important for me is her compassion. She loves. Humanity could use more people like her. A few million more."

The funny thing is that Ruth, word for word, offers the same vaulting praise for Raymonda. That's what makes them friends.

"Yes, Raymonda, I understand that. I'd like to go back to the book . . ."

"We've already talked a hundred times about the mission Father Michel gave me as a little girl."

I didn't see the connection. "How can you fulfill your mission here on Malta?"

"With this book, of course." From the expression on her face, she couldn't believe I had never figured this out on my own.

Raymonda's tenacious "mission" remains the same, to break the forced silence between the two peoples. Letting people know just how much she loves and admires Ruth is her way of leaping over Uzi's wall in her mind, and going home.

Notes

1 In 1972, a Mossad bomb blew the novelist and playwright to shreds, along with his seventeen-year-old niece.

2 Ruth describes the family bliss this way: "The cat was asleep, the dog waiting for her dinner, and all in all it was a cozy domestic scene."

3 Once the British forces were gone, predicted General D'Arcy, commander of British forces in Palestine, the "Haganah would take over all Palestine tomorrow."

4 The real reason for the bombing was retribution for an Arab terror attack on the refinery in Haifa in which forty-seven Jews died; the other motivation, in the words of the planner, was to "force the Arabs out of the quarter and change the psychological climate in the city."

5 Deir Yassin

6 The plan, called *Tochnik Dalet* or Operation Danny, called for controlling as much of Palestine as possible before May 15. The only way to do so was first to score a decisive victory over the guerrilla fighters, and then to clear out large swaths of territory of the Arab population. The Israeli historian Benny Morris considers Operation Danny to be an expulsion plan. See Benny Morris, *The Birth of the Palestinian Refugee Problem* (Cambridge University Press, 2004), p. 163 ff.

7 Ben-Gurion spoke of "cleansing" the country of Arabs, and the introduction of Jews in their place. Yehuda Slutzky, *Summary of the Hagana Book*, pp. 486–7. Cited from Ilan Pappé, The Ethnic Cleansing of Palestine 2006, p. 128.

8 A reporter from the *Chicago Sun-Times*, a witness on the ground, writes of Dayan's men in jeeps and half-tracks surging through the towns in "blitz tactics." With a huddle of Jordanian troops firing madly down at them,

Moshe and his men returned fire and "practically everything in their way died," including scores of civilians.

9   Lea came from an ultra-Orthodox Jewish family, and she ended up leaving her husband for a British officer. Heart-broken, during the war Dr. Bey rented the house to Ethiopian Emperor Haile Selassie.

10 Other more or less permanent guests were Moshe's sister Aviva, her husband Israel Geffen, and their son Jonathan, who was Assi's age.

11 His name was Reuven Shiloah.

12 His name was Yigael Yadin.

13 Digging also backed up Zionist "claims to the land," writes Yael Dayan about her father, which can explain the "wonderfully primitive bond between him and the archeological artifacts he was pulling out of the ground."

14 Yael Dayan, *My Father, His Daughter*.

15 Avi Shlaim, "Israel's Dirty War," London Review of Books (August 8, 1994). Review of Benny Morris's *Israel's Border Wars, 1949–1956: Arab Infiltration, Israeli Retaliation and the Countdown to the Suez War*, Clarendon Press Oxford, 1993.

16 Ariel Sharon wrote about Dayan that he "was the greatest revolutionary the IDF ever had. Dayan's imagination absorbed and encouraged every daring operational plan, and he breathed a spirit of battle into the army."

17 Mordechai Bar-On, *Moshe Dayan: Israel's Controversial Hero*.

18 Avi-Shlaim, *The Iron Wall: Israel and the Arab World*.

19 Avnery published an article exposing details of a retaliatory raid by a commando Unit 101 against the Arab village of Qibya. Terrorists had killed a Jewish mother and her two children by tossing a grenade into their house a few kilometers from the frontier with Jordan. In response, Sharon had orders to make "Qibya an example for everyone." Ben-Gurion, praising Dayan and Sharon for the operation, said that it would teach the Arabs a lesson and "give us the possibility of living here." (See Avner Falk, *Fratricide in the Holy Land: A Psychoanalytic View of the Arab-Israeli Conflict* [Terrace Books, 2005], p. 46.)

20 Yael Dayan, *My Father, His Daughter*, p. 99.

21 Interview with Raymonda Tawil.

22 In Raymonda's words, "There had to be separation; the regime didn't want us to know one another. And it wasn't because the nuns tried to push their religion on Jews, because they didn't. Anyway, many of the Jewish girls were

now Catholics. But this didn't matter to the bureaucrats in the Ministry of Education." Interview with Raymonda Tawil.

23 The friend's name was Marie-Louise.

24 Urquhart was a founder of Amnesty International.

25 Sahar Khalifeh would go on to write the novel *The Image, the Icon, and the Covenant*.

26 For more on Raymonda's claim that the IDF used napalm, see comments by the British commander Glubb Pasha who reported that the Israeli army employed napalm during the war. See Arthur C. Forrest, *The Unholy Land* (1971), p. 16.

27 Raymonda's son-in-law Ibrahim Souss co-authored the book with General Elpeleg, *Dialogue entre Israel et la Palestine*.

28 Dayan reversed his order. Interview with Raymonda Tawil.

29 *Time* praised Yael's account of the war as "an exhilarating chronicle of the Israeli victory over the Arabs," while the American-Jewish journalist Tony Judt lashed out at her for her "self-satisfied arrogance."

30 Not long after the 1967 war, Dayan laid out what he wanted in the West Bank: the permanent borders would be the ceasefire lines; there would be peace talks with the Arab governments; the government would prevent a bi-national state; and there would be no Arab majority in the conquered territories. See Bar-On, *Moshe Dayan*, p.145.

31 According to Dayan, the Open Bridge was a "breathing spell enabling us to create additional facts on the ground, and so it will go on. I believe that this way we shall be able to achieve a part, or even most, of the goals we want to accomplish."

32 Shlomo Goren wanted to erect a synagogue on the Temple Mount.

33 Mercouri had done a film with Yael's former boyfriend Michael Cacoyannis and was best known for her role as a prostitute in *The Children of Piraeus*.

34 "It was not one of [Dayan's] more glorious victories. . . . We did not consider ourselves defeated."

35 Amos Kenan, "Those of us who couldn't restrain ourselves would go into the prison compounds to fuck Arab women." Quoted in A. Clare Brandabur, "Reply to Amos Kenan's 'The Legacy of Lydda' and An Interview With PFLP Leader Dr. George Habash," in *Peuples & Monde* (April 11, 2007).

36 See Chaim Herzog and Shlomo Gazit, *The Arab-Israeli Wars: War and Peace in the Middle East from the 1948 War of Independence to the Present* (Vintage Books, 2005), p. 205.

37 *New Outlook* was founded by Polish-born Simha Flapan, a legendary leftist and author of *The Birth of Israel: Myths and Realities.*

38 Ibrahim Souss was Palestinian Delegate General to France from 1978 to 1992.

39 See Ahron Bregman, *Israel's Wars: A History Since 1947* (Psychology Press, 2002), p. 147.

40 According to an interview with Raymonda Tawil.

41 Abu Nidal, nom de guerre for Sabri Khalil al-Banna, grew up in a family beachside mansion in Jaffa (it now serves as the Israeli military court). In 1948, the family ended up in a refugee camp in Gaza.

42 See *Haaretz*, February 12, 2014, p. 3.

43 "Once we were grown, he owed us nothing, and in his egotistical, self-centered pattern it was not his duty to contribute to our happiness when he was alive or consider our pain and distress when he was gone."

44 See Amnon Barzilai, "Golda Meir's nightmare," *Haaretz*, October 2, 2003.

45 The film is a spoof on the 1954 patriotic classic *Hill 24 Doesn't Answer.* In contrast to the drunken escapades of *Halfon Hill*, *Hill 24* presents Israeli soldiers as humane, generous, and merciful, and their foes as little better than genocidal Nazis. In fact, there is one scene in which a soldier captured by the Israelis during a fight against the Egyptians turned out to be a former SS officer bereft of human morals.

46 The reserve officer was Motti Ashkenazi.

47 Based on an interview with Raymonda Tawil.

48 Set up in the sixties, the aim of the organization, to quote one of its presidents, Sir Paul Reilly, was "to support the aspiration of the world's craftspeople, whether in maintaining honorable inherited traditions or in extending frontiers by experiment and innovation."

49 Based on an interview with Raymonda Tawil.

50 The official invitation came from the "Committee on New Alternatives for the Middle East." Its members included the likes of Noam Chomsky, I. F. Stone, and Moshe Menuhin, the father of the violinist who had gone to school with Ruth's parents at the Herzliya Gymnasium.

51 "I was released thanks to the intervention of a decent military man named Amnon Cohen, a professor and scholar." Interview with Raymonda Tawil.

52 See Freda Guttman, "Imwas 1967, 1968, 1978, and 1988 Canada Park: Two Family Albums," in *Positions: East Asia Cultures Critique* 13, no. 1 (Spring 2005): 49–54.

53 Interview with Raymonda Tawil.

54 See Tom Segev, "When a shy but stubborn Israel first went to the Olympics," *Haaretz*, July 7, 2012.

55 Marshall J. Breger, Yitzhak Reiter, and Leonard Hammer (eds.), *Sacred Space in Israel and Palestine: Religion and Politics*, (Routledge, 2013), p. 184.

56 Issam Sartawi, *My Friend, the Enemy* (1986).

57 Interview with Raymonda Tawil.

58 Avishay Braverman

59 Lilly Rivlin, journalist, writer, and filmmaker, introduced Raymonda to Letty Pogrebin. Rivlin is the first cousin of the president of Israel. The Israeli human rights lawyer Leah Tsemel defended Raymonda during the event.

60 Pogrebin credits Raymonda's belief in dialogue, negotiation, and compromise in helping her go "from anger to activism, from silence to dialogue, from passivity to protest."

61 In a letter to the Hebrew poet Haim Gouri in the 1960s, Ben-Gurion accused Begin of being a "racist along the lines of a Hitler" and, even worse, a man willing to exterminate all the Arabs "for the sake of a Greater Israel." See Yehiam quoted in Weitz's article "Begin's Sharp Points, Blunted," in *Haaretz*, June 27, 2003.

62 Begin was a leader in the Irgun attack on the village of Deir Yassin in April 1948.

63 Interview with Raymonda Tawil.

64 Yael's transformation in her attitude toward Ruth was hastened by the reading of Dayan's will. His archeological treasures and his various properties ended up with the new wife who announced that Assi was a "worthless playboy, Udi a corrupt, lazy no-good," and Yael a "cunning, dominating bitch."

65 In 1981 Raymonda won the Bruno Kreisky award for advocating "dialogue and reconciliation."

66 Anthony H. Cordesman and Jennifer Moravitz, *The Israeli-Palestinian War: Escalating to Nowhere* (Greenwood Publishing Group, 2005), p. 130.

67 "P.L.O. Aide Killed in Paris Bombing," *New York Times*, July 24, 1982. Fadl was assassinated in retaliation for the PLO's killing of Yacov Barsimantov, an Israeli diplomat in the Paris embassy.

68 Begin ordered the invasion after Abu Nidal's group attempted to assassinate Israel's ambassador to the UK, Shlomo Argov.

69 Interview with Raymonda Tawil.

70 The Arab League's Ambassador to the UN told Raymonda that the "Zionists use your name in all their attacks against us and our Arab mentality."

Um Jihad, the wife of Arafat's right-hand man Abu Jihad and the head of the PLO women's organization, ordered her to "stop doing propaganda against the Palestinian people."

71   This story is based on an interview with Raymonda Tawil. Henry Kissinger noted the way "sentences poured forth from him in mellifluous constructions complicated enough to test the listener's intelligence and simultaneously leave him transfixed by the speaker's virtuosity."

72   Based on an interview with Raymonda Tawil.

73   Based on the interview with Raymonda Tawil.

74   Interview with Raymonda.

75   Joining them was an Arab-Israeli doctor and secret PLO member named Ahmed Tibi. He and Weizman had become friends when as an intern Tibi took care of Reumah and Ezer's son Saul following the Egyptian sniper attack.

76   The note said, "Raymonda, if you do not leave within three days, you will end up like Aziz Shahadeh." Aziz, the father of the writer Raja Shahadeh, was killed by an unknown assassin, probably a member of a rogue Palestinian faction.

77   As reported by Raymonda.

78   Abu Nidal was eventually shot to death in Baghdad on orders of Saddam Hussein.

79   Interview with Raymonda Tawil.

80   Her decision to have the child in Paris was criticized as anti-nationalistic. She struck back: "Our child was conceived in Gaza, but sanitary conditions there are terrible. I don't want to be a hero and risk my baby."

81   Edward Said, America's most influential Palestinian, lampooned Arafat to Christopher Hitchens as the Palestinian "Papa Doc."

82   The other architects of Oslo were the Israelis Ron Pundak and Uri Shavir.

83   Based on an interview with Raymonda Tawil.

84   See also Dafna Linzer, "Netanyahu Rejects Call by Weizman for Early Elections," *Associated Press*, June 30, 1998.

85   Weizman was cleared and returned to office. He later retired.

Index